WALKING IN THE
DOLOMITES

Last stretch climbing towards Bocca di Brenta

WALKING IN THE
DOLOMITES

by

Gillian Price

CICERONE PRESS
2 POLICE SQUARE, MILNTHORPE

To Nicola, with all my love.

*"walking is not simply therapeutic for oneself but is a poetic activity
that can cure the world of its ills" (Bruce Chatwin).*

My thanks go to Betty and Dave who taught me how to walk.

Acknowledgements
Thanks also to Piero D'Este for his helpful suggestions on
the itineraries and to all my walking companions
Nicola, Paola, Giorgio and Egidio in particular.

All the photos were taken by Gillian Price and Nicola Regine
unless otherwise indicated.

Contents

Introduction

THE LEGEND OF the "Monti Pallidi" or "Pale Mounts" as the Dolomites were first called, has it that the prince from the western slopes of the Alps wanted desperately to visit the moon. His wish was granted, and while he was there he fell in love with and married the princess of the moon whom he brought back to earth. She in turn pined for the pale mounts of her homeland. Her earthly husband on the other hand would have gone blind had he stayed on the moon any longer. Luckily Providence took a hand, and a group of homeless gnomes turned up - in exchange for permission to dwell in the upper mountain reaches they wove the rays of the moon into an extremely fine white gossamer covering for the rock faces. These splendoured in the sun and were illuminated at sundown turning wondrous hues of pink. So the princess settled down and lived happily ever after with her earthly husband.

The Dolomites were renamed after the French geologist Déodat de Dolomieu. As a result of his trip there in 1788, he discovered and analysed their mineral composition and differentiated between dolomite (calcium magnesium carbonate) and calcite (calcium carbonate), the two types of limestone which are the main ingredients of these mountains.

The geological origin of these mountains dates back some 230 million years to when they were deposited in the form of marine sediments and coral in a low open sea. This material, rich in calcium carbonate, was to form the base of the mountains. Much later, around 65 million years ago, the rocks, also containing fossilised sea life, were forced and lifted high up by various tectonic events, and the Alps came into existence. More recently - only 2 million years ago - the ice ages covered the mountains with successive ice sheets that on retreating sculpted out deeper valleys and lake beds, leaving morainic (glacial) debris. The ongoing process of weathering by snow, rain and wind has done the rest. It is not unusual to find fossilised shell and marine remains along the path, but enthusiasts should not miss a visit to the Natural History Museums of Verona and Cortina d'Ampezzo.

The Dolomites, which take on breathtaking hues of pink at sunset, known as the "enrosadira" ("alpenglow"), are famous worldwide for their soaring peaks, dramatic walls and towering heights. Landscapes range from sweet alpine meadows to deciduous and evergreen woods and high altitude lunar-like terrain where you are dwarfed by soaring peaks and glaciers and may catch sight of fleet-footed chamois or comical marmots.

Mountaineers have been coming here attracted by the peaks since the 18th century but accessibility for walkers is relatively recent. World War One made the area a war zone, with many hard fought battles between Austrian and Italian troops contesting borders that often ran along mountain crests. Military mule tracks were constructed to supplement existing shepherds' paths for supply and accessibility and they comprise a valuable part of the network of pathways today. Remains of fortifications, trenches, barbed wire and even the occasional rusty tin can are still seen along paths in some areas.

These splendid mountains have been discovered by nature lovers and tourists alike. People now come from all over the world and there is not much room left for fairy tale castles - particularly in those valley resorts where indiscriminating local councils continue to give the go-ahead for excessive hotel complexes and a seemingly infinite number of ski lifts. Many of the Dolomite villages were once dramatically impoverished and large-scale postwar immigration overseas was common. Since then the whole area, like the rest of Europe, has had its own tourist boom, bringing with it an improvement in life style and the return home of many immigrants who could now rely on secure jobs. The time has now come, however, to restrain development. The Dolomites are already well trodden and environmental problems are not unknown - yet in the midst of the degradation of the European environment the area still represents a paradise and will hopefully continue to do so with more responsible valley management as well as environment-conscious walkers.

How to get there & when to go

THE DOLOMITE MOUNTAINS are in the northeast of Italy, and form a parallelogram enclosed by the towns of Fortezza - San Candido - Feltre - Trent. This guide also includes a brief area east of the River Piave, and the Brenta Dolomite Group northwest of Trent.

By car, approaching Italy from the north, (ie. driving south from Innsbruck), via the A22 (Brennero-Modena) motorway (autostrada) take any of the exits between Bressanone and Trent. Otherwise, if you arrive from the west on the A4 (Torino-Trieste), exits can be made east of Verona. Shorter useful motorways are the A31 (Vicenza-Schio) and the relatively quiet A27 (Mestre-Vittorio Veneto) - work is presently under way to extend it eventually all the way to Austria.

International trains run down the main north-south artery from Munich and Innsbruck to the Isarco valley with Bressanone and Bolzano, then the Adige Valley with Trent and Verona. Alternately, from the east, through Lienz in Austria, a single line runs along Val Pusteria connecting San Candido, Dobbiaco and Brunico to Fortezza just north of Bressanone on the previous line. Other secondary lines provide convenient connections from the Po plain in the south with Feltre, Belluno, Longarone and north as far as Calalzo.

The nearest useful airports are at Verona, Treviso and Venice. Ongoing coach or train connections can be made from the relevant town centre.

A host of private coach companies from major northern cities such as Milan, Parma, Bologna, Verona, Padua and Venice, provide direct links with Dolomite centres all through the summer. The main companies covering the internal Dolomite area itself are Dolomiti Bus - Headquarters in Belluno, tel:(0437)941237-941167; S.A.D. - Headquarters in Bolzano, tel:(800)846047 (nb. this is a "green number" ie. the caller is only charged the equivalent of 1 local call); Holzer - Headquarters in Sesto, tel:(0474)710309; Atesina - Trent Bus Station, tel:(0461)983627; and the Ferrovia Trento-Malè (small electric train and buses) - Headquarters in Trent tel:(0461)822725.

Even if travelling by car, once you arrive in the Dolomite area get hold of as many local bus timetables as possible. These will enable you to organise transfers from one village to another to link itineraries, facilitate a 'return to base' after a crossing route, and help you time your return to civilisation. The Dolomiti Bus Company, for example, puts out a pocket size summer edition for a small charge; and sheets or booklets are available (usually free of charge) from the other companies. Ask at bus stops (often a bar or restaurant), depots or tourist information offices.

What's more, use of public transport in preference to private car travel can help reduce, or at least not contribute to a further increase in air pollution levels in mountain localities.

Because you are dependent on refuge opening periods and local weather conditions, plan on going between mid-June and late September/October. Typical summer weather can mean blazing hot sun on the exposed stretches, or breezes through the woods with a cool respite, but snow storms with poor visibility are not rare occurrences in these ranges, even at the height of summer. September - October is a superb time to go as you've a good chance of crisp clear days and excellent visibility without the usual valley mist of the summer. However days will be colder

11

and shorter (Italy goes off daylight savings late September) and there is the risk of early snow covering. In compensation, you'll hardly meet anyone, particularly important for popular zones such as the Tre Cime di Lavaredo. But in autumn there will only be a limited number of high altitude huts open to choose from (though one-day walks will be feasible), and while autumn colours (larches and beech in particular) are magical, the fresh spring greens and carpets of wild flowers in bloom in summer should not be missed.

Flora & Fauna

A BRIEF NOTE on wild flowers: some areas in nature parks and reserves feature unusual flora identified by experts and these are mentioned wherever relevant in walk descriptions. Otherwise, depending on the altitude and exposure of the slopes, walkers in late spring are most likely to see snowdrops, crocuses and the alpine saffron, butterburs, primroses, cyclamens, lily-of-the-valley, heather and violets. Late summer-autumn, as well as the more common meadow flowers, will include the more unusual gentians, a myriad of orchids, rosebay willow-herb, the artistic-looking carline thistle, saxifrage clinging precariously to rock faces and crannies, colourful lilies, pasqueflowers, alpenrose and edelweiss.

Most local tourist offices and refuges display informative posters to help you identify local flora, especially the protected species. Even if not on the protected list, wild flowers are better not picked so as to guarantee their regeneration.

Your chances of finding fresh supplies of wild fruits along the track are good, especially in late summer-autumn. However, as there are many deadly poisonous as well as stomach-upsetting varieties, stick to the internationally known ones that you are already familiar with. There are raspberries, tiny sweet strawberries and bilberries. Hazelnuts are plentiful, and you occasionally find red currants and wild cumin (in open grassland).

There is a vast range of mushrooms and edible funguses (completely different varieties from British ones) to be found. Again, clear informational posters are on display in most refuges, as well as valley localities. They show all the types growing in the area and whether or not they are edible ("commestibile") or poisonous ("velenoso"). However, non-residents need a permit to collect as well as a basket which allows the spores to drop back to the ground and keeps mushrooms well-aired. Plastic bags cause spoiling in a short space of time. Most villages have

Rhaetian poppies

Devil's claw

a resident expert to check the mushrooms - usually to be found at the First Aid station or Municipality. Unless you actually have the chance to prepare and cook the mushrooms yourself, you will be much better off ordering them for dinner in a refuge or valley trattoria, where they will undoubtedly be prepared in the most enhancing and delicious manner.

Bears are now virtually extinct in the Dolomites, apart from the surviving few in the Brenta Group, and foxes make an unusual sight too. Many of them are afflicted with rabies, but the picture is reasonably optimistic nonetheless. Some hunting is still allowed in Italy, but there are strict regulations governing and limiting its practice. As well as the successful introduction of small herds of ibex in the Croda del Becco area of the Fanes-Sennes-Braies Nature Park, other areas actually report increases in sightings of animals. It is quite common to see roe deer in

13

Hungry crows on the edge of the Latemar

forest environments, as well as chamois grazing in light wood or climbing nimbly, totally at home in their rock habitat above the tree line. Herds are usually led by a female, and they have a sharp, almost human-like warning whistle. The marmot is another delightful inhabitant of the Dolomites, and can be seen after its October-to-April hibernation. Usually found on a sloping, mixed rock-earth terrain, it is easily identified by the piercing cry of alarm it utters - when you hear it scan the landscape for a marmot trying to look unobtrusive by freezing in an upright position, and keep an eye out for burrow entrances. Rodents such as the squirrel and dormouse are commonly seen in woods, and more rarely, ermine on rockscapes.

Birds include, among other game types, the capercaillie; a large European wood grouse which relies heavily on conifer needles for its nest and food, except for late summer when it gorges itself on bilberries. There is also a range of small song birds, finches and the occasional wall creeper, gliding hawks, scavenging crows and ravens and, if you are lucky, an eagle or two in the Pale di San Martino area, for example. Vultures feature in legendary tales feasting on corpse-strewn mountain sides after battles, but since these are no longer in fashion and peace has come to the area, they have presumably become extinct through lack of carrion, though persecution by man was also a significant factor. Projects are now successfully underway to reintroduce the bearded vulture (Lammergeier) and the griffon vulture to the Alps and there have already been reports of sightings in the Dolomites.

The only potentially dangerous encounter you are likely to have with the wildlife is with snakes. Hot days on exposed terrain, particularly in the Belluno area, could mean vipers sunning themselves on the path. In the relative areas, posters with clear colour photographs are on display in refuges and public places. They show the differences between the harmful and otherwise snake types (including protected ones!). It is not an easy matter however to distinguish them when you meet them on the path. They do not tend to attack, but slither away in fear. A serum is available from most chemists, but it requires storage at refrigerator temperatures, and is not therefore suitable for rucksack travel. Elementary precautions that you can take to avoid, or at least minimise the possibility of being bitten, are to (literally) pull up your socks in an 'infected' area and tread heavily on the ground as you walk, to warn the snakes you are coming and frighten them away first. Opinions on how to treat snake bites vary enormously - from the latest and most widely-accepted technique of extensive bandaging and immobilisation of the affected limb, to attempted removal of the venom by aspiration with a small hand operated suction device.

The individual walk descriptions that follow include references to plants and animals likely to be seen along the various routes.

Walks & Walking

THERE IS AN extensive network of interconnecting numbered footpaths all through the Dolomites, within easy reach of the averagely fit walker.

For one-day walks, in addition to those described, longer itineraries can easily be adapted by doing the early stages then returning the same way, or following an alternate descent to the valley where available. Times for descents tend to be about ⅔ of the ascent time. As will be seen, it is feasible to link up a series of tracks to form a circular route, overnighting in the refuges and high-altitude bivouac huts. In this way you can immerse yourself in this unique atmosphere. In this guide, preference has been given to these ring routes or others crossing a mountain group and thus connecting different valleys, as they are more rewarding than a simple up and down walk. Where relevant, there is cross referencing to enable walkers to link up or vary itineraries.

Dolomite walking distances are usually measured in terms of metres up and down rather than kilometres to be covered. A day of 4-5 hours walking is probably quite sufficient for the average walker without rushing and allowing extra time to look around and having energy enough to go on the next day! Walking times given are for a person of average fitness, and are based on the Italian Alpine Club outlines - ie. in 1 hour you cover 4-5km on level ground, approx. 300m uphill, and 500m downhill. Rest stop times are not included.

Footpaths are well-marked with painted stripes of red and white on prominent rocks and trees at regular intervals. Their numbering and maintenance is the responsibility of the section of the Italian Alpine Club (CAI) of the nearest refuge or local valley authority.

While following a track you will often come across unmarked side-tracks which are usually detours around fallen trees or muddy patches, alternatives to a difficult passage, or short cuts which can be particularly useful in descent. Follow them at your own discretion, but ensure that they do return to the main track. Areas such as the Cadore are criss-crossed with old paths still used by hunters, woodcutters or mushroom collectors. CAI junctions are signposted.

SOME IMPORTANT DO'S AND DONT'S: read the walk description beforehand to get an idea of what to expect and select an itinerary that suits your state of fitness. Never start out on a walk when weather is uncertain, particularly if you plan on walking a high altitude route. Should there be an electrical storm with lightning, keep away from metallic fixtures, remove any metal objects (chains, necklaces, keys etc.) from your body and put them in a heap away from you, don't shelter under trees or overhanging rocks, and at worst curl up on the ground to avoid attracting the lightning. Advice on weather forecasts and track conditions can always be obtained from the nearest refuge. Furthermore, it is advisable to plan your walk so as to arrive at your destination in daylight and with time to spare, to allow for unforeseen circumstances. Don't set out alone on tracks that are particularly long or not well trodden or known.

Learn the international rescue signal. The call for help is **SIX** visual or audible signals per minute to be repeated after a minute's pause. The answer is **THREE** visual or audible signals per minute to be repeated after a minute's pause. Anyone hearing a call for help is obliged to contact the nearest refuge or group leader.

The following arm signals could be useful for communicating at a distance or with a helicopter:

- help needed
- land here
- YES (to helicopter pilot's questions)

- help not needed
- do not land here
- NO (to helicopter pilot's questions)

Do help preserve the natural environment taking all your rubbish back down to the valley where you brought it from. Respect all nature areas, as well as prescribed nature parks and reserves. Don't pick any wild flowers or light fires. Walkers, particularly in nature parks, should refrain from straying from public paths to avoid damaging vegetation and causing erosion. For toilet stops along the way, avoid areas near natural water courses, and if toilet paper (unbleached preferably) is unavoidable, bury it, so nothing unsightly is left. Leave only footprints.

Last but not least, do greet the walkers you meet on the path. The Italian people always do, and typical greetings are "buon giorno" (good morning) or the less formal "salve" (hello) between young people. You will usually get a "Grüss Gott" (sounding a bit like "scot") from German-speaking walkers. It's considered rather impolite to enter a refuge (or a valley shop for that matter) without saying "buon giorno" or "buona sera" (good evening), and "arrivederci" when you leave. "Ciao" is only to be used with people you know well.

Refuges & Bivouac Huts

THERE IS A conveniently situated series of mountain huts ("rifugi" in Italian) with mostly walker-only access. Strategically placed with the original scope of acting as a base for climbers, they nowadays provide walkers with basic overnight accommodation and warm meals at very reasonable prices. Supplies are brought up by aerial cableway, helicopter, mule, or, more rarely these days, on someone's back! They are run by the Italian Alpine Club (CAI), local councils, clubs and families, and are also essential contact points for rescue operations. They range tremendously in terms of facilities. You will come across some akin to modest guest-houses, offering the option of 2-bed rooms with freshly-laundered sheets, (at a higher price of course). Others will have a large attic level dormitory with bunk beds ("cuccette"). Blankets and pillows are always in abundant supply, but you may prefer to take your own sheet sleeping bag, without overloading your rucksack. Should you arrive in Italy by train, remember that the couchettes on Italian trains are usually supplied with disposable lightweight sheets, re-usable. In 1991 bunk bed accommodation cost 10,000 lire for members, and 17,000 lire for non-members, though there are some slight price variations due to refuges belonging to different categories in terms of access and facilities offered and some price rises are forecast.

Do remember to change a reasonable amount of foreign currency before you set out walking, as the refuge staff cannot be expected to accept anything but Italian lire in cash.

As far as bathrooms go, you will nearly always find an inside toilet. There is often cold running water outside the buildings, whereas the occasional refuge will have a sign saying "doccia calda" ie. hot shower, at a modest price. Water may be in short supply at the height of a dry summer, and there will often be a sign requesting users to go sparingly, for example "non sprecare acqua" (don't waste water). On the other hand, a sign may say "acqua non potabile" ie. water not fit for drinking. This is rarely due to the presence of harmful bacteria in high altitude locations, but more likely points to a mineral composition unsuitable for human consumption (local health authorities carry out regular analyses). Such water will not, of course, be improved by the addition of water purifying tablets. It is not necessarily dangerous to drink it in small doses, but will probably lead to upsets such as loose bowels and cramps, so be warned! Check with the refuge staff if in doubt. Safe bottled mineral water is always on sale.

As far as food goes, for both lunch and dinner, every refuge will provide substantial Italian style first courses of home-made vegetable soup ("minestrone") or a pasta dish, as well as meat, cheese or eggs for second course, with extra vegetable side dishes. Breakfast is essentially continental style, ie. coffee (small Italian black "espresso" or "cappuccino" with frothy milk) or tea with bread rolls, butter and jam - not particularly cheap or energising food for walking on. Eggs and bacon ("pancetta / speck con uova") can be ordered as a feasible alternative. Otherwise, carry your own supplies of biscuits, cheese and so on, and just order hot drinks.

A few remarks on behaviour in refuges: hiking boots are not worn inside, but taken off and left on appropriate shelving, usually just inside the front door. Some places provide rough slippers, otherwise take your own gym shoes or similar. The refuge's generator is turned off at 10pm, in line with Alpine Club regulations for 'lights out' and silence from 10pm to 6am.

Opening periods do vary, depending on position, weather conditions and accessibility, but unless specifically mentioned, refuges operate from mid-late June to the end of September. Refuges with extended opening periods are marked thus (*) when listed. If walking at the beginning or end of the season, it is essential you contact the refuge in question (relevant telephone numbers are listed at the end of each walk) or the nearest main Tourist Office to check on opening. Remember though that many refuges on motorable roads and mountain passes are open all year round, and though they often lack the cosy isolated refuge atmosphere being geared toward providing bar-restaurant service, they can be extremely handy.

Anyone is welcome to stay in a refuge, and discounted rates (for accommodation only) are available to members of other clubs with reciprocal agreements - Alpine Clubs from English-speaking countries are those of Canada, England and New Zealand. Regulations state however, that members should be of the same nationality as the club they belong to in order to qualify for the special rates.

It is advisable to phone to book your sleeping arrangements beforehand, particularly in high season, and at least the day before if you intend to overnight on a weekend in refuges on Alta Via routes. Remember as well to cancel such arrangements should your plans change, as bed-space is precious. It is a reflection of inconsiderate walkers in recent times that some refuges - in the Catinaccio and Brenta Group in particular - may not accept phone bookings on weekends or peak periods, though foreign walkers do not seem to be penalised. The glossary at the end of the book provides useful phrases in Italian for such conversations.

The Practical Information section at the end of every itinerary described comprises a list of all the refuges touched on, including telephone numbers and accommodation details. Unless mentioned otherwise, all refuges listed provide both meals and accommodation. Refuges which do not provide sleeping arrangements are not included. Relevant Tourist Offices have also been listed.

Bivouac huts ("bivacchi" in Italian) are unmanned, smaller permanent structures placed in even more inaccessible points often only reachable by climbers. They are however, open all the year round and usually contain bunks (though not always blankets) some food supplies (to be replaced as far as is possible or payment left), basic cooking and heating facilities (e.g. a wood stove + wood hopefully) and information on where to find water nearby. Several are referred to, where accessible.

All Alpine Club refuges should also have a separate 'winter shelter' ("ricovero invernale") adjoining the main building, but exclusively for use in an emergency during the winter period when the refuge is closed.

Maps

A COMPREHENSIVE ROAD map covering all the Dolomites is the 1:200,000 scale 'Trentino Alto Adige', put out by the Italian Touring Club (TCI). It shows some refuges, but not walking tracks. The widely available Italian TABACCO mountain maps "Carta Topografica per escursionisti" have been referred to here - the 1:50,000 scale version is clear and easy to follow, though some are out of date now. Those of the more recent 1:25,000 series, where available, give even more detail and have improved art work. However, the larger scale means that each one covers a more restricted area, so you may need more than one map for a given itinerary. Details of maps and numbers are given under each individual walk heading.

KOMPASS and GEOGRAFICA also put out good walking maps on various scales, using slightly different criteria for path difficulty and conditions, and are therefore not referred to for the sake of uniformity.

Many local tourist offices also distribute walking maps, with varying degrees of detail and reliability, often showing the mountains in relief - a great help for understanding the lay of the land and for putting the various peaks and groups into perspective.

The easiest tracks are clearly marked with an unbroken red line and

slightly more difficult ones with a broken red line − − − . A dotted line ....
indicates some difficulty such as a particularly steep stretch or a passage
along a ledge with a metallic cable fixed permanently in the rock face, but
it can also be a path with poor waymarking, such as those crossing
mobile scree slopes. Tracks indicated with ++++ are "ferrate", mountaineering passages with or without fixed ladders and various aids, but they
are usually very exposed and only for experienced climbers, equipped
with a helmet, length of rope and karabiner. They should not be
attempted by those who are inexperienced or afraid of heights. This
guide however, deals solely with walking routes. Should you wish to try
some climbing with help, contact a qualified Alpine Guide through the
nearest Tourist Office.

In this guide, names of mountains, places and refuges are in Italian
for the most part, though the practice on recent maps is to return to
original dialect names. Furthermore, the many valleys inhabited by a
majority of Ladin speakers for whom Italian today is a second (or third)
language, means place-naming is by no means uniform. Maps for the
South Tyrol (predominantly German-speaking) give names in both
Italian and German, as they are often distinctly different, not just a
translation. This holds true for names of refuges too. In general, place
naming as per the TABACCO 1:25,000 maps has been followed.

Equipment

Experienced walkers will have their own preference for gear, but for
those who are inexperienced the following is suggested:

Clothing

* Walking boots with ankle support, cushioning, and thick rubber soles
with good Vibram-type grip. Training Shoes are not sufficient for heavy
walking over rocky terrain because your feet will tire too quickly. As well
as traditional style boots with leather uppers, the market nowadays
features an extensive range of good quality synthetic models, which you
may find more flexible. If you don't have time to break your boots in before
arriving in the Dolomites, then protect the sore points as soon as they
appear with band aids. Should a blister appear, thread a small length of
sewing cotton through it using a sterilised needle, and leave the ends of
the thread protruding to ensure it drains gradually, and the skin is not
broken.
* Training shoes or light footwear to change into in the evening in the
refuge.

* Down jacket with hood (OR thick woollen sweater + windcheater + woollen hat)
* Woollen sweater   * Woollen shirt
* Warm long trousers (corduroy are suitable). Italian and German walkers prefer a down-to-the-knee type worn with long woollen socks. Jeans are unsuitable as they are too cold and inflexible.
* Lightweight rain gear eg. poncho, preferably to cover your rucksack as well
* Track suit for relaxing evenings in the refuge, doubling as pyjamas
* Woollen or cotton socks   * Shorts
* Sun hat   * T-shirts and underwear
* Swimming costume for those alpine lakes

Miscellaneous

* Spacious rucksack - possibly waterproof - if not, remember to pack everything in plastic bags
* Lightweight sleeping sheet (optional)
* Sleeping bag (for stays in bivouac huts)
* Ski stocks are good for getting down steep scree slopes or snow, and testing snow depth (telescopic if possible so they can be carried easily and don't get in the way when not needed)
* Swiss pocket knife   * Torch + batteries
* Camera   * Sunglasses
* Compass, altimeter (optional but handy)
* Binoculars   * Water bottle
* Personal toiletries
* Small repair kit - safety pins, needle, thread, buttons, string etc.

First Aid

* Water sterilising tablets   * Sun block cream
* Band aids   * Chapstick
* Personal first aid kit

Food

* Lunch supplies
* Tea bags, powdered milk, lemon etc (boiling water is available in most refuges if you want to economise)
* Fresh fruit, dried fruit   * Muesli bars, chocolate
* Tinned meat, tuna etc to save on evening meal expenses

Walks

WALK 1 (see sketch map A, page 24)

SORAPISS / TONDI DI FALORIA
via Passo Tre Croci - R. Vandelli (2h) - Forcella Ciadin -
R. Capanna Tondi (2h45mins-3h) - R. Faloria (30mins) -
R. Mandres (1h30mins) - Cortina (30mins).
TABACCO MAP NO.03 scale 1:25,000
TABACCO MAP NO.1 scale 1:50,000
(1 day possible but 2 days suggested)

Coach lines service the resort township of Cortina (1226m) all year round. However, walkers with their own transport can either leave their cars here or park at Passo Tre Croci itself, then do a round trip (see the alternative in Stage Four). Starting out from Cortina's lovely old bus (ex-railway) station, catch the Misurina bus (runs July to mid-September) or a taxi the winding 8kms east to Passo Tre Croci (1809m). The three crosses ("tre croci") are in memory of an Ampezzo mother and her two children who perished here in 1709. There was no road over the pass until the end of the 19th century.

Stage One: to R. Vandelli (2h)
Just down the road east, facing away from Cortina, after the large hotel on the right is the start of track n.215. There is a handy sign that says whether the refuge is "aperto" (open) or "chiuso" (closed). You set off towards the Marcoira peaks (south) on what was previously a military mule-track. It narrows a little and goes through a wood of larch and wild flowers, across a water course, then climbs gradually coasting the mountain. Don't neglect to turn around to appreciate the splendid vistas this track affords of the surrounding mountain groups. Ahead are the often snow-covered Marmarole and soon the waterfall known as "píss", that gave the Sorapíss Group its name, ("sora" means "over" in dialect). You're about two-thirds of the way when the path turns right and up, and is cut into the rock base of the Laudo. A series of wooden stairs and short

23

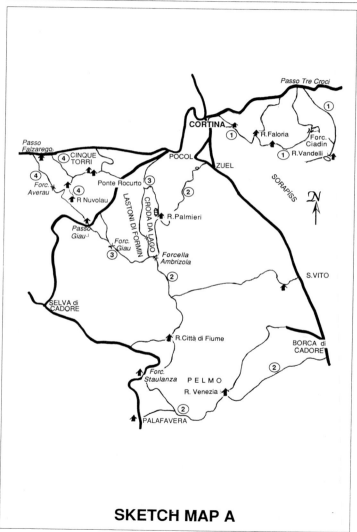

SKETCH MAP A

metallic ladders have been fitted as well as metallic fixtures on some slightly exposed rock-faces to make this section trouble-free. Continue a little longer on south through the woods of mountain pine (Pinus mugo) and you'll soon arrive at R. Vandelli (1928m) with its quaint blue and white shutters. First constructed by an Austrian Alpine Club in 1891, slightly uphill from the present site, it was swept away twice by avalanches and rock slides, and rebuilt in 1924 only to burn down in '59! Hopefully the present owners, the Venetian branch of the Italian Alpine Club, will have better luck. It is situated right in front of the northern wall of the Sorapíss giant with its two small frontal glaciers. On good days too you can look northeast straight onto the Cadini Group as well as Misurina and its glittering lake backed by the Tre Cime di Lavaredo.

Sorapíss, in fact, was said to have been a king in ancient times. He had a capricious daughter, Misurina who longed to possess a wondrous mirror belonging to a local witch. The witch agreed to give up her mirror for the girl's birthday, but in exchange required permanent shade for her house which was completely exposed to the sun. The king had no choice but to transform himself into the massive towering mountain which bears his name today. It took some time for Misurina to fully appreciate her father's sacrifice, and when, regretful at last, she was moved to tears, her copious crying formed the Misurina lake - right in front of her father Sorapíss.

If you stay the night here and have time to spare, stroll over west behind the refuge to the exquisite milky-blue lake. It's also worth continuing on track n.242 up the scree slope for an hour or so until you're at least on a level with the protruding end of the western glacier to your left. Early in the season, you'll probably hear ricocheting snow fall sounds and see powdery falls from the Dito di Dio ("God's Finger") point and rock walls high above the lake. Keep an eye out for chamois here too.

Stage Two: via Forcella Ciadin to R. Capanna Tondi (2h45mins-3h) and R. Faloria (30mins)
Even if you're walking in early July, expect to find snow on this stage. With destination R. Capanna Tondi and R. Faloria, start off by going back down track n.215. After about 100m in descent when the refuge is finally out of sight, is the turn-off n.216 left that climbs in zigzags up through the thinning vegetation to above the tree line. If you don't see at least a small herd of chamois here you should at least see their droppings. Vultures, on the other hand, now extinct, once inhabited these mountains. A legend tells of a maiden and artist who was under a spell and turned into

Tondi di Faloria looking towards Forcella Ciadin

a vulture. She used to spirit young boys away to her nest in the Marcoiras and keep them as songbirds in ornate silver cages.

There are good views looking back south at the refuge. After about an hour from the refuge there is a good rest spot on a crest. Following it is a brief descent along a rock ledge underneath, with the aid of a fixed cable. Late in the season when the snow's melted and waymarking is clearly visible, you can follow the path around to the left across the scree - it will lead straight to Forcella Ciadin (2378m) in about 30mins. Late-lying snow could, however, obscure waymarking and mini-avalanches could be provoked, so the longer variant to the right and across the middle of this silent amphitheatre is safer earlier on in the season. This latter takes you up to Forcella Marcoira (2306m) in 45mins.

Alternate descent to Passo Tre Croci
At this point it is possible to descend via n.213/216 to Passo Tre Croci in another 1h30mins. Very steep with loose rubble at first and possible snow, it hugs the rock and bearing left joins up with n.213 coming up through delightful woods from the pass.

From Forcella Marcoira go left and follow n.223 up the ridge to Forcella Ciadin (20mins). Fixed cables help you up the rock face and over the top. Snow permitting, follow this down left and across under the rocks as the path (now n.213) traverses the lower northern reaches of this offshoot of the Sorapíss. This last hour consists of gentle ups and downs and goes via Forcella Faloria (2309m), where n.215 turns up left to Punta Nera. Continuing straight ahead, brace yourself for a brusque return to 'civilisation' with the unexpected sight of the elevated metallic space-age construction ahead. It actually landed some years ago and is the arrival station of one of the many ski lifts on these slopes. R. Capanna Tondi (2310m) (no accommodation) with its glorious panorama, is just west over the hill. This area between the two refuges is rather scruffy and unattractive in summer as ski slopes and chair lifts have been given precedence. The cable-car linking the two refuges and still shown on maps is no longer in function though. However the view on a clear day does tend to make up for it - just about all the principal Dolomite groups are visible - apart from the Cristallo Group close by and due north across the valley. In the northeast are the Tre Cime di Lavaredo, ranging around to the Croda Rossa, Tofane, Sella Group and Marmolada in the distance, and the Pelmo and Civetta south. You can also see your next destination R. Faloria (2138m), another 30mins down the slope (northwest). The occasional chamois in small herds or lone males, can often be seen grazing here.

Stage Three: descent via R. Mandres (1h30mins) to Cortina (30mins)
An alternative to this 650-metre descent is the cable-car (if working) down to R. Mandres then Cortina. Otherwise take the steepish route down the western flank on path n.212. It is clearly signposted slightly uphill behind the refuge, and coasts along right for 10mins to where the large concrete shell of a building stands in an unnamed forcella. Some transmission relay equipment is visible just up to the left. The red and white waymarking points you down right for a tricky oblique crossing of a rough stretch of loose stone and scree flow at the top part of an open gully. Take special care on the mobile rubble. Where painted waymarking is missing, a few small stone marker heaps (cairns) have been placed. The path very soon enters low scrubby vegetation with springy dwarf mountain pines, and chamois are often sighted here. Zigzags are tight as you descend west and the wood starts to thicken. An unmarked path (left) leads across and down to Baita Fraina (1304m), soon visible with its horses and restaurant. Keep right on n.212. Further down, a short section

27

of the path has crumbled away crossing a dried-up water course, but nothing more than a little extra care is needed. The pine forest is tall and silent now and you soon reach a path junction (1h30mins from R. Faloria): by all means keep straight ahead to come out at the intermediate station of the cable-car and R. Mandres (1480m). Continue down west on foot to Cortina by way of the rough track that runs directly under the cable-car. From the path junction for a more pleasant route (some 30mins) turn right and follow n.210 straight down. Waymarking is clear and you come out at a car parking area and a large hotel-type building. Further down at the road intersection, either go straight ahead or, to come out directly at Cortina's bus station, turn right, keep on and take the downward left fork of the next road. Continue down by road - a few short cuts are possible without trespassing on the innumerable "proprietà privata". After a brief meadow crossing bringing you out on a footpath, turn right and cross the ex-railway bridge, past the Faloria Funivia station, and the bus station you started out from in Stage One is straight ahead.

Alternate descent: to Rio Gere (1h15mins) and Passo Tre Croci (15mins)
Should you wish to complete a round trip and return to Passo Tre Croci then from R. Faloria take path n.212 down west then north to Rio Gere. The 1h15min walk is an easy if not particularly interesting route, as it follows ski pistes for most of the way or a wide white gravel base vehicle track which is used for winter access for the ski and chair-lifts (closed to unauthorised traffic). It passes through a lovely tall pine forest and you get good views over the valley north to the Cristallo Group and the long fortress-like eastern extension of the Pomagagnon. You come out at the departure station of the chair-lift at Rio Gere and it's another 15mins (northeast) to Passo Tre Croci. After the large parking zone, take the side track up to the right. You join the main road for a very brief stretch before a path bears off right and straight over to the pass.

PRACTICAL INFORMATION:
R. FALORIA TEL:(0436)2737-868346. Private, accomm.
R. MANDRES TEL:(0436)866688. Private, limited accomm.
HOTEL TRE CROĊI TEL:(0436)867141.
R. A. VANDELLI TEL:(0435)39015 Alpine Club, Venice Section. Sleeps 60.
TOURIST OFFICE CORTINA TEL:(0436)3231/3232.

WALK 2 (see sketch map A, page 24)

CRODA DA LAGO / PELMO
via (Cortina) Zuel - R. Palmieri (3h) - Forcella Ambrizola (45mins) -
R. Città di Fiume (1h45mins) -
Forcella Staulanza (1h) - R. Venezia (2h45mins) -
Borca di Cadore (2h30mins).
TABACCO MAP NO.1 scale 1:50,000
TABACCO MAP NO.03 & 015 scale 1:25,000 (only partially)
(2-3 days suggested)

This straightforward walk is well within the capabilities of all walkers, and has several possibilities of overnight stops in refuges. As well as views over Cortina's wonderful valley there are sights ranging east to the line-up with the Sorapíss to the Antelao, then south to include the massive Pelmo giant. It is sometimes referred to as the "throne of the Gods", and is almost completely circled in this itinerary, giving the walker the chance to appreciate the various aspects such a mountain presents from different angles. The walk can easily be adapted into shorter sections with, for instance, the possibility of an interesting, relatively unused return track descending to San Vito di Cadore (see the end of Stage Two). Other accesses or exits are given where relevant, offering the walker a wide range of choices.

Stage One: to R. Palmieri (3h)
Starting out from the village of Zuel on the southern outskirts of Cortina (just before the Olympic Ski Jump coming from Cortina), follow the road to the right (west) down and across the Torrente Boite to the Camping ground. Further along turn left to Hotel Tiziano. Local bus n.1 from Cortina also runs this far. Now go left up the signposted (n.432) jeep track, asphalted at first. You pass turn-offs to Lago Pianoze (left) then Lago d'Aial (right), and after 20 mins there is a barrier for unauthorised vehicles. You wind upwards and southwards through the woods, steeply at times. Forestry work has led to recent track improvement but hopefully the hillside scars will heal quickly. There are several walkers-only short cuts but also many confusing logging vehicle side tracks, so always make sure you are actually back on the main track (red and white waymarking and n.432 are frequent). About halfway up, with cascades nearby, the track crosses the river (Rio Federa), then goes on to grazing meadows

and the summertime dairy farm Malga Federa (1816m) (tap with drinking water). This is a scenic and photographic vantage point over the Cortina area and, according to legend the site of an ancient castle, its subterranean cavern housing the marvellous Rajetta jewel, guarded of course by a terrible dragon. Many were the courageous cavaliers who sacrificed their young lives for their beloved in vain attempts to gain the jewel.

The magnificent Croda da Lago mountain is visible ahead (west), and some 200m more in easy ascent will see you at the delightful R. Palmieri (2046m) and Lago Federa. The hut was originally constructed pre World War 1, then since 1919 has belonged to the CAI, Cortina section, who named it in honour of a partisan from Bologna. Good spot for a rest, invigorating swim in the lake or overnight stay.

Stage Two: to Forcella Ambrizola (45mins) and Malga Prendera (30mins)
Take the wide white gravel track n.434 across the lake outlet and wind up the old mule-track to Forcella Ambrizola (2277m) in 45mins.

At this point you can link up with walk 3 to Passo Giau. Furthermore, on a clear day, stop for a rest and admire the magnificent views ranging southeast from the Pelmo (virtually straight ahead), then around west to take in the Civetta, the Pale di San Martino and possibly even the Marmolada and its glacier.

Thus refreshed, take the furthest left fork (south) n.436 coasting beneath the sheer and awesome Becco di Mezzod (2602m). Should you see a golden-clawed eagle circling overhead, it will be in search of its daughter, a princess (actually a white marmot) lost in these whereabouts on the flight home after the customary exchange of offspring with its allies, the legendary people of Fanes.

After walking amongst scattered boulders and fallen rock, and passing Forcella Col Duro (2293m), in another half hour or so, you'll come to abandoned Malga Prendera (2148m) and a junction.

Alternate descent to San Vito di Cadore (3h)
N.436 turns off left (east) to descend to the Alpe di Senes and San Vito (about 3h). A quiet path, it crosses some scree and waymarking is unclear on this first stretch so take care not to go off the track, particularly if cloud cover is low. There are several junctions with other paths, but the direction is essentially east, and down. Careful map-reading will be necessary as you cross meadows (waymarkings are easy to lose here) and sweet-smelling forests of tall pines and

larch. There are several *tabià* (shepherds' huts) still in use. The path continues along a wooded crest to Passo della Sentinella (1639m) and descends steeply. You come out at the upper limit for vehicle access slightly uphill of R. Senes (1214m) (meals only). It is well-placed for appreciating the majestic form of Monte Antelao which rises up on the other side of the valley (east). A side path (or road) leads straight down to the small lake and the township of San Vito di Cadore (1010m). Buses pass along the main road to Cortina or Calalzo (train connections) and southern destinations.

Stage Three: to R. Città di Fiume (1h15mins)
Continuing the route south towards the Pelmo and R. Città di Fiume, from Malga Prendera the path number becomes n.458. It traverses detritic ground and across a brief valley bottom to the next small forcella and crest, Col Reon, then it is n.467 the rest of the way. There are further changes in terrain as well as scenery as the track passes Forcella de la Puina at 2034m and bears southwest towards more grazing land, descending gradually along the grassy western flank of Col de la Punia. Mid to late summer walkers will be rewarded with fruitful bilberry patches here. With a brief curve around to the left (southeast) the track comes down to R. Città di Fiume at 1918m. Fiume, as well as meaning "river", is in fact the Italian name for Rijeke in Yugoslavia. The refuge is set (northeast) above Forcella Staulanza (referred to as Passo Staulanza on some maps), at the head of the pastoral and picturesque Val Fiorentina to the west and Val di Zoldo south. More importantly, however, it is right in front of the imposing northwestern wall of the Pelmo.

Cows from nearby dairy farms roam around quite freely, often eating rubbish and whatever they can get their teeth into, so watch out for your washing!

Access is also possible from Val Fiorentina in about 45mins on either n.467 (vehicle track) starting from a bend in the main road a few kms uproad ie. south of Selva (or 4km down from Forcella Staulanza), or an unnumbered track starting from about 2km south of Selva via R. Aquileia (camping ground nearby) and Malga Fiorentina. The summer bus service connecting the northwestern reaches of the valley (Selva di Cadore and Colle Santa Lucia) with Forno di Zoldo and other localities in Val Zoldana could be useful here.

Stage Four: to Forcella Staulanza (1h) then R. Venezia (2h45mins)
The path for this whole stage is n.472. Head down from the refuge south

31

to a small torrent. Continue down alongside the small watercourse then through a brief wooded flank to a pasture valley. You are now on the lower fringe of the frontal scree spread of the Pelmo. Here it opens out with Val d'Arcia and its permanent snow-field is higher up, beneath the 3168m summit. The path curves around southwest circling the lower reaches of the Pelmetto (little Pelmo), crosses a zone of low mountain pine then climbs to a crest over the road. Unless you wish to link up with the Civetta itinerary (see walk 27), it is not necessary to drop right down to Forcella Staulanza, as the track originating there soon joins n.472. This far will take you 1h or so.

Should it happen to be a quiet day without other walkers, deceive yourself not - others were here before you - in fact fossilised footprints have been found on the lower southwest corner of the Pelmetto and identified as those belonging to small dinosaurs living something like 200 million years ago! Signposting points up towards the area with the relevant rock slabs but they're not easy to find.

The itinerary from here on is still known by its old name of "Triol dei Cavài", from when it was used for taking horses up to grazing. Now, climbing very gradually the path coasts in a southerly direction through lightly wooded areas, and there are several clearings and pasture where you get superb panoramas back to the Pelmo itself as well as the Civetta's unmistakable mass southwest over the valley. Then, as well as a couple of path junctions including n.474 from Palafavera (with 2 private refuges and camping ground), there are often muddy tracts especially after rain, but it's easy going. Curving around east, the track crosses the Le Mandre pasture area and meets yet more paths coming up from Val Zoldana. Now the last stretch north much closer to the rock wall of the Pelmo, descends slightly to cross the Ru Torto stream and there's more rock and grass and a final ridge to be crossed to R. Venezia (1947m). A spacious and comfortable refuge (with lovely eiderdowns), in an enviable position, it looks across east to (right to left) the Antelao and Sorapíss, and west to the rugged Civetta. The Pelmo itself should turn an interesting shade of pink-orange in the morning, should you happen to secure a bedroom on that side to see it.

Stage Five: descent to Borca di Cadore (2h30mins)
While not strictly the shortest way back to the Boite valley to complete the round trip, this path scores well on scenery. Leave R. Venezia down the slope on its southern side then briefly up a clear track to a signboard which shows all the route numbers with relative destinations in the area.

Misurina lake and Sorapíss (Walk 1)

Becco di Mezzodì (seen from the path towards Passo Giau) (Walk 2)

Path junction near head of Val Travenanzes (Walk 5)
Refuge Locatelli with Sasso di Sesto (Walk 6)

Turn left (southeast now) along the gentian-studded grassy ridge on n.475 and head for the modest meteorological measuring station visible nearby. The path then curves left and along to an excellent Pelmo viewing spot. Now the descent begins down earth banks and across fields. Waymarking is in the form of small red and white painted metal plaques nailed to trees, and takes you gradually down past ruins of farm buildings and across an open cleared grazing area with marshy tracts crossed by small wooden trunk bridges. More wood where roe-deer may be seen, then it's out at an active summer dairy farm at 1440m - about halfway down. There are a couple of gurgling springs and drinking water.

Clear signposting indicates the rough driveable track right (n.477) to Vodo, and the continuation of n.475 which passes left between the buildings. You're shortly down at a junction and jeep-width track where you essentially go straight ahead, but waymarking is clear. At the next junction keep right (the left variant n.475 comes out at Villanova) on what is now n.476.

At a new log cabin the track becomes a walkers-only path again. Though the woods are thicker now they continue to allow for spectacular views of the dazzling white mountains straight ahead over the valley - namely Antelao, the triangular shaped one right, and the Sorapíss furthest left. Several more old abandoned dry stone buildings as well as new huts are passed before the path winds down a rocky section. It then moves closer to the rushing torrent which features a waterfall - a sign for "cascata" points off right further down. On the final stretch approaching the valley floor, the path crosses the torrent, which at the time of writing had recently had its banks reinforced but was still lacking in a bridge - so hope for a low flow level! Shortly down to the river and it's across the road bridge then straight up to the village of Borca di Cadore (909m) with shops, buses, and so on.

Alt. descent a) to San Vito di Cadore (2h15mins)
Slightly faster and with the possibility of coming right out in the township of San Vito di Cadore - only 8kms from the starting point at Zuel - the disadvantage of this route is its very steep gradient which makes it more tiring. After the meadows surrounding the refuge, path n.470 descends more steeply and mostly follows the course of a stream, with several worthwhile raspberry patches about the middle stretch. It is a jeep track most of the way through wild flowered fir and larch woods which become thicker with the descent and are inhabited by small dark squirrel-like dormice and roe deer. You descend to a

R. Venezia with the 'east shoulder' (spalla est) of the Pelmo

path junction and small bridge in Val Orsolina: n.468 left connects with Forcella Forada and R. Città di Fiume (about 2h30mins from here). Take the right branch (still n.470), which later becomes a wider vehicle road. There is soon a signposted junction with the left fork leading to San Vito di Cadore, and right (n.460) through Villanova continuing on surfaced road to Borca di Cadore on the opposite side of the valley. (Done in the opposite sense, ie. in ascent from the valley floor, this itinerary takes around 3h30mins).

b) to Zoppé di Cadore (1h)
The briefest descent from R. Venezia is about 1h on path n.471 south to Zoppé di Cadore (1461m), from where the occasional bus (Sundays excluded) will take you down to Forno di Zoldo in Val Zoldana - onward connections southeast to Longarone and the train line.

c) to Vodo di Cadore (3h15mins)
Otherwise, a somewhat longer and less-frequented route, coming out in the Boite valley at the township of Vodo di Cadore, goes via the small privately-run R. Talamini (1582m) at Forcella Ciandolada. It will take just over 2h as far as the refuge, then another 1h15mins (6km) down to Vodo di Cadore.

PRACTICAL INFORMATION
R. CITTA DI FIUME TEL:(0437)720268. Alpine Club, Fiume section. Sleeps 45.
R. MONTE PELMO (PALAFAVERA) TEL:(0437)789359. Private. Accomm.
R. PALAFAVERA TEL:(0437)789133. Private, accomm. + camping ground.
R. PALMIERI TEL:(0436)862085 Alpine Club, Cortina Section. Sleeps 35.
R. PASSO STAULANZA TEL:(0437)788566. Private, sleeps 35.
R. TALAMINI. Closed.
R. VENEZIA TEL:(0436)9684. Alpine Club, Venice section. Sleeps 74.
TOURIST OFFICE BORCA DI CADORE TEL:(0435)482015 seasonal.
TOURIST OFFICE CORTINA TEL:(0436)3231/3232.
TOURIST OFFICE SAN VITO DI CADORE TEL:(0436)9405.
TOURIST OFFICE VODO DI CADORE TEL:(0435)489009 seasonal.

> **LASTONI DI FORMIN / CRODA DA LAGO**
> via Pocol or Ponte Rocurto - R. Palmieri (1h45mins-2h) -
> Forcella Ambrizola (45mins) - Forcella Giau (1h15mins) -
> Ponte Rocurto (1h40mins).
> TABACCO MAP NO.03 scale 1:25,000
> TABACCO MAP NO.1 scale 1:50,000
> (1 day suggested)

Walkers equipped with a car can make this a feasible round trip by driving 5kms up the Passo Giau turn-off from Pocol, as far as Ponte Rocurto and starting the walk from there. As this road is not served by public transport, other walkers who wish to avoid the accompaniment of traffic, would be better off beginning the walk from just beneath the village of Pocol. Furthermore, several alternative links are referred to - from Forcella Ambrizola south to the Pelmo or towards Passo Giau connecting with Passo Falzarego, so as to extend the itinerary. Otherwise you can hitch-hike back down to Pocol, but it is not always a good bet as passing traffic will usually mean holiday makers, ie. full family cars.

Stage One: to R. Palmieri (1h45mins-2h)
Walkers can take the local Cortina bus the 6kms to Pocol (1530m), then set off left (southwest) on the Passo Giau turn-off. After a brief descent and 1.5kms (15mins or so) down the road take track n.434 leading off left. It crosses the Rio Costeana stream, said to be the haunt of the mythical Anguanas - water women who would counsel local people on their most pressing problems if sought out. The track narrows and climbs through the wood, eventually joining n.437 in about 45mins.

Drivers likewise should take the Passo Falzarego road west from Cortina and at Pocol, turn left towards Passo Giau. About 5kms up, at 1700m, just before the road crosses the Rio Costeana, ie. at Ponte Rocurto, are prominent signposts for path n.437. The right hand branch (west) connects with R. Cinque Torri, R. Scoiattoli, R. Nuvolau (2h30mins) - see walk 4 - and yours on the left (east), with R. Palmieri. As the road widens here road-side parking is no problem. Path n.437 takes you very briefly in descent to cross the Rio Costeana stream, before winding and climbing gradually through larch and mixed conifer woods. A few more rustic wooden bridges and 30mins later is a largish stream, crystal clear

(From lookout point on path to R. Palmieri),
view east over Cortina to Sorapíss

and with a gushing cascade if you're in luck - very inviting for a dip. Just above this, near a log cabin, is the path junction with n.434 from Pocol.

Side trip: at this point, the right hand branch (n.435) leads due south and in ascent across scree, rubble and irregular boulders behind the coloured western flanks of the Croda da Lago. In 2h you reach the magnificent Forcella Rossa del Formin (also known as the Forcella dei Lastoni di Formin) at 2462m. Then, if the weather and your energy warrant it, it's worthwhile going off the main track for the elementary ascent to the summit of the Lastoni di Formin at 2657m. Make your way west, up and across the enormous rock slabs. There is a series of large 'steps', and some care is needed to avoid the occasional deep crevice. Allow up to 1h for this last stretch in ascent. To rejoin the main itinerary, back on path n.435, continue southwest to the junction slightly below Forcella Ambrizola (see Stage Two), allowing about 40mins from Forcella Rossa del Formin.

With another 1h to go to R. Palmieri, keep straight ahead (south at first) on n.434 and it soon climbs quite steeply. After some 45mins more keep an eye out for a brief detour left (north) to a rocky outcrop and excellent panoramic lookout point over the Cortina valley with views ranging from Nuvolau right around to Sorapiss. Back on the track, you come out shortly onto a wide grassy ledge with yet more good views. A little further on, level ground now, is Lago Federa - non-polluted with no feeder streams supplying it, and very tempting for an envigorating swim. At the far end of the lake stands R. Palmieri (2046m), under the eastern wall of the gracious Croda da Lago mountain. Access is also possible from Zuel on the outskirts of Cortina - see walk 2.

According to legend it was on the sunny slopes facing the Croda da Lago that the first larch trees were said to have grown. They were created by dwarves from the many beautiful flowers sent to the wedding celebrations of the local queen who reigned over the wood and the water spirits. The fact that the larch, unlike other conifers, is not evergreen but deciduous, is explained by the fact that it was made from many different plants and flowers, thus incorporating their different qualities. Furthermore, the delicate light green covering it generates in spring is the veil the bride covered them with to stop them from drying out.

Stage Two: to Forcella Ambrizola (45mins) and Forcella Giau (1h15mins)
Cross the lake outlet stream next to the refuge on path n.434, and start the easy, gradual 45min climb to 2227m and Forcella Ambrizola (also referred to as Forcella da Lago). From here, on a clear day, you can see the unmistakable mass of the Pelmo before you (southwest), and, bearing right (west), the Civetta just behind it, then the Pale di San Martino and even a glimpse of the Marmolada's glacier further around.

Walkers at this point wishing to proceed to the Pelmo can pick up walk 2 at Stage Two.

There's a newly-signposted track n.466 which leads ultimately down to Pescul in Val Fiorentina (about 3h). It is named "Mesolitico" as a reminder to modern man that Val Fiorentina was a site of seasonal summer settlement for Mesolithic hunters (10,000-6,500 years ago). In 1987 the burial pit of a 25-year-old adult male, accompanied by 60 pieces of flint, bone and deer antler instruments was unearthed on the Mondeval di Sora plain just under the forcella. The skeleton and finds are on display in the library in Selva di Cadore, down in Val Fiorentina.

Follow n.466 down right briefly to a junction - keep right on n.436 - then at the next junction (with n.435 to Forcella dei Lastoni di Formin) keep left. The next stretch crosses a sort of gently rolling high grassy tableland; a good spot for picnics, crows, edelweiss and gentians. The path climbs gently up grassy slopes, (popular alpine winter cross-country skiing route) following the southern wall of the Lastoni di Formin. It crosses a stream with black plastic piping supplying water to the (signposted) Malga Mondeval di Sopra just below, and further on is Lago della Bastes (2281m) down to the left. In 1h15mins from Forcella Ambrizola you reach Forcella Giau (2360m). This time the pancrama includes the Cernera Group directly south (left), and the magnificent Sella Group in the distance west as well.

Stage Three: descent to Passo Giau road and Ponte Rocurto (1h40mins)
The road from Pecol to Passo Giau is now visible, and the track direction quite clear. The descent is not difficult, but the terrain is loose and subject to mini landslides particularly after heavy rain or snow melting, but you'll come out with no worse than thick mud caked on your boots. Shortly after the end of the stony part of the descent, a track left (n.436 same as yours) branches off to coast round, up and over to Passo Giau (2233m) - it is signed by 'Passo Giau' painted on a prominent rock. Unless you intend to come out at the Pass (no accommodation at R. Passo Giau) and perhaps continue over to Nuvolau or Cinque Torri linking with walk 4, keep on straight down in a northerly direction.

If walking late in the season, leave plenty of time for bilberry gathering in the low bushy area. The large morainic boulders around here are said to have been deposited by a primordial glacier. Be wary of short cuts as the area is deceptively swampy and you must cross the stream to reach the road (1h). This point, at about 2000m on the map, used to be a very active mining zone for galena (lead) and blende (zinc). It's another 40mins down the asphalted road to where you left your car, but in late summer you'll be rewarded with luscious raspberries all the way!

About halfway down, and clearer on the maps than in real life, is the "Muraglia di Giau" (Wall of Giau), a dry-stone wall built at the end of the 1700s to separate the Giau pastures belonging to the Cadorini people (nb. Selva di Cadore is down on the south side of Passo Giau) and the lower grazing lands of the Ampezzo people. Evidently this is but one of the examples of feuding between the two groups.

PRACTICAL INFORMATION
R. PALMIERI TEL:(0436)862085 Alpine Club, Cortina. Sleeps 35.
ALBERGO CIMA PASSO GIAU TEL:(0437)720130.
R. PASSO GIAU TEL:(0437)720118.
TOURIST OFFICE CORTINA TEL:(0436)3231/3232.

WALK 4 (see sketch map A, page24)

AVERAU / NUVOLAU / CINQUE TORRI
via Passo Falzarego - Forcella Averau (1h10mins) -
R. Averau (20mins) - R. Nuvolau (1h) - R. Scoiattoli (45mins) -
Passo Falzarego (1h30mins).
TABACCO MAP NO.03 scale 1:25,000
TABACCO MAP NO.1 scale 1:50,000
(1 day)

When you look west from the township of Cortina, or back from the road leading to Passo Tre Croci these are the low-set mountains that rise up from that faraway slope. They're not that impressive compared to the majestic Tofane group to their north, but are of special significance for rock-climbers, and offer some worthwhile walking, particularly suitable for starters.

This walk is easily done in one day (preferably with good visibility), and is within easy reach of Cortina and Val Badia (San Cassiano and beyond), making it well-trodden. However, an overnight stay at R. Nuvolau, a wooden hut perched right on top of its mountain, definitely beats the crowds and sleeping in town.

A brief note on Passo Falzarego: being one of the most strategically situated road passes in the Dolomites, it was a central arena for fierce Austrian-Italian battles during the First World War. All the surrounding mountains and valley areas still bear evidence of fortifications, artillery positions and strongholds. Unfortunately, both sides embarked on what seem today to be inordinate amounts of mine laying and explosive activity, and made a significant contribution to speeding up mountain erosion. Two obvious examples are clearly seen from the pass - look straight up (north) to the arrival station of the Lagazuoi cable-car - the enormous cone-shaped mound of detritus directly under the cables was caused by the Austrians, and a similar one further right is of Italian production.

Passo Falzarego is an ample pass, and is an excellent mountain viewing point: the view starts with the Piccolo Lagazuoi directly north, the Tofane northeast, Sorapíss east behind Cortina, Antelao further south, then the Croda da Lago, Cinque Torri, Nuvolau, Averau, and it even goes as far as the Marmolada southwest then Col di Lana. That strange pyramidal rock sticking up between the road south to the Cordevole valley (Andraz and Livinallongo) and the Valparola-Val Badia road is known as the Sasso di Stria. The name means Witch's Rock, and whereas now the area provides shelter for a thriving marmot colony, it was once the abode of a wicked witch in exile.

Disguised as a nurse she had worked for a count in the castle of Andraz in the valley below (the ruins are worth a visit by car). She was blindly jealous of her master's new young bride, and succeeded in tricking the count into believing her stories of infidelity - although he had already confined his wife to an isolated tower. The hapless victim, the Countess of Andraz was cast into a ravine, and sucessively 'saved' by a pair of ill-intentioned wizards. When the count realised his mistake, he had to overcome all sorts of evil magic spells to get her back. The story concludes in an enchanted wood, with a wizard in the shape of a bear chasing the count who is riding a horse (his wife under a spell). He is helped by magical phenomena including walnuts thrown to the ground creating large holes (known locally as "buse", actually glacially formed cirques), and a mirror turning into a black lake.

Yet another particularly interesting legend from here refers to the name of the pass itself - Falzarego, from "falso re" ie. false king, the one-time king of the legendary Fanes people. Despite the prosperity of his kingdom he desired more riches and decided to 'sell' (betray) his kingdom to this end. Needless to say, his pact with the enemy turned sour on him, and while waiting on the Lagazuoi mountain to hear the news, he was turned into rock. From the pass, look north to Lagazuoi and you might be able to make out the outline of his petrified face with his long beard and crown of rocky points, (see walk 10 for more legends about Fanes).

Stage One: via Forcella Averau (1h10mins) to R. Averau (20mins) and R. Nuvolau (1h)
Passo Falzarego (2105m) is served by summer buses from both Cortina to its east and Val Badia (San Cassiano) northwest. When you can drag yourself away from the fascinating range of typical alpine souvenirs and good selection of maps, look for path n.441 - signposted behind the large, blue shuttered bar/restaurant building (no accommodation). Heading off southeast, it climbs gently across grassy hillsides. These are important winter skiing slopes, but red clay is usually exposed and they tend to be muddy when wet. You pass to the right of the top point of the chair lift from Col Gallina, and bear right (southeast).

The terrain becomes rockier with the occasional grass and wild

41

flower patch, and you shortly cross an indented gully curving left. Waymarking is regular, with red and white painted stripes on rocks. If you look back down now, the Laghetto de Limides can be seen. There are a couple more debris-filled gullies and a brief clearing with "cima" (peak) painted on a rock - it points right (northwest) and up to Punta Gallina. The path here goes left and climbs very steeply but briefly up a rough gully, where you are required to clamber up an easy boulder (about 1m in height). Continuing on a level path you are soon joined by another n.441 - the junction is marked by a metallic signpost anchored down by rocks. Straight ahead and you come out shortly at Forcella Averau (2435m). The name is painted on a rock. Now turn left (southeast) and take the lower path. It is mostly level walking cutting across scree, skirting the crumbling southern wall of Monte Averau, and it's another 20mins to Forcella Nuvolau and privately-run R. Averau (2416m). This hospitable timber-lined refuge has some excellent photos of local animal life on display, a pleasant change from the more usual stuffed specimens. There's also a great terrace looking south taking in the Marmolada to the Pale di San Martino, Civetta and the Monti del Sole. Should you wish to cut out the next ascent, turn left (north) here to exclude R. Nuvolau - see next Stage.

Alt. descent to Passo Giau

At this point there is also an alternative southward making it possible to reach Passo Giau in just over one hour (no accommodation available). The path (n.452) coasts across the loose rubble beneath Nuvolau and, on the last part, just as the path bears south approaching the grassy slope leading down to Passo Giau, there are several groups of marmots. They appear to be quite used to humans, and let you take their photograph almost submissively.

Otherwise, proceed on n.439, the popular and well-marked way southeast straight up the strange rock crest of Monte Nuvolau. It's only another 150m or so up to the refuge. The first R. Nuvolau (2575m) dated back to the late 1800's, and was the property of the Alpine Club of Cortina, which was part of Austria in those days. There was also a special track for horses to enable the well-off to visit the area on horseback, as was the fashion. The present hut is more recent, as the first one had been destroyed by Austrian artillery. The atmosphere is unique, and the panorama, on those days when the refuge doesn't keep true to its name ("nuvola" = cloud), ranges from the graceful shape of nearby Monte

Averau, the Tofane massif and the Cristallo east over Cortina and as far west as the Ortles Group and southwest to the Marmolada. Sunrises and sunsets are incomparable. Even the usual water shortage, meaning you probably can't have a wash, doesn't detract from the delights. The refuge also scores well on hospitality and quality of the catering.

Stage Two: descent to R. Scoiattoli (45mins) and Passo Falzarego (1h30mins)

Return the way you came on the preceding stage (n.439), as far as the forcella where R. Averau stands, then follow signposting in a northern direction to R. Scoiattoli (2225m). This private refuge is named after the famous Cortina-based rock-climbing team, the "Squirrels". There is a chair lift link with the main road a couple of kms downhill from Passo Falzarego (R. Bai de Dones). An alternative descent east to Ponte Rocurto (1h) enables you to connect with walk 3 to R. Palmieri.

Leave plenty of time to explore around the squarish blocks of the Cinque (5) Torri - the lowest one is the 'English Tower'. Despite their continual erosion they are still of great importance for rock climbing practice, and you'll undoubtedly be treated to demonstrations. The other refuge in this area, R. Cinque Torri stands on a white dirt track just 15mins below at 2137m.

A return on foot to Passo Falzarego is possible via the jeep track that branches off north from R. Cinque Torri, later becoming a walking path to the lower station of the chair lift. From there take path n.442, virtually parallel to the main road, as far as another path junction at the road, in a swampy area where the path crosses a stream.

Otherwise, walk back just past R. Scoiattoli to the path junction where n.440 branches off northwest (2280m) on a crest. You cross the rocky mountain side amongst evidence of wartime trenches and enormous boulders, on a stone track which soon narrows. It winds up and down a little and goes through thinnish wood with mixed conifers and dwarf pines on the final stretch. Wild flowers include dwarf rhododendrons called alpenrose, white and yellow pasqueflowers, heather and globe flowers. It should take you around an hour to get down to the stream and road approx. 2.5 kms downhill from the pass. Keep on the left hand side of the road on an unnumbered path which crosses the meadows and cuts the road bends. About 30mins more, via R. Col Gallina (the only available accommodation in the vicinity of Passo Falzarego) and you're back over at the pass, where you started from. A suitable follow-up is walk 5 via R. Lagazuoi to the Tofane and Val Travenanzes.

PRACTICAL INFORMATION

R. AVERAU TEL:(0436)4660. Private, sleeps 21.
R. CINQUE TORRI TEL:(0436)2902. Private, sleeps 20.
R. COL GALLINA TEL:(0436)2939. Private, sleeps 15.
R. NUVOLAU TEL:(0436)867938. Alpine Club, Cortina branch.
Sleeps 26.
R. SCOIATTOLI TEL:(0436)867939. Private, sleeps 20.
TOURIST OFFICE CORTINA TEL:(0436)3231/3232.

* * *

WALK 5 (see sketch map C, page 74)

LAGAZUOI / TOFANE / VAL TRAVENANZES
via Passo Falzarego - R. Lagazuoi (5mins-2h) -
Forcella Travenanzes (30mins) -
ex. Malga Travenanzes (1h) - [alt. to R. Giussani (2h30mins) -
R. Dibona (1h) - Passo Falzarego (2h-2h30mins) or
Pocol (1h30mins)] - Ponte Outo (Valle di Fanes) (2h) -
Fiames (1h) (Cortina).
TABACCO MAP N.03 scale 1:25,000
TABACCO MAP N.1 scale 1:50,000
(2 days suggested)

Covering terrain that saw drawn-out fighting during WW1, this walk can feasibly be made into a round trip by either following directions for the ascent to R. Giussani then back to Passo Falzarego, or more simply by branching off south at Forcella Travenanzes or Col dei Bos and returning to the pass. If you have the time and energy though, Val Travenanzes is well worth walking down. See walk 4 for information about Passo Falzarego.

Stage One: via Passo Falzarego to R. Lagazuoi (5mins-2h)
Having arrived in the fashionable all-year round resort centre of Cortina by car, coach or private plane, proceed the 13kms west to Passo Falzarego at 2105m (bus service runs July - early September only). The last cable-car up to R. Lagazuoi is usually just before 5pm. It is, of course possible to walk up the 650m, but the terrain tends to be a little

monotonous, with innumerable steep zigags on fine scree. The advantage in walking lies in the fact that you can acclimatise more gradually, as the altitude of the refuge (2752m) might take some getting used to, perhaps causing you difficulty sleeping.

On foot then, from Passo Falzarego. Facing the cable-car station, to its right is path n.402 which heads up northeast towards Forcella Travenanzes at 2507m. Look up left to the ledge under the Piccolo Lagazuoi known as the Cengia Martini - it was held by the Italians for two years during WW1 while the peak was under Austrian control. You soon pass the turn-off to the wartime tunnel (see side trip later in this stage). As the valley opens out there is a cut up left instead of going all the way to Forcella Travenanzes. Otherwise, from the forcella, (a good 1h so far) and the signposted path junction, the path is n.401 and it turns decisively left (west). Allow around another 30mins up to Forcella Lagazuoi, left again and a further 30mins via the cable-car top station and to the refuge itself, visible for some time now. Then settle down to a peaceful evening with the flocks of crows, and hopefully with good visibility for the extensive panoramas - there are handy name plates on the refuge's terrace railing pointing to the important mountains.

Note that the water at R. Lagazuoi is classified not suitable for drinking purposes.

Alternate side trip to visit the WW1 mountainside tunnel
Lower down, at the cable-car arrival station, is the start (marked with a black "G") of the descent path which returns to Passo Falzarego via the wartime tunnel. In an attempt to reach the summit and the Austrian positions, the Italians undertook the construction of a tunnel 1100m long connecting with the Cengia Martini. It has since been completely restored and equipped with a cable hand rail running its length. It can make for a fascinating visit, but it is very steep with exposed ledges, and is recommended in descent, for walkers who preferably have some "via ferrata" experience. Torches for illumination are available from R. Lagazuoi. Allow about 1h30mins all the way down to the pass.

Stage Two: descent to Forcella Travenanzes (30mins) and ex Malga Travenanzes (1h)
Path n.401 zigzags down scree or late-lying snow to a path junction directly below R. Lagazuoi - yellow and black signposting points winter skiers left for the Armentarola (Val Badia) or right to Falzarego. Go right,

and you'll be above the rugged Alpe di Lagazuoi (down to your left), and war fortifications up right. The long mountain running directly ahead (north) of you now is Monte Lagazuoi Grande. You soon reach another path junction - Forcella Lagazuoi at 2573m. Take the middle level path, (not the one right in descent to Falzarego), which will bring you coasting around under hefty anti-avalanche and rock slide barricades and in slight descent to the signposting at Forcella Travenanzes (2507m) (about 30mins this far).

You should start seeing chamois about here, the sure-footed wild mountain antelopes. In fact, on virtually the whole of this stage you can indulge in chamois spotting, as the area is chock-a-block with herds of them, despite the presence of large numbers of people in both summer and winter.

Don't be tempted by path n.20b to Biv. della Chiesa, but take n.401, virtually straight ahead (east) now, across red earth (mud when wet) and a grassy clearing amid boulders and, in another 20mins you'll arrive at a signposted path junction - right for Forcella Bos overlooking the Cortina-Passo Falzarego road, and yours left for Fiames (Cortina). Straight ahead of you (east) now is the majestic Tofane di Rozes (3225m), and the Castelletto, the lower front protruding part, better viewed from points later on down the valley. Turn left on n.401 and thus begins the gradual descent of Val Travenanzes. There are interesting geological aspects on this west side: you can clearly see clay and dark red calcareous marly soil layers. This is a very soft and fragile base for the overlying dolomitic rock mass which often slides down it. Soil colours range through red, green, grey and white. Erosion is continuous and there are many crumbled tracts of path, particularly where a watercourse is crossed. Modelling by ancient glaciers gave the valley its U-profile.

The area seems barren, littered with scattered boulders, but there are tiny pink and white alpine rock flowers. Another 20mins or so down from the last forcella in light wood with twittering birds and splashes of colour from the dwarf rhododendron or alpenrose, and you will reach the stone foundations of a previous refuge. Shortly below this is a signposted path junction - right for the "via ferrata" Scala del Menighel. Keep on the left hand side of the valley. Continuing down there are several more streams (or dry beds), the second of which is crossed by a collapsed series of old timber supports. Path n.17 comes down left from Monte Cavallo, and you reach the grass and secondary growth clearing with the ex malga Travenanzes (1965m). There's quite a comical marmot family here. After they utter their shrill warning whistle which will alert you

R. Lagazuoi

to their presence, they use the "freeze not be seen" technique, so look out for rigid animals perched on rocks trying to seem unobtrusive. The small abandoned shepherd's hut has been recently lined with wood panelling and equipped as a rough bivouac hut (for emergency use only), with a stove and a couple of metal mattress bases.

Alternative: ascent to R. Giussani (2h30mins), descent to R. Dibona (1h) then to Passo Falzarego (2h-2h30mins) or Pocol (1h30mins)
This variant takes you right (southeast) up between the magnificent Tofana di Rozes and the Tofana di Mezzo to a silent forcella where R. Giussani stands. It is a very steep and tiring 600m ascent (much worse in descent though!) but highly recommended.

Just back (slightly uphill) from the hut you'll need to look for n.403 which crosses the stream then joins up with n.404 (from Forcella Col dei Bos). It starts climbing steeply across grass and scrub to the left of the waterfall, then sharp right to climb along a rather exposed natural ledge - take care your rucksack doesn't catch on the rock and put you off balance. You come out at the top of the waterfall where a path from the Scala del Menighel (a pre-war ladder with 270 metal rungs) joins up. You are now at the bottom of a wondrous lunar-like gully to be ascended in zigzags up its left hand side. It is the Masarè gully, and is filled with scree and rubble, and closed at its head by the rock barriers of the Tofana di Mezzo and Punta Giovannina. Your destination is Forcella di Fontananegra (2580m) where the modern R. Giussani shelters (2h30mins this far). Just downhill on the other side amongst scree are the ruins of an older refuge, R. Cantore, named after a courageous WW1 General of the Italian Alpine Forces.

On n.403 leave this zone in descent (southeast) passing between pointed rock needles. The narrow gully opens up a little then you drop down across a good scree slope in tight zigzags, or running short cuts if you prefer. Should you wish to continue straight down to the road, then bypass R. Dibona and on path n.442 go down into the cool wood where there are gentians and bilberry shrubs. Keep parallel to the gushing stream all the way to the road at 1730m (about another 1h). This is some 6kms downhill from Passo Falzarego, and 5kms uphill from Pocol, so the choice is yours.

A preferable alternative for returning to Passo Falzarego on foot, would be to take path n.412 - it branches off just before R. Dibona and coasts along beneath the Tofana di Rozes joining the military mule-track under Forcella Col dei Bos (about 1h30mins this far). You can then re-join the road or with a slight ascent continue under Col dei Bos to come out right at the pass in another hour or so. Otherwise follow signposting to R. Dibona (2083m) then take the more gentle descent alternative (n.403) which will bring you out at Pocol, with a few road corner cuts on the final stretch.

Stage Three: descent Val Travenanzes to Ponte Outo (2h) then Fiames (1h) (Cortina)

From ex Malga Travenanzes, continue north straight down the valley on n.401. It crosses the white gravel bed and stream and there are several points subsequently when the path follows the same course as the torrent and waymarking may have washed away. Look out for cairns, (one has a good timber upright), heaped up by passing walkers to indicate the way, and add a stone yourself. Check your map if in doubt about the direction, but after this first crossing, the path stays on the right side for a longish stretch, dipping in and out of the scrub and mountain pines.

The valley is a perfect habitat for the frail yellow Rhaetian poppies which pop up between the white scree and rubble, and there are the

Descending Val Giralba, Marmarole in background (Walk 8)
Alpe Fanes Grande area with M. Cavallo (Walk 12)

occasional larch trees courageously dotted on the lower scree slopes, daring the rock and landslides. There is a continual series of cascades (early in the season or after heavy rain) and the Tofana flank on the right (east) is particularly impressive, as is Monte Cavallo up left (west).

As you descend further the rocky walls manifest strange weathering in the form of holes in the cliff sides. Lower down, as the sides become steeper and closer, the valley takes on a canyon form. There is another crossing left, then later, approximately under the fine orange scree and earth flow of the *Grava* (landslide), you cross right once more on a bridge of tree trunks wired together (about 1 h to here). The valley and path curve sharp right (east) here and the descent steepens somewhat. At several points where a watercourse is crossed the path has crumbled right away and brief detours are necessary. Take care on the friable terrain. The torrent is now crashing away wildly far down to your left, but there is a lovely waterfall that comes down from your right onto the rock slabs you cross.

If you're lucky on this lower part in amongst low scrub with mountain pines, you may see a rare specimen of the protected Lady's-slipper orchid, with its large yellow 'slipper' and dark brown petals. The mountain ahead now, to the north, is the Croda Rossa.

Down into thicker woods the path is lined with pine needles, soothing for tired rock-battered feet. A signed path turns up right to Passo Posporcora, but you keep left and descend steeply to a wooden bridge (Ponte dei Cadoris) high over the torrent. The track is now jeep width, and essentially level. This area is excellent for the delicate early-purple orchids and further down are more alpenrose and the (poisonous) dark purple monk's-hood that grows profusely in shady wooded areas here, along with the delicate white wood anemones.

In 20mins after passing the turn-offs left to Fanes (see walk 10 for a feasible link), you come out at the Ponte Outo bridge over a dramatic chasm. It's a good hour now on track n.10/401 to Fiames, (watch out for speeding mountain bikes). Don't be surprised on the way down if you see pine trees sprouting light blue flowers - it's the alpine clematis which twines and climbs all through the trees. When you come out on the valley floor and turn south towards Cortina, the road is barred to traffic. At the parking area, keep right on the dirt track by the river. After 10mins or so

At the head of Val Setus with Puez-Odle group in the background (Walk 15)

49

bear left through the forest and you'll come out at Fiames and the hotel and bus stop - both the Cortina urban service and the line from Dobbiaco pass by. Should you have to walk, allow another hour - across the road from the hotel is a CAI path sign for the "Via Ferrata" to Punta Fiammes - shortly up into the wood, turn right and follow the ex-railway track which will bring you out directly at Cortina's bus terminus (see walk 9 for information on the ex-railway line).

PRACTICAL INFORMATION

R. COL GALLINA (PASSO FALZAREGO) TEL:(0436)2939. Private, sleeps 15.
R. DI BONA TEL:(0436)860294. Private. Accomm. (*)
R. GIUSSANI TEL:(0436)5740. Alpine Club, Cortina branch. Sleeps 70.
R. LAGAZUOI TEL:(0436)867303. Private, sleeps 70. (*)
TOURIST OFFICE CORTINA TEL:(0436)3231/3232.

(*) possible extended opening.

✳   ✳   ✳

WALK 6 (see sketch map B, page 51)

TRE CIME DI LAVAREDO
via Misurina - R. Auronzo (2h) - R. Lavaredo (20mins) -
R. Pian di Cengia (1h30mins) - R. Locatelli (1h) -
Forcella Col di Mezzo - R. Auronzo (2h15mins).
TABACCO MAP NO.010 scale 1:25,000
TABACCO MAP NO.1 scale 1:50,000
(1 day suggested)

Some brief comments pertinent to all walks in the area of the Tre Cime di Lavaredo (Drei Zinnen) and the Sesto Nature Park. First of all, try to avoid coming here at the height of summer, ie. mid-July - late August, as it is usually swarming with groups of all shapes and sizes. The 'hot' points tend to be R. Auronzo, the entry point from Misurina in the southwest, and Val Fiscalina (Fischleintal) which affords access from Val Pusteria (Pustertal) to the northeast. Even at non-peak times it's unusual to be

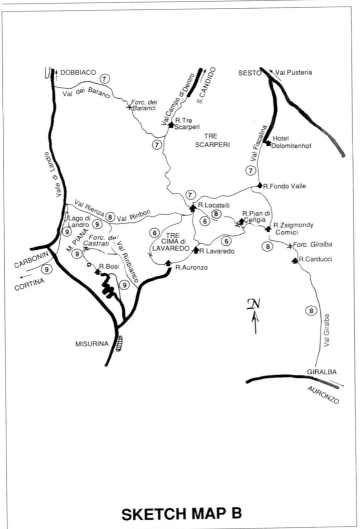

SKETCH MAP B

able to contemplate the magnificence of the central part of this area in absolute solitude. Remember though that the majority of visitors arrive mid-morning and have gone by evening, so plan on overnighting in a refuge. Despite this, it is undoubtedly worth a visit, and is justifiably considered to be one of the most awe-inspiring places in the Dolomites, with guaranteed dramatic alpine scenery.

Secondly, due to its strategic position, it was another of the WW1 hot spots. The front in fact, ran right through the area, so, as well as the soldier-made mule-tracks you'll be walking on, there are ruined military fortifications, huts, tunnels dug out of the mountain side, as well as 'rubbish' in the shape of rusty barbed wire, tin cans and even boot soles lying around. Most of the refuges were used as ammunition depots and barracks so were all virtually destroyed or damaged in some way, and rebuilt of course in a great hurry and with great enthusiasm immediately after the hostilities ceased.

Don't expect to see much in the way of animals, but reports of golden eagle sightings are frequent, and there is an enormous range of small song birds such as warblers. Plenty of interesting butterflies too, and you won't be disappointed by the variety of wild flowers.

Stage One: to R. Auronzo (2h)
From July to mid-September coach services connect Cortina, Auronzo and Dobbiaco (Toblach) with Misurina (1745m) and its picturesque tarn. From there on, by bus, car or on foot, you'll need the road northeast towards the Tre Cime di Lavaredo. A few kms up is Lago d'Antorno (1866m) with its private refuge and 200m further on, the start of path n.101 to R. Auronzo which takes around 2h all the way up, starting from Misurina. Otherwise, drive on a little further to the toll booth and either pay for the remaining 7.5kms, or take the track that branches off right here and joins n.101. You can also start out from Misurina itself, but, quite frankly, it is worth saving the time and energy and going all the way to R. Auronzo by bus or car and spending more time walking once you're up there.

Stage Two: to R. Lavaredo (20mins) and R. Pian di Cengia (1h30mins)
Don't waste time at R. Auronzo (more an unfriendly hotel than an alpine refuge). The spectacular Cadini Group directly south, with its rock spires and strangely formed needle-points can be admired along the way. Start straight out east, around the south side of the Tre Cime di Lavaredo, along the wide jeep track, n.101/104. In 20mins you'll reach R. Lavaredo

R. Lavaredo and Croda Passaporto

(2344m) under the Croda Passaporto (Passportenkofel) (north). Continue on 10mins up the main track with the masses to a ruined building and turn right on n.104. (N.101 continues left up to Forcella Lavaredo (Paternsattel) at 2457m with its excellent panorama). There will definitely be fewer tourists from now on. You drop down southeast past a small lake. Don't be tempted by short cuts to the left, but keep to the wide stone wartime mule-track which winds down and around left some 200m into a pasture zone. Path n.107 from the Valle di Cengia joins up, and you climb into a silent unworldly amphitheatre of debris with Lago di Cengia (2324m) and a monument.

North now, (n.107 branches off right to Biv. de Toni) cutting across a barren rocky slope, then another series of steep zigzags leads to a stony amphitheatre, on the edge of which stand extensive WW1 fortifications (2414m). 15mins up ahead, northwest, is the Forcella Pian di Cengia (Büllelejoch) (2522m) - junction with n.101 from R. Locatelli. Turn right along the crest (n.101 now) and enjoy the marvellous views all around - particularly fascinating is the small glacier visible virtually due east on Monte Popera. There is a brief stretch along a wide rock ledge with wooden planks, then around left to where the tiny cosy R. Pian di

53

Cengia (Büllelejochhütte) nestles at 2528m. (1h50mins this far).

At this point, a connection with walk 8 is feasible (see Stage Two).

Stage Three: R. Locatelli (1h)
Return to the saddle of Forcella Pian di Cengia and the exceptional view of the Tre Scarperi (Dreischuster) group northwestish, and take path n.101. It descends (northwest) a steep rocky valley for the first stretch, then, almost horizontally cuts across the vast scree flows. Beneath is an almost unreal bluish alpine lake, fed by snow melt, and providing a pleasant dramatic contrast with its grey rock surrounds. There's a brief climb, and more small lakes on the last leg to R. Locatelli (Drei-Zinnen-Hütte) at 2405m. Among other sights - which could include the Cristallo Group southwest, the Croda Rossa west and the distant ranges in Austria - this is a good viewing point for the Tre Cime di Lavaredo, particularly at sunrise or sunset. The characteristic division between the peaks is due to erosion along the fracture lines.

Alternatives at this point are;

a) descent east to R. Fondo Valle (Talschlusshütte) (1548m) in Val Fiscalina - allow 1h30mins-2h and see Walk 7, Stage One in the opposite direction;

b) descent northwest to Val Campo di Dentro (Innerfeldtal) and R. Tre Scarperi (Dreischusterhütte) - see Walk 7, Stage Two;

c) descent west to the Valle di Landro (Höhlensteintal) - allow 2h45mins and see walk 8, Stage One in reverse.

Stage Four: to Forcella Col di Mezzo and R. Auronzo (2h15mins)
There is a faster return route on n.101 that cuts across the scree beneath Monte Paterno (Paternkofel) then goes via Forcella Lavaredo, R. Lavaredo and R. Auronzo taking about 1h. However the long way back to R. Auronzo on n.105 is usually less crowded. The path descends briefly under a rocky outcrop, and where path n.101 goes straight ahead, you keep descending in a southwesterly direction in gradual wide curves and bear left into a valley in a diagonal descent. Shortly after a small stream crossing, track n.102 to the Valle di Landro forks off right (see walk 8). Your path (still n.105) climbs up and across barren rock and there is the possibility of late-lying snow. Waymarking may be difficult to follow as you skirt around the impressive West Peak and Sasso di Landro (Zinnenkopf) among toppled rock masses and detritus. There's a small

stone shepherds' hut (equipped as a bivouac but with a rather over-riding animal smell!) then another scree traverse, but on a good path. This gives you yet another marvellous perspective of the Tre Cime di Lavaredo, before you arrive at the Forcella Col di Mezzo (2315m) virtually on the same level. Around another curve southeast with visions of Sorapíss, Antelao, Marmarole and the Cadini group, and you're soon back at R. Auronzo and 'civilisation' (2h15mins).

PRACTICAL INFORMATION

R. AURONZO TEL:(0435)39002 Alpine Club, Auronzo Section. Sleeps 125.
R. LAGO D'ANTORNO TEL:(0436)39148. Private, accomm.
R. LAVAREDO TEL:(0336)494617. Private, sleeps 30.
R. PIAN DI CENGIA TEL:(0337)451517 or c/o (0474)710258. Private, sleeps 11.
R. A. LOCATELLI ALLE TRE CIME TEL:(0474)972002. Alpine Club, Padua Section. Sleeps 180.
TOURIST OFFICE AURONZO TEL:(0435)9359.
TOURIST OFFICE CORTINA TEL:(0436)3231/3232.
TOURIST OFFICE MISURINA TEL:(0435)39016 (seasonal).
TOURIST OFFICE SESTO (SEXTEN) TEL:(0474)710310.

✳   ✳   ✳

WALK 7 (see sketch map B, page 51)

TRE SCARPERI / BARANCI GROUP
via Sesto - Hotel Dolomitenhof, Val Fiscalina (10-45mins) -
R. Fondo Valle (20mins) - R. Locatelli (2h30mins) -
R. Tre Scarperi (2h30mins) - [alt. to San Candido or Sesto 1h-
1h45mins] - Forcella dei Baranci (2h30mins) -
Valle di Landro (2h30mins) - Lago di Dobbiaco (20mins).
TABACCO MAP NO.010 scale 1:25,000
TABACCO MAP NO.1 scale 1:50,000
(2-3 days suggested).

German-speaking Val Pusteria (Pustertal), a northwesterly extension of Italy, was part of Austria until the aftermath of WW1 moved the borders. Its peaceful townships are well worth a visit for their beautiful churches, and Sesto (Sexten) also has a cemetery where many famous local guides are buried.

If from the township of Sesto you continue further on towards Moso (Moos) and look southeast along Val Fiscalina (Fischleintal), the so-called Sesto sun dial comes into view - some of the mountain peaks were named according to their position as on a clock face - starting with Cima Dieci (ten) (otherwise known as the Croda Rossa di Sesto or Sextener Rotwand), then Cima Undici (eleven) (Elfer), Cima Dodici (twelve) (otherwise known as Croda dei Toni or Zwolferkofel) and Cima Una (one) (Einser).

This itinerary begins by following the popular Val Fiscalina then ascends to the very heart of the Sesto Nature Park (see the introductory comments to walk 6). After descending into Val Campo di Dentro (where a shorter exit route is feasible), it climbs once again into the less-frequented and wild Val dei Baranci and finally descends in a westerly direction coming out near the peaceful waters and restful atmosphere of the lake just south of Dobbiaco.

Val Pusteria can be reached by bus from virtually all directions, and there is also a west-east train line between Fortezza (just north of Bressanone) and into Austria (Lienz and beyond).

Stage One: via Hotel Dolomitenhof, Val Fiscalina (10-45mins) and R. Fondo Valle (20mins) to R. Locatelli (2h30mins)
A local bus service connects San Candido (Innichen) with Sesto, Moso then enters Val Fiscalina, going as far as the Hotel Dolomitenhof (1454m). This far on foot from Sesto will take around 45mins on path n.1a (Alta Via 5 waymarking). Unauthorised vehicle access ends at this point, and the Sesto Nature Park begins. There is a large car park (payment) and a small kiosk with a helpful notice board listing each refuge in the area and whether it is *(aperto)* open or *(chiuso)* closed . From here, there are good views west up into the immense Tre Scarperi Group (Dreischuster), which has the highest peak in the park - 3152m.

Path n.102/103 (south) follows the wide rough road up the valley floor, and as the bus no longer continues its run up the valley, there is actually a rattling quaint cart drawn by draught horses - a very ecological alternative. It could save you the bother of a very pleasant and mere 20min stroll through woods and flowered clearings (an unusual profusion of the tiny ice blue speedwell flowers). R. Fondo Valle (Talschlusshütte) (1548m) is at the valley head. From there, following clear signposting fork right and up Val Sassovecchio (Altensteintal). In 15mins you reach a path

Tre Cime di Lavaredo, north aspect

junction and painted pictorial map, (n.103 off left to R. Zsigmondy-Comici in 1h30mins - possible link up with walk 8). Keep straight on (n.102) under a seemingly solid rock wall above you on the northern side of the valley. As it turns out, the first section is virtually a separate point - Cima Una in fact, flanked by the Crode Fiscaline. Quite superb. Such brilliant sights ease the climb, which is gentle but steady. The winding path is frequently reinforced with timber traverses.

The vegetation of the lower reaches of the valley consists mostly of low mountain pines interspersed with climbing roses and short deep red and purple orchids. Ahead, the valley is blocked by an ancient landslide which formed a wall, down the middle of which a waterfall cascades. You climb to the right of this, up into an ample grassy hollow. There is a good view over to the wide amphitheatre and immense scree crossing (south) beneath Monte Paterno, leading to the Forcella Pian di Cengia.

A plateau with several picturesque tarns follows, and those spectacular world-famous Tre Cime di Lavaredo (Drei Zinnen) peaks are soon visible to the southwest. The Sasso di Sesto (Sextnerstein) is on your right (north) with its wartime rock-hewn tunnels, as you climb the final stretch up to R. Locatelli (2405m) (Drei-Zinnen-Hütte) on its rock and thin grass terrace. On a clear day the panorama is breathtaking, and takes in the Cristallo Group southwest, Croda Rossa west, and the strange squarish shape of the Torre dei Scarperi (Schwabenalpenkopf) (northwest) looking like an incongruous transplant from Arizona. Both sunsets and sunrises get top rating here, as the Tre Cime themselves are illuminated.

Alternatives at this point consist in connections with walk 6 for either R. Pian di Cengia (1h) or circling the Tre Cime and return to R. Auronzo (2h15mins). Otherwise you can descend to the Valle di Landro (Höhlensteintal) - allow 2h45mins and see walk 8, Stage One in reverse.

Stage Two: descent to Val Campo di Dentro and R. Tre Scarperi (2h30mins)
From R. Locatelli the new path is n.105. After other paths branch off immediately to the left, you skirt northwest under the western base of the Torre Toblin (Toblinger Knoten) to a saddle (20mins) at 2457m with numerous ruins of WW1 trenches and fortifications. Two wonderful rock towers are nearby - Torre dei Scarperi to the west and Monte Mattina (Morgenkopf) to its north. At this point you start getting good views of the Tre Scarperi massif due north, in addition to the unique form of the Rocca dei Baranci (Haunold) slightly to its west with its jagged teeth-like points. It's 10mins more to where path n.11 branches off left, and faraway mountains in Austria are visible.

N.105 is signposted for Val Campo di Dentro (Innerfeldtal) and descends several rock gullies (no difficulty), then becomes a more typical winding mule-track. Some way down, bearing right, the path crosses a wobbly short wooden bridge and there is evidence of a wartime goods cable-lift. Vegetation gradually starts again with thin mixed woods and pink alpenrose shrubs. You go left under a cascade then down more steeply in tighter zigzags. The terrain is loose stones and tends to be tiring. Soon, after nearly 800m in descent, you reach the wide shingle bed of the torrent where a series of large wooden poles show the way across to the left-hand side and to a path junction. Keep on down (n.105) through the low wood, and 10mins more will see you in the proximity of a waterfall, at the path junction (1661m) for n.8 to Forcella dei Baranci (Birkenschartl). R. Tre Scarperi (Dreischusterhütte) (1626m) is only 15mins further north down the main valley, making a total of 2h30mins.

Alternative descent to San Candido / Sesto (1h-1h45mins)
One choice from this point is to continue on down (north) to Val Pusteria. It's 5kms from the refuge down the pretty valley (20mins to the car parking area) with its dark timber hay sheds and barns to the Lanziger sawmill and intersection with the San Candido-Sesto road (allow 1h this far). The local bus connecting the two townships stops close by, just to the right at the Alte Sage guesthouse (1259m). You're 3.5kms from San Candido and just less from Sesto, so on foot allow another 45mins.

This next stage becomes rather long and very tiring if done straight after Stage Two, so consider an overnight stay at R. Tre Scarperi.

Stage Three: ascent to Forcella dei Baranci (2h30mins), descent via Val dei Baranci to Valle di Landro (2h30mins) and Lago di Dobbiaco (20mins)
From the afore-mentioned path junction, n.8 climbs steeply west in tight zigzags. There is the occasional slippery stretch with loose gravel on the surface. Luckily the trees shade you from the sun beating down on your back - if possible, do this early morning. After about 30mins you'll reach the top of the cascade, (plastic water pipes divert a part of the flow) and from then on up that's the last you'll see of flowing water in this valley. The terrain becomes drier but the gradient less steep, and there are alpenrose and bilberry shrubs until half way up. A rock and boulder strewn bowl-shaped area is next, under the Cima Piatta di Mezzo, left. Walkers are relatively few and far between in this wild and solitary valley, but with luck you'll see some of the chamois which are well-known inhabitants of the valley.
The path narrows and is bordered by low springy pines, the *baranci*, the name given to the 2 main mountains separated by this valley - Rocca dei Baranci (north) and Croda dei Baranci (southwest). At rest stops, look back (east) to the massive Tre Scarperi Group with its jagged top profile. The scrubby wood gives way to grass then loose rock and several sections of the path have slid or crumbled away. Follow faint traces or look for the (sometimes faded) red and white markings further up and aim for them. The valley opens out a little and the fallen squarish boulders are enormous now, and in a few spots you have to clamber over them. The path continues in wide zigzags and the forcella high above with its wooden signpost soon comes into sight. It's still a good 200m up - a relentless haul over monotonous scree, with a couple more tricky narrow crumbled-away spots. Allow 2h30mins all the way to the top at Forcella

Looking southeast onto Sesto Dolomites (from Forcella Baranci)

dei Baranci (2540m). Wonderful sights await you, west all the way through the central Dolomite area and northwest to the Austrian Alps, while behind, views range from the Tre Scarperi Group (east), to the unmistakable Tre Cime di Lavaredo (southeast). Brilliant.

There are strangely eroded spires just down over the forcella. Path n.8 descends some 350m on rough scree, (not suitable for running descents). Some extra care is needed on the initial steep stretch as there are several crumbly angles and there may be snow covering part of the track. If you are the first to cross it, test the hardness and depth first. If you decide to detour it, be careful not to loose sight of the path ahead. Soon it becomes a series of regular zigzags, and waymarking is somewhat erratic as the slope is rather mobile. There is a small snow-melt waterfall to your left under a rock outcrop, then after more barren loose rocky terrain in this cirque, you move down onto grassland then light wood once more in Val dei Baranci.

Further down, in what becomes a taller shady wood, there are entire banks of pink alpenrose for the enjoyment of July walkers. Then follow a couple of watercourse crossings on blinding white stones and low dwarf mountain pines with the occasional lone lightning struck ex-larch. Around

1700m the path runs down the middle of the valley on rocky terrain and painted waymarking disappears for a brief stretch. Follow the cairns intended as markers, past another small cascade where a strange scree flow curves down from the left.

The descent becomes much steeper and more tiring now, through woods but with loose stones underfoot as you approach the valley floor. After some 2h30mins from the forcella, you will hopefully reach the Cortina-Dobbiaco road. Even if you intend to go south from here, you're better off continuing north to Lago di Dobbiaco because that's where the nearest bus stop is. So, just left and across the road is a dirt track - the ex-railway line which runs slightly below and parallel to the road. Turn right (north) along it, and 20mins will see you at the main lake area complete with trout fishermen, bus stop (right, in front of the picturesque hotel) and camping ground (left, across the bridge).

PRACTICAL INFORMATION

R. FONDO VALLE (TALSCHLUSSHÜTTE) TEL:(0474)710606.
Private, sleeps 24.
R. A. LOCATELLI ALLE TRE CIME (DREI ZINNEN HÜTTE)
TEL:(0474)972002. Alpine Club, Padua section. Sleeps 180.
R. TRE SCARPERI (DREISCHUSTERHÜTTE) TEL:(0474)966610
AVS (South Tyrol) Alpine Club, San Candido section. Sleeps 56.
TOURIST OFFICE DOBBIACO (TOBLACH) TEL:(0474)972132.
TOURIST OFFICE SAN CANDIDO (INNICHEN) TEL:(0474)913149.
TOURIST OFFICE SESTO (SEXTEN) TEL:(0474)710310.

* * *

WALK 8 (see sketch map B, page 51)

MONTE PATERNO / CIMA DODICI / VALLE GIRALBA
via Landro - Val Rinbon -
R. Locatelli (3h30mins) - R. Pian di Cengia (1h) - R. Zsigmondy-
Comici (1h) - Forcella Giralba (45mins) - R. Carducci (20mins) -
Giralba (Auronzo) (3h).
TABACCO MAP NO.010 scale 1:25,000
TABACCO MAP NO.1 scale 1:50,000
(2 days suggested)

This itinerary involves an easy if longish initial 1000m ascent into the wonderful arena of the Sesto Dolomites, crossings with ups and downs to several refuges, then a long solitary 1500m descent to Auronzo in the Ansiei valley. Though the total walk time does not seem excessive, it is recommended in short doses as these magnificent surroundings need slow savouring, and the continual steep ups and downs can be tiring. It can of course be split up into shorter sections and linked with other itineraries in the area - these are referred to where relevant. There is a series of well-run refuges, each in a uniquely panoramic position. See the introductory remarks to walk 6 as a general preface to the area.

Stage One: to R. Locatelli (3h30mins)
The Valle di Landro (Höhlensteintal) connects Cortina with Dobbiaco (Toblach) in Val Pusteria (Pustertal), and regular bus services run along it all year round. 1km north of the Lago di Landro (bus stop) is the Hotel Bauer Tre Cime (Drei Zinnen Blick) at 1406m - the sole restored building of what used to be the small township of Landro. Signposting for n.10/102 points you east up the wide dirt track (authorised traffic only) into Val della Rienza. The 3 peaks of the Tre Cime di Lavaredo (Drei Zinnen) are visible right from the start. After a stretch of low trees and flowered clearings, you enter the valley bounded by Monte Rudo north, and Monte Piana south and follow the left side of the white bleached torrent bed. Some 30mins up near a small hut, is the Sesto Nature Park signboard - n.103 turns off right (see walk 9). Keep straight on n.102 east into Val Rinbon. At about 1700m n.10 turns off north (to Passo Grande dei Rondoi), and the valley narrows somewhat. Continue the gentle climb up to the head of the valley, where the last 1h consists of a series of zigzags up a rocky face amongst dwarf mountain pines. You emerge into the barren, wide bowl-

*At Forcella Pian di Cengia looking east to Croda dei Toni (right)
and M. Popera and its glacier (left)*

shaped Pian da Rin under the northern side of the immense Tre Cime peaks, where you are joined by n.105. There's a further climb to the junction under Monte Paterno (east) with 'main road' n.101. Keep left and follow signs for R. Locatelli (2405m) just a little further up and right.

The commanding and strategic position the refuge occupies cost it destruction by fire during WW1, (the first building dated back to 1883), and further damage during WW2 hostilities. Evidence of its proximity to the front is also seen in the rock-hewn tunnels in the Sasso di Sesto behind the refuge (north).

Alternate routes from here are:

a) via path n.101 - see walk 6 for exit via R. Auronzo (1h) and Misurina.

b) descent to R. Fondo Valle (Talschlusshütte) (1548m) in Val Fiscalina (Fischleintal) - allow 1h30mins-2h and see walk 7, Stage One in the opposite direction;

c) descent to Val Campo di Dentro (Innerfeldtal) and R. Tre Scarperi (Dreischusterhütte) - see Walk 7, Stage Two;

R. Pian di Cengia

Stage Two: to R. Pian di Cengia (1h) then R. Zsigmondy-Comici (1h)
Path n.101 leaves the refuge in a southeasterly direction, descends briefly then coasts beneath the northern flanks of Monte Paterno and traverses its immense scree flows almost on a level. After the Laghi dei Piani (Bödenseen) are left behind, another small vivid blue tarn comes into sight below. Later on the path climbs steeply up a barren rocky valley to the Forcella Pian di Cengia (Büllelejoch) (2522m) and junction with n.104 from R. Auronzo.

   Turn left (east) now along the brief crest with far-ranging airy views including a glimpse of the small glacier on Monte Popera due east. After a rock ledge with a passage over wooden planks, it's around left to R. Pian di Cengia (Büllelejochhütte). In its protected position at 2528m it is a welcome sight on a chilly windy day and their hot soups are hard to resist.

   A possible *alternate exit* route at this point is via n.104 (back at the forcella) to R. Auronzo and Misurina. Allow about 1h30mins - see walk 6, Stage Two in reverse.

N.101 continues along a lovely rock ledge to Passo Fiscalino (Oberbachernjoch) at 2519m (10mins) and more wartime ruins. The Croda dei Toni (Zwolferkofel) is the highest peak to your right (southeast), Cima Una (Einser) to your left (north), whereas Monte Popera (Hochbrunner Schneid) is ahead slightly right (east) with Cima Undici (Elfer) to its left. The path, still a wartime mule-track, drops down quickly now (east) and winds through thin grass and rock. You pass plastic water pipes and a storage tank supplying the refuge from a spring (marked on map) about 200m down. Some 50mins down from the pass on a grassy terrace is another good example of a well-run alpine refuge - R. Zsigmondy-Comici (named after 2 famous mountaineers). It can alternately be reached on path n.103 from R. Fondo Valle in Val Fiscalina (1h30mins) - also a feasible exit route.

On the immense mass of Monte Popera in front of you a rock ledge is visible about halfway up - this is part of the "Strada degli Alpini", (referring to the intrepid WW1 Italian Alpine soldiers), said to be one of the most dramatic and scenic "vie ferrate" in the Dolomites. It is an incredible rock-climbing route as the dramatic postcard scenes you'll find in the refuges in the area testify. It dates back to the winter of 1915-16 when it was literally hewn out of the rock face, the work being done at night time. Some stretches were then equipped with cables to facilitate access and supply for the Italian forces who then advanced to take over Austrian-occupied peaks in the Sesto area.

Stage Three: ascent to Forcella Giralba (45mins), R. Carducci (20mins) and descent to Giralba (Auronzo) (3h)

Follow signposting for n.103. After a brief descent to cross the valley head, the path starts the 200m climb southeast, skirting the base of the sheer orange-black-grey northern flank of Croda dei Toni. The lilac-coloured flowers that blossom in the midst of the calcareous scree are called round-leaved penny-cress. Looking back north you can see right down Val Fiscalina (the Tre Scarperi Group is lower left) to the township of Sesto in Val Pusteria, with the Austrian Alps in the background. After 20mins of oblique climbing, path n.101 to the "Strada degli Alpini" (experts only) branches off to the left. Keep straight on up and into the delightful cirque with the tiny Lago Ghiacciato (frozen) under Monte Popera, then the final stretch on darker earth and mixed rubble amongst tangles of discarded wartime barbed wire to Forcella Giralba (2431m). There may be late-lying snow here, but the saddle is wide and passage should not be a problem. You now leave the Sesto Nature Park. Below southeast now another brilliant landscape opens out - the marvellous vast grey amphitheatre bounded by the Croda dei Toni and Cima Auronzo and nestling in which is another alpine lake - Lago Nero. On the eastern edge stands the solitary R. Carducci (2297m) which you can reach in just another 20mins easy descent on the clearly marked path.

Ahead of you now is the long tiring descent towards the resort township of Auronzo in the Ansiei river valley. Relative to the number of walkers and visitors in the Sesto Dolomites though, this stage is comparatively desolate and the peaceful valley is ablaze with an incredible variety of wild flowers. The surrounding mountains include Monte Giralba on your left (east), then the imposing Croda di Ligonto further down. The far-off Marmarole range is visible ahead of you (south) most of the way down.

Path n.103 winds down easily and the successive transitions from one habitat to the next are particularly marked as you descend the valley. The loose scree soon gives way to grassland, and there are bursts of secondary growth (knee-high large-leaved plants and docks and nettles) testifying to previous human occupation as the area used to be pasture. You pass on to dwarf mountain pines, mixed wood interspersed with alpenrose, lilac orchids, dark red martagon lilies, wine red columbines, the occasional cyclamen, climbing roses, and blue round-headed rampian flowers, just to mention a few.

Lower down the path curves around right under a rocky outcrop and crosses cascades several times at about 1500m then enters a narrowish gully then beech wood.

Some 2h from the refuge will see you at the confluence of Val Stallata and Val Giralba and the path junction with n.109. This gnat-ridden clearing is the Pian de le Salere (1412m).

Continuing due south now, in another 15mins are the timber traverses of a bridge somewhat precariously balanced in 2 sections on boulders high off the torrent bed. Now follows a series of cascades and inviting small ice-blue pools. The houses in the hamlet of Giralba are soon visible, not so far below.

The next brief section of track was in a very bad state of repair at the time of writing. The path follows the left-hand side of the valley which has landslided at several points making the going rough. A little care is needed detouring crumbled-away sections. Back in the wood again you curve left, away from the torrent and exit on the main road just under Giralba. The local Auronzo bus will stop at this point, but as you should be equipped with a ticket beforehand, it's less than 5mins along the road left to the inn called Pensione Cacciatori where tickets and timetable information (and bus stop) are available. Auronzo is only 4kms away by road, for further long distance bus connections. Furthermore, a link with the Marmarole mountain range is possible - at the far (southernmost) end of Lago di S. Caterina (bus), is the start of the ascent to R. Ciareido - see walk 29, end of Stage Three.

PRACTICAL INFORMATION

R. CARDUCCI TEL:(0435)400485. Alpine Club, Auronzo section. Sleeps 40.
R. A. LOCATELLI ALLE TRE CIME DI LAVAREDO
TEL:(0474)972002. Alpine Club, Padua section. Sleeps 180.
R. PIAN DI CENGIA TEL:(0337)451517 or c/o (0474)710358. Private, sleeps 11.
R. ZSIGMONDY-COMICI TEL:(0474)710358. Alpine Club, Padua section. Sleeps 72.
TOURIST OFFICE AURONZO TEL:(0435)9359.
TOURIST OFFICE DOBBIACO (TOBLACH) TEL:(0474)9772132.

* * *

WALK 9 (see sketch map B, page 51)

MONTE PIANA / VALLE DI LANDRO
via Misurina - R. Bosi (1h30mins) - Capanna Carducci (20mins) -
Forcella dei Castrati (30mins) - Val Rinbianco (1h15mins) -
Val Rienza (30mins) - Lago di Landro (45mins) -
Cimabanche (1h15mins) - Ospitale (1h) - Cortina (2h).
TABACCO MAPS NO.03 (& 010 partially) scale 1:25,000
TABACCO MAP NO.1 scale 1:50,000
(1-2 days suggested)

The first stage of this itinerary involves an easy, mere 500m of ascent, and could be a good 'first' walk in the Dolomites, with a return by the same route. As well, from the top of Monte Piana, you get a marvellous 360° panorama which is enormously helpful in putting the groups and ranges of this part of the Eastern Dolomites into perspective in relation to each other. An added extra is the open air First World War museum, an experience in itself; a moving silent testimony to man's wartime follies.

First World War trench on M. Piana

Furthermore, the itinerary can easily be made into a round trip by taking the variant in Stage Two as you reach Val Rinbianco, to return to Misurina. Otherwise, followed in its entirety, its third stage goes through woods, along the track of the Dobbiaco-Cortina ex-railway line.

Stage One: to R. Bosi (1h30mins) and Capanna Carducci (20mins)
Monte Piana (which means 'flat'), is used here to refer to the whole of this humble mountain, whereas during WW1 Monte Piano, the northernmost part, was the Austrian stronghold and the southern part, Monte Piana, was Italian. It is possible to drive all the way up, as far as R. Bosi, though the final section of the road is rather rough and not asphalted and corners are tight.

On foot from the lake at Misurina take the main road north then the first turn-off right, signposted to the Tre Cime di Lavaredo (Drei Zinnen). Monte Piana is the flat-topped oversized hill directly north, with the Italian wartime access road clearly visible climbing the south side in wide zigzags.

Go past the camping ground, and at the signposted (R. Bosi) fork in the road, where the Genzianella guest-house and restaurant stands, take the left branch. This first section of road is asphalted and climbs very gently through pleasant conifer woods. After a trough with piped drinking water and some 30mins, turn right up a wide dirt track. It carries no signposting but can't be missed. After a curve to the left where another track comes in, is the first of the regular and evident signposting for R. Bosi.

In the wood here sweet conifers are interspersed with wild flowers such as heather and protected trumpet gentians and dwarf alpenrose. You rejoin the road (now dirt) briefly before a series of short cuts. The wonderfully panoramic road isn't that much longer and in the absence of traffic gives you ample time to appreciate the changing aspect of the Cristallo Group southwest and the Tre Cime di Lavaredo northeast. Then at 2205m stands the refuge with its chapel.

Don't follow signs for n.6a to the left past the parking area, but take path n.122 from behind the refuge, and in about 20mins over the exposed and often windswept top you'll reach the Capanna Carducci hut (no accommodation) and monument at 2325m. There are marvellous all-round views, ranging from the unmistakable blood-red Croda Rossa directly west, Cristallo southwest, Cadini southeast, Tre Cime di Lavaredo and other Sesto Dolomite peaks east to north. There is also a lot to see in the way of WW1 remains, and this was the Italian stronghold during the fierce fighting that took place during the terrible winter of 1916/17. Extra time should be allowed for exploring here. In the late 1970's an Austrian group "Dolomitenfreunde" together with various local organisations and volunteers from all over Italy set about restoring many of the trench systems, artillery positions, fortifications and tunnels, as well as mapping out a historic itinerary or "sentiero storico" (yellow and black signposting). It takes a couple of hours to complete but involves several exposed and difficult aided sections along the former front lines.

Stage Two: via Forcella dei Castrati (30mins) and descent to Val Rinbianco (1h15mins), Val Rienza (30mins) and Lago di Landro (45mins)
It should only take about 20mins if you manage to get to the Forcella dei Castrati straight off. The difficulty in finding it is caused by the lack of waymarking compounded by the confusing series of trenches and the like. From Capanna Carducci head north in the direction of the further end of this plateau and it's less than half way, a mere shallow earth depression at 2250m. There is a steep rough short cut here that heads straight down to join the main path 100m or so below (shown with small black dots on Tabacco map n.010). The path on the left instead takes you

along an exposed aided cliff-side route (6a variant) to explore the "Galleria delle mine" (Italian) but it is recommended only for the more adventurous and is shown as "via ferrata" on maps.

The third and easiest option is to climb up and over slightly north to near a barbed wire enclosure and a small monument. Look down to the right for the grassy basin where the mine gallery finishes. Make your way down to it through dwarf mountain pines and scrubby vegetation, and onto path n.6 signposted to Val Rinbianco and Landro. The first stretch is a little tricky as the terrain is crumbly, descending past man-made rock caverns and collapsed tunnel entrances. Among the scree in this small silent amphitheatre directly below the Forcella dei Castrati, is all sorts of war debris in the shape of rusty cans, timber, metal sheeting and barbed wire, and even leather boot soles. A lower path from R. Bosi joins from the right. This specially constructed mule-track was the main Italian access and supply route. After the path bears left and descends through low trees and scrub, it narrows somewhat to descend a rocky gully in tight zigzags. Where huts once stood in the levelled clearings, chamois have taken over now. As you reach the valley floor there is a delightfully typical gushing alpine stream and rustic wooden bridge to greet you.

Should you prefer to return to Misurina at this point, take the right branch of this path n.103 and in about 30mins you'll come out at Malga Rinbianco on the road up from Misurina to R. Auronzo and the Tre Cime di Lavaredo.

Otherwise, turn left on n.103. The path narrows shortly and climbs briefly up right as the stream crashes and cascades down left in its narrowing rocky valley. As you begin to descend again, several seemingly inaccessible rock caverns (Austrian positions) come into view on the steep side of Monte Piana. There is soon a short section of path that has crumbled away, but is easily passed with a little attention, then you wind down through taller trees and bilberry shrubs to the wide bleached rock bed of the Rienza. Past the enormous boulders across it, under the power lines and pylons and you join the wider white gravel track n.102 and a Sesto Nature Park signboard.

From here the Tre Cime di Lavaredo peaks are visible. Left again past a small timber hut then alongside the torrent with dramatic scree flows left from Monte Piana. There are plenty of grassy openings carpeted with tiny bright blue (protected) Bavarian gentians. The track is barred to traffic. 30mins or so will see you at Landro ie. the main road and hotel, and another 10mins to the lake. The green-white waters of the Lago di Landro (which has been known to dry up during rainless summers) have the Cristallo Group as backdrop (south). Here, outside the Rasthaus Alpenflora (no accommodation) are the bus stops for Cortina (south) or Dobbiaco (north) and occasionally for Misurina, should you wish to finish the walk at this stage.

There are several plaques and lakeside monuments which testify to the WW1 activity, and the black wheel on display belonged to the Austrian mechanised cableway for supplying their positions. Access for the soldiers was by way of what is now known as the "Sentiero dei Pionieri", an extremely steep and dizzy path virtually straight up the mountain's south flank and with several aided sections.

Stage Three: via Cimabanche (1h15mins), Ospitale (1h) to Cortina (2h)
The path in this last stage follows the ex-railway track Dobbiaco-Cortina and is a particularly pleasant stroll affording superb views of the mountains that flank the valley. Begun by Austrian soldiers during WW1, this narrow-gauge railway line was completed by the Italians in 1919. It was electrified in 1929 and operated until the early sixties when bus transport took over. The railway track itself and sleepers have been removed, but the numerous bridges and station buildings are still standing and the route has become popular for cross-country skiing in winter and mountain bikes virtually all year round. There is no waymarking as such, but when in doubt, go straight ahead and look for the concrete blocks on the side of the track.

From the bus stop, the track runs alongside the lake then as the road curves right, it moves away and follows a white gravel river bed, going off into mixed conifer woods. The Cristallo group is that spectacular massif directly to your south. As the track crosses the road along Val Popena Bassa (to Misurina and the Tre Cime di Lavaredo) you leave the Sesto Nature Park and climb gradually with views of the Croda Rossa ahead. The highest point on this final stage, Cimabanche at 1530m, constitutes an important watershed. The ex-railway station here is still lived in, and there's a small bar for refreshments and a bus stop, but no accommodation. As well, the Fanes-Sennes-Braies Nature Park begins on the other side of the road (see walk 11 to Pratopiazza and further). The next stretch runs past a couple of lakes featuring wild ducks, through meadows and closely parallel to the road and slightly lower than it, as far as Ospitale (1490m) (bus stop), site of a 10th century hospice for pilgrims (now a hotel) and a chapel dating back to the 13th century. Then, far away from traffic once more, there's more mixed conifer wood, and views west to Monte Vallon Bianco and Fanes, before a short section of tunnel as you bear south and the Austrian wartime Felizon bridge comes into view.

Though not much to look at nowadays, its position is quite impressive as it straddles the sheer sides high above the narrow torrent bed. According to legend, the chasm below was once inhabited by a strange woman and her son, always clothed in green, who slept half-immersed in the rushing water with a moss-covered rock for a pillow. This scrubby rock area is also a well-known haunt of chamois, often to be seen effortlessly sauntering up the steep valley sides.

Straight after the bridge is a long, dark and often muddy tunnel, better avoided by taking the path detouring right, using only a short section of tunnel permanently lit by electric bulbs. Now you look down onto the milky-blue of the Torrente Boite, and beyond it to the back part of Col Rosa, then the Tofane. The track traverses areas of typical dwarf mountain pine interrupted by vast flows of scree and rubble from rockslides. Where these enormous volumes have come away from the towering west flanks of the Pomagagnon, the newly-exposed rock high up is still fresh and pink, in contrast to older dark shades of black, grey and white. After half an hour or so you'll be above Fiames, a small centre, and the road and bus can be easily reached if necessary. Otherwise (with a good 1h to go) continue on past the railway station (drinking water available) and through the larch forest alive with colourful twittering finches.

The final half hour is asphalted track through meadows and the not unpleasant residential zone, and has become a 'promenade', coasting right into Cortina (1210m) at the bus (ex-railway) station.

PRACTICAL INFORMATION
R. A. BOSI TEL:(0435)39034. Private, sleeps 32.
HOTEL BAUER DREI ZINNEN / TRE CIME (LANDRO)
TEL:(0474)972633.
HOTEL OSPITALE - no accommodation.
HOTEL PLONER (CARBONIN) TEL:(0474)977111.
TOURIST OFFICE CORTINA TEL:(0436)3231/3232.
TOURIST OFFICE MISURINA TEL:(0435)39016 seasonal.

* * *

WALK 10 (see sketch map C, page 74)

FANES
via (Cortina) Fiames - Ponte Outo (Valle di Fanes) (1h20mins) -
R. Fanes / R. La Varella (3h) - R. Pederü (1h15) -
R. Fodara Vedla (1h15mins) - R. Ra Stua (1h20mins) -
Botestagno (45mins) - Fiames (30mins).
TABACCO MAP NO.03 scale 1:25,000
TABACCO MAP NO.1 scale 1:50,000
(2 days suggested)

This lovely and easy walk will take you into the former realm of the glorious Kingdom of the Fanes, which is infiltrated with legends, and the present-day realm of the Fanes-Sennes-Braies Nature Park which has been infiltrated by four-wheel-drive vehicles in some parts. The area is, furthermore, a stronghold of the ancient Ladin language and you'll see signs written in Ladin, German then Italian - in that order!

In legendary times the valley locality of Fiames was the site of a fierce battle against the hereto victorious Fanes people. The evil organiser was the wicked wizard Spina de Mul - a ghastly mule-like apparition, half skeleton and half putrefied body. To regain possession of the precious jewel, La Rajetta, worn by the Fanes warrior princess Dolasilla, he co-opted the prince Ey de Nèt (Eye of the Night). The prince subsequently fell in love with and devoted himself to the protection of the princess Dolasilla, who was seriously injured in spite of her magical ermine fur and silver armour forged by dwarves. This battle was actually the turning point (in a downwards direction) for the kingdom of Fanes, ultimately betrayed by its false king (see walk 4 and Passo Falzarego) in exchange for the buried treasures of Aurona said to lie below the Padon mountain group touched on in walk 19.

A final note: due to the karstic (limestone) nature of the rock, water drains straight through and goes underground, so there is normally very little to be found on the surface. Lakes and rivers carry water only when snow melts or after persistent heavy rain. For walkers, this signifies that adequate supplies of drinking water should always be carried, particularly when crossing the high reaches of the plateau.

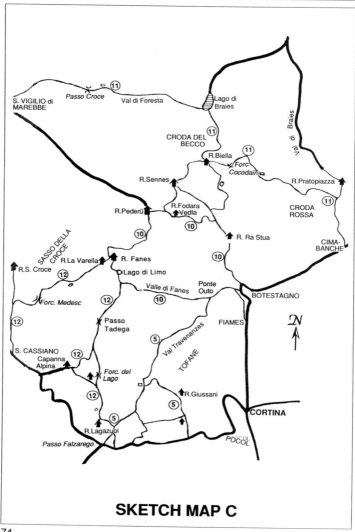

SKETCH MAP C

*In Valle di Fanes,
waymarking and shrine*

*Stage One: via Ponte Outo (Valle di Fanes) (1h20mins) to R. Fanes / R.
La Varella (3h)*
This walk begins 5kms or so north from Cortina on the Dobbiaco road at
Fiames (1292m, local bus service this far). At the end of the bus line, at
Albergo Fiames, take the forestry track to your left (facing uphill) - it is
barred to unauthorised traffic. It runs north, parallel to the Torrente Boite,
just below the main road. It travels through wooded and picnic areas and
after a couple more bars across the road (25mins or so) you'll meet up
with a tarmac side road. (If you arrive by car take the turn-off left shortly
after Albergo Fiames and park here). Another bar and you're on track
n.10.

This soon becomes a dirt track, crosses a couple of rushing white
streams and curves left (west) around the mountain Col Rosa. It's a good
50mins on to where you cross Ponte Outo ("outo" is Ladin for "alto", ie.

75

high) self-explanatory when you look down into the ravine below! You traverse mixed wood with a predominance of larch, especially noticeable in spring with their delicate fresh light green foliage, and in autumn with yellow and orange colours in contrast to the dark evergreens. Soon afterwards, the jeep track bears left, and n.401 up Val Travenanzes subsequently branches off.

Take the short cut (signposted to Alpe di Fanes) which climbs somewhat steeply west up through the woods with plenty of squirrels. A delightful gushing waterfall is audible from the right, and an unmarked narrow but well-worn side-track detours briefly to its base. Your path rejoins the main jeep track and soon afterwards reaches commemorative rock plaques marking the Austrian 1916 front, near Lago di Fanes. Shortly after this is the entrance to the Fanes-Sennes-Braies Nature Park and an area thick with typical alpine dwarf pines. Further uphill you are under the awesome mass of Monte Vallon Bianco to the left (south) with its fascinating white rock folds and waves as the valley opens out into a wide amphitheatre with woods of spruce and Arolla pine.

After a stretch accompanied by a wide merry gushing stream, the jeep track continues on to Malga Fanes Grande towards Lagazuoi, and you take n.10 as it short cuts up to the right (west) following the zig zags of a wartime mule-track to 2100m. Continue past a white military building on your right, over the flat top to the lake and Passo di Limo (2172m), with its carpets of indigo blue and purple gentians. Clearly visible now, below to the left is R. La Varella (2042m) next to Lago Verde, and R. Fanes (2060m) to the right, 10mins away.

This tableland is geologically characterised by its rock slabs and soluble limestone, modelled over the years by the effect of water. Once you're down on a level with the refuges and various dairy huts and chalets dotted around, you can appreciate the wide amphitheatre of the Sasso della Croce and Cunturines groups. Horses and cows graze here in summer. Curiosities include the docile St. Bernard and bits of WW1 bombshells and shrapnel, and the decorations on the counter of the bar at R. Fanes which depict various episodes from the kingdom of the same name, which had its castle on the Cunturines.

There is also an interesting horizontally stratified rock face with solitary pines dotted on its surface, directly left (west) of the vehicle track from the R. Fanes turn-off going to R. La Varella. The area is known as the "Marmots' Parliament".

At this point in the Nature Park you can link up with walk 12.

Stage Two: descent to R. Pederü (1h15mins), ascent to R. Fodara Vedla (1h15mins)

Track n.7 follows another jeep track down this bare valley in an easterly then northerly direction, and although this is part of the Nature Park, a private jeep-taxi has been allowed to operate here. There are, however, a good few walkers-only signposted short cuts and the easy stroll frees your attention to appreciate the great variety of erosion phenomena in this unusual valley. Rock and earth colours include tones of grey striped with red on the flanks of Col Becchei (2793m) up right (southeast). Conglomerates are present as well as extensive moraine and debris from ancient glaciers on the right-hand side.

Down at R. Pederü (1548m) there's a parking area, local summer bus service 12kms northwest to San Vigilio di Marebbe, the jeep-taxi service to R. Fanes / R. La Varella as well as R. Fodara Vedla, your next destination.

The next section consists of path n.9 in an easterly direction. It should be taken in slow puffs, slowly particularly on a sunny day. This feat of civil engineering with compact zigzags has recently been surfaced mostly with concrete and conglomerate. The sheer rock face right is multicoloured. 45mins later, and shortly into the lovely wood as the track levels out, is the turn-off left for R. Sennes and R. Biella (n.7). Keep straight on, and further on, up and over to the quiet depression, a lovely setting for R. Fodara Vedla (1980m) and a cluster of old dark wood chalets with the occasional rabbit scuttling about. M. Lavinores is up to your right (southeast). In line with the karstic nature of the terrain, several springs (marked on the 1:25,000 map) can be found at the base of rock slopes in the vicinity, being the surface water from higher reaches which has run straight through to a natural exit here.

Stage Three: descent to R. Ra Stua (1h20mins), Botestagno (45mins) and Fiames (30mins)

On the left side of the refuge is the continuation of track n.9 leading up and over to Lago Fodara - or what would be a lake in case of abundant rain! Keep to the left-hand alternative of n.9 (the right branch leads up to a rocky itinerary). A comfortable white gravel track with neat stone borders - another thanks to Austrian WW1 soldiers - now starts gently descending east accompanied by a gurgling stream. The mule-track continues on a slightly longer route than the left branch you soon take. The next stretch is one of the most delightful, descending through a wooded area (dwarf pines, firs, larch mostly) and as the path actually has a rock base, there are many examples of strangely eroded textures on a small-scale, but interesting close up. In autumn the track is softly carpeted with the yellow larch needles which gently rain down during even the lightest winds.

After 1h you're down at 1758m at Campo Croce in the valley of the Boite (Cortina's river) and its source is just uphill from here (see map). Cross the boggy summer grazing land and winding stream - it has been suggested that shepherds divert such streams into meanders to slow the flow and facilitate cattle drinking - then turn right (southeast) down the jeep track from R. Sennes and you'll reach R. Ra Stua (1669m) (meals only) and other summer dairy buildings in 20mins. Car parking used to be possible here, but the road has recently been closed to unauthorised traffic. Unless you opt for the link with walk 11 (Stages Two and Three) by ascending to R. Biella (allow 2h from here on path n.26), continue on down.

The now peaceful asphalted road traverses mostly larch forest and runs alongside a typically alpine stream that cascades and rushes down rock gullies. It's 45mins to the main road (1513m), and this area is known as Botestagno (Potestagno on many maps). To avoid the traffic, take the forest track down right at the intersection, and you'll very shortly join up with the asphalted stretch of n.10 in Stage One, just upstream of the car parking area. Allow another 30mins to Fiames where there are buses to Cortina.

PRACTICAL INFORMATION

R. FANES TEL:(0474)501097 Private, sleeps 70. (*)
R. LA VARELLA TEL:(0474)501079 Private, sleeps 40. (*)
R. PEDERÜ TEL:(0474)501086 Private, sleeps 25.
R. FODARA VEDLA TEL:(0474)501093 Private, sleeps 30.
TOURIST OFFICE CORTINA TEL:(0436)3231/3232.
TOURIST OFFICE SAN VIGILIO DI MAREBBE TEL:(0474)501037.

(*) possible extended opening.

✳   ✳   ✳

WALK 11 (see sketch map C, page 74)

CRODA ROSSA / CRODA DEL BECCO / COLLI ALTI
via Cimabanche - Pratopiazza (2h) - Malga Cavalli (2h30mins) -
Forcella Cocodain (1h30mins) - R. Biella (30mins) -
Lago di Braies (2h) - Val di Foresta - Passo Croce (3h) -
San Vigilio di Marebbe (2h30mins).
TABACCO MAP NO.03 scale 1:25,000 only as far as R. Biella.
TABACCO MAP NO.1 scale 1:50,000
(2-3 days suggested)

This itinerary constitutes a diagonal (southeast to northwest) crossing of the entire Fanes-Sennes-Braies Nature Park, with a spectacular section below the northern face of the Croda Rossa mountain. There is only one brief difficult tract (see Stage Two), so the walk is generally straightforward, though walkers should avoid setting out on the long and lonely stretches in Stages Two and Four if there is any risk of the weather turning bad, as possibilities of shelter are virtually non-existent.

Pratopiazza, in an idyllic pasture valley far from traffic, between the Valle di Braies (Pragser Tal) (south of Val Pusteria/Pustertal) and the Valle di Landro (Höhlensteintal) north of Cortina, is probably the best vantage point for viewing the Croda Rossa (Höhe Gaisl), so-called for its blood-red rock due to the presence of iron oxide.

The mountain evidently turned red in legendary times to express solidarity with Princess Moltina. A timid newly-wed, she was subjected to spiteful ridicule when a jealous noblewoman exposed her humble origins - she had been brought up by marmots. Moltina's embarrassment and bright red blushing were experienced directly by the mountain, (Croda Rossa), which has retained its sanguine colouring to this day.

Stage One: to Pratopiazza (2h)
The Valle di Landro connects Cortina with Dobbiaco (Toblach) in Val Pusteria. Get off the bus at Cimabanche (Gemärk) (1530m) and try not to be tempted by the barbecued sausage smells that waft over from the outdoor restaurant. Across the road from the ex-railway station building is drinking water and the start of the Fanes-Sennes-Braies Nature Park.

Take path n.18 north up the Valle dei Canopi - a name evidently derived from the German "Knappenfusstal" referring to the miners who once trod this valley as they travelled south for work. After 15mins through low scrubby mountain pines the path crosses a wide white shingle torrent bed. Next is a steady 45min climb, gentle at first, through prettier mixed conifer wood with wild flowers. At signposting, keep straight on n.18 and you cross the water course right once more, marked with scattered timbers from a ruined bridge.

The path climbs more steeply now in wide zigzags and is reinforced with cross timbers. Past a cascade down a sheer rock slab (left) and, a little further on, as the path turns sharp left above the rock wall, you get a good view south over to the small Cresta Bianca glacier on the Cristallo Group. Soon left over a crest (another 45mins) you enter the lush green rolling pastures of Pratopiazza (Plätzwiesensattel) dotted with small dairy farms and log cabins for hay storage. You go briefly down to a stream crossing and path junction - the one left (west) - signposted Malga Cavalli and R. Biella - heads off towards the Croda Rossa, and after a brief stretch of wood it is joined by n.3a from R. Pratopiazza - see next stage.

At this point, you can move straight off on path n.3 without going up to Pratopiazza itself, but a brief detour to (or even an overnight stay) to the Pratopiazza refuges can be recommended. In 15mins climbing across the flower-carpeted meadows obliquely left (northeast) on a wide timber-lined track you come up to the classical chalet-style hotel and next to it R. Pratopiazza (1991m). They are positioned uniquely directly opposite the main face of the Croda Rossa. As well, behind them (northeast) is the gentle slope of the Picco di Vallandro, the 2839m summit of which can be reached in an easy 2h30mins.

Being a Nature Park, traffic access is restricted - from Braies (north) via Ponticello you can drive up to a parking area about 5mins walk before R. Pratopiazza - there is also a summer bus line this far. From Carbonin (south) limited access is possible via the dirt track or walkers-only short cuts, coming out at R. Vallandro (2040m). From this refuge it's another 30mins northwest to Pratopiazza coasting along the dirt track with cattle-proof gates. R. Vallandro stands next to an old Austro-Hungarian fort, and offers excellent views onto the Cristallo Group (south).

Stage Two: via Malga Cavalli (2h30mins) then Forcella Cocodain (1h30mins) to R. Biella (30mins)
From the signposted path junction in front of R. Pratopiazza, leave this picturesque valley echoing with cow bells by path n.3a. 15mins later in the wood, path n.18 branches off right to Ponticello. N.3 keeps straight on, over a stile in the cow fence, across a couple of water courses and

begins climbing west. Plenty of wild flowers and the possibility of seeing wood grouse in the conifers. Soon the rocky mountain side path has timber protection on the exposed side. In another 20mins of gentle climbing west you come over a rise to enter the grassy hollow valley with magnificent outlook onto the principal Croda Rossa peak with its small glacier and frontal moraine - the immense mound with a base of ice and fine gravel with some earth then larger stones and debris heaped on top, all of which is gradually pushed down valley by the advancing movement of the glacier. Twenty minutes more climbing out of this valley to the highest point on this route - 2358m where there is a cairn. You coast the sloping barren rock and scree flanks of the Piccola Croda Rossa and descend very gradually in a series of ins and outs of a couple more moraine valleys - lesser in dimensions compared to the first one, but equally dramatic. About 2h since the start of this stage at a sharp left turn (southwest), marked as Gaiselleite on the map, the terrain becomes more earthy and crumbly and there are several exposed passages rendered trouble-free by well-secured guiding cable. Soon you're back to grass, scrubby vegetation and Arolla pines and coast around north before a slight descent through alpenrose to the path junction with the jeep track and path n.4 from Ponticello. Carry on the path straight ahead and over a rise among thick carpets of buttercups and forget-me-nots are the low timber buildings of Malga Cavalli (Ross Alm) the shepherds summer 'residence' - so don't expect anything more than drinking water, picnic tables and a crucifix here.

Heading north you follow the track steeply uphill and there are cushions of the tiny pink moss campion flowers alongside. Over another crest to the first of 4 signposted path junctions (about 30mins from the malga). Keep left (southwest) on n.3 for R. Biella until the 4th junction, shortly down left, when the path for Forcella Cocodain becomes n.28. Ahead you can see the north face and regular rock layering of the Remeda Rossa peak and the unusual rock slope composed of thin horizontal rock strata which you are about to traverse obliquely to reach the forcella. The path as such is virtually nonexistent, but waymarking is excellent in the form of frequent white and red painted stripes on prominent rocks. You head due south and climb some 100m to Forcella Cocodain (2332m) (total 1h30mins from the malga). Below (southwest) in a rocky depression is the Lago de Fosses.

The most direct way now is right (northwest) along the rock crest (well marked) where edelweiss grow. After 20mins you descend left for the final 10mins on the undulating stone and grass plain where there's

From Forcella Sora Forno, R. Biella and cone-shaped Col de Ra Siores; Tofane in background (right)

a good chance you'll surprise snow grouse which nest in the stone depressions and clumps of grass. As they take flight they show dark brownish-black and white summer plumage and may utter a cry which sounds a bit like a pig snorting. This terrain also favours the strange seemingly dried-up stemless carline thistles said to forecast bad weather when closed-up, and vice versa. Watch out for mad sheep as well as the alpine ibex which were reintroduced here some two decades ago.

The grey stone building of R. Biella (Seekofelhütte) (2325m) is dominated by the imposing mass of the smooth sloping triangle of the Croda del Becco to its north. In the Ladin language the mountain is known as "Sass dla Porta", ie. entrance rock, due to the presence of a huge rock door, now buried, providing access to the depths of the mountain where the last of the legendary Fanes people lay in suspended sleep waiting to return to the sunlight and the former glory of their kingdom to be reinstated.

On a clear day from R. Biella you can see as far south as Monte Pelmo, with the Tofane to its right, and even a glimpse of the snow-capped Marmolada further west. R. Biella is an old style hut, run in a very friendly and helpful manner - no home comforts like hot water though. As it serves as the first stopover on Alta Via n.1, it is advisable to book in advance if you plan to sleep there. Should it be full, the private R. Sennes is a 1h detour on path n.6 along the jeep track southwest.

Alternate descent via Campo Croce, R. Ra Stua to Fiames (Cortina) (3h)
A feasible return in the direction of Cortina, enabling you to make the itinerary a round trip, is via path n.26. Heading south across the rocky plain past three lakes, you will zigzag down to come out at Campo Croce (1772m) in just over 1h. From here it's another 20mins in descent on jeep track to R. Ra Stua, and 1h15mins to Fiames (Cortina) - see Stage Three of walk 10 for this description.

Stage Three: descent to Lago di Braies (2h)
From the refuge in 10mins on path n.1 you climb up to the saddle Forcella Sora Forno (2388m) and its shrine. With an easy gradient the path descends northeast into the silent rock amphitheatre - the "Forno" (oven), of greater significance for walkers in ascent on a hot summer's day. Some low mountain pines follow, and in 30mins there is a path junction (n.3). Shortly below this is an aided passage down an easy rock face. Going north now, you traverse left under cliffs and soon enter a wood of mixed conifer. Down to another path junction (n.4 from Ross Alm/Malga Cavalli) in a saddle. Here the official path goes straight ahead and slightly upwards before the final descent through light wood, while left is a steeper short cut down a loose scree and debris gully. They join up at the cliff base. Val di Foresta opens up to the west, bordered by immense scree flows anchored by low vegetation. You meander a little in the bleached stone bed of a water course (follow waymarking carefully here) and path n.1 brings you out down at the lake side in some 45mins more. (The lovely old hotel, visible at the northern end of this delightful lake, can be reached in another 45mins or so.) Turn left at the signposts and following the lake edge in 5mins you'll reach some information boards where you turn-off up n.19 for Val di Foresta (Grünwaldtal), destination San Vigilio di Marebbe.

Should you wish to do the Lago di Braies-R. Biella path in ascent, allow 3h30mins. Furthermore, a bus service connects the Lago di Braies with Val Pusteria (Dobbiaco via Villabassa and Monguelfo railway stations), providing access or an easy exit at this point.

Stage Four: via Val di Foresta, Passo Croce (3h) to San Vigilio di Marebbe (2h30mins)

In contrast to the popular Lago di Braies-R. Biella path, this next section is relatively less-trodden. Many animals and birds as well as plants inhabit this lovely valley. You pass under the squarish top back block of the northern reaches of the Piccola Croda del Becco with a high rock amphitheatre, and the first stretch of n.19 is a jeep track leading to the dairy farm Malga Foresta (1590m) 20mins up the valley. N.23 branches off left, and at the drinking water tap and trough you move over to the right-hand side of the valley and continue on n.19 west, through alternating wood and pasture clearings with the occasional stretch up the torrent bed. After a good 1h from the lake is a small log cabin and path junction (n.25 goes (left) up the wild and lonely Val dei Larici [Valley of Larches] headed by the red-tinted Monte Sella di Sennes).

The valley narrows and the path climbs briefly right, crosses a gushing cascade and continues through noisy woods with tiny darting birds such as finches and greys, as well as the cuckoo. A squirrel or two might also appear. The climb is hot going under strong sunshine, but after about another 1h of zigzags, a stretch alongside the torrent with low scrubby vegetation then a curve right and up with plenty of pink alpenrose shrubs, and you will be rewarded by an idyllic flowered pasture valley dotted with dark timber hay sheds and summer dairy huts. These are the Tabià di Colli Alti (2114m). This miniature amphitheatre is complete with its own waterfall, resident chamois and marmots. Proceed in a westerly direction on the jeep track following the stream and at the path junction (10mins) keep straight on - still n.19. The terrain in this green valley becomes more eroded and crumbly. Yellow Rhaetian poppies grow profusely among the calcareous stones in the watercourse. Go past a low sloping-roofed cow shed, left, and the wide saddle of Passo Croce (Kreuzjoch or Summa Munt) is not far ahead now at 2283m (2h30mins-3h so far), with another wooden crucifix and clear signposting.

The descent via Val Foscedùra to the township of San Vigilio di Marebbe follows the white gravel jeep track (access limited to dairy farm vehicles) most of the way, so it's an easy, if rather long 1000m and 2h30mins down. Shortly under the pass there are views southwest to the Puez-Odle plateau and the Sella massif. Vegetation is scrubby and woods thin at first, but alpenrose abound, and late summer walkers should find bilberries. Monte Paraccia on the left, with its ridges, has some strangely eroded rock needles almost growing out of the scree. A good 1h down at the car barricade is thick sweet forest carpeted with heather. You pass another path branch-off right (n.12) but keep on the road. Shortly, waymarking (n.19) indicates the beginning of steeper short cuts left through the woods and 30mins later is the surfaced road. Signposting continues to the outskirts of San Vigilio (total time 2h30mins). If you decide not to stay in one of the numerous hotels, bus connections are possible with Val Pusteria (Brunico) and Val Badia (La Villa) and beyond.

PRACTICAL INFORMATION

R. BIELLA TEL:(0436)866991. Alpine Club, Treviso section. Sleeps 50.
MALGA CAVALLI (Ross Alm) - basic accommodation.
HOTEL LAGO DI BRAIES TEL:(0474)748602.
R. PRATOPIAZZA (BERGGASTHOF PLÄTWIESE) TEL:(0474)748650. Private, sleeps 50. (*)
R. SENNES TEL:(0474)501092. Private, sleeps 40. (*)
R. VALLANDRO TEL:(0474)972505. Private, sleeps 40.
TOURIST OFFICE CORTINA TEL:(0436)3231/3232.
TOURIST OFFICE DOBBIACO TEL:(0474)972132.
TOURIST OFFICE SAN VIGILIO DI MAREBBE TEL:(0474)501037.
(*) possible extended opening.

* * *

WALK 12 (see sketch map C, page 74)

SASSO DELLA CROCE / LAGAZUOI
via San Cassiano - Forcella Medesc (3h30mins) -
R. La Varella / R. Fanes (2h) - Passo di Limo -
Malga Fanes Grande (1h) - Passo Tadega (20mins) -
alt. a) Capanna Alpina (1h30mins) - San Cassiano (45mins) or
alt. b) Forcella del Lago (1h45mins) - R. Lagazuoi (1h45mins) -
Passo Falzarego (1h30mins).
TABACCO MAP NO.03 scale 1:25,000
(except the first part of Stage One)
TABACCO MAP NO.2 scale 1:50,000
(2 days suggested)

One of the best places to appreciate the flesh pink and white rock of Sasso della Croce, the graceful rounded mountain that forms the lower eastern edge of Val Badia, is from the Passo Campolongo road that connects Arabba with Corvara. Another is from the Gardenazza part of the Puez plateau (see walk 13). Legends depict the mountain as the abode of a terrible dragon who used to make frequent visits to the valley to terrorise the inhabitants. A courageous knight Prack, from Marebbe, is said to have slain it, so present day walkers can venture there with no fear of attack.

This itinerary is of average difficulty, and requires an especially good measure of stamina for the steep sections in alternative (b) in Stage Two. Rugged mountain scenery features in this very worthwhile detour to R. Lagazuoi high above Passo Falzarego, but it should only be attempted by fit and experienced walkers, and avoided in bad weather.

As well as far-ranging views, one of the strengths of this itinerary lies in the marvellous variety of terrain it covers, particularly the fascinating high level karstic area crossed in descent to the refuges in Stage One. The practical significance of this phenomenon for walkers is that as all the water drains straight down through the top rock strata, surface water is non-existent so plenty of drinking water should be carried up from the valley.

Stage One: via Forcella Medesc (3h30mins) to R. La Varella / R. Fanes (2h)

San Cassiano (1537m) in the southeastern extension of Ladin-speaking Val Badia, has year-round bus connections with La Villa, a few kms northwest and beyond, in just about all directions, as well as summer connections southeast with Passo Falzarego and Cortina.

After a visit to the local bakery with its delicious range of cereal breads, cross the road and look for n.15 painted on the corner of the local Alpine Guides' building, slightly to the left. It quickly takes you out of the hotel zone and bearing left starts coasting through flowered pastures and across rushing streams. There are small groups of picturesque dark timber farm buildings and several cattle gates with old style wooden latches which you should always close after you. There are many drinking water points and rustic troughs on the way. After about 35mins you enter a light, predominantly larch wood and the confines of the Fanes-Sennes-Braies Nature Park. 10mins or so further on is a junction with n.12 (from La Villa).

(N.15 continues north on to the private refuge and hospice Santa Croce (2045m) in 1h15mins more, following an ancient Via Crucis with the traditional wooden stations of the cross along the way).

Ascent to Forcella Medesc, Sella group in the background

Turn up right (east) on n.12. There's more wood, then some grassy clearings with different types of gentians and sweet perfumed daphne. A dry white torrent bed is followed. The conifer wood gradually gives way to more scrubby vegetation and the characteristic low-lying mountain pines as you move up towards a wide white rubble valley. You have the flesh pink rock face of Sass dla Crusc (Sasso della Croce in the Ladin language) left (north). Another path junction arrives shortly, but keep on n.12, clearly marked and curving up to the right, to start the climb towards the forcella. The path is clearly visible ahead crossing the slope with hues of red, orange and white. There is plentiful evidence of chamois here. Looking back, when you pause for a breather, you'll see from the Sass Putia northwest, to the Puez-Odle Group west (virtually straight ahead), then the Sella massif southwest and even the Marmolada with its gleaming snow-covered glacier further south. High above the tree line the path climbs gently but steadily and the monotony of the scree is broken by the lilac clumps of tiny round-leaved penny-cress flowers. Piz d Lavarela is the peak to your right (south) as you move over to the left side of the valley, and puff a lot more on the final narrower 200m (1h30min) stretch. After a low rocky spur, you come out to a wide flat opening on the top and wooden signposting at Forcella Medesc (2584m), sometimes also referred to as Forcella La Varella. (3h30mins this far).

Follow n.12 waymarking northeast now with special attention in descent, as orientation can be confusing here particularly in conditions of low visibility. Furthermore, with late-lying snow, if it is not possible to bypass snow patches, then test their depth (with your ski stock or alpenstock) before crossing, as this karstic terrain is characterised by narrow fissures, splits and narrow mini-gullies gouged out by running water, and hidden by snow. While not wide or deep enough for a person to fall completely into in most cases, they could cause sprained ankles or worse.

The landscape is most unusual, perhaps the best in the Dolomites for understanding the karst phenomenon. As you cross this sort of uneven plateau and gently descend towards the Fanes pasture area, you'll see more examples of what running water can do to such smooth soluble Jura limestone, in channelling, wave-like formations and dolina depressions. The water soaks straight through, goes underground and comes out later on at the foot of some slopes as powerful springs and cascades.

The mountains around you now are the Sass dla Crusc, left (northwest), Lastrone Verde is that sheer flank gleaming north, and the red you glimpse behind it (northeast) is the Furcia dai Fers (the name referring to iron). Alternating with the rock are grassed areas with yellow alpine and spring pasque flowers and gentians. About 1h from the forcella is a path junction with n.7, but keep right on n.12 and it takes you down and over a crest to view black and orange rock walls above Lago di Parom, which you coast high above. After a brief rock and boulder-strewn clearing with resident marmots, there's a short ascent left over a ridge, where mountain pines accompany you once more. R. Fanes and the nearby Lago Verde now come into view in the valley below. The lake is said to have been tinted its characteristic dark green when an enchanted but highly poisonous mirror that was said to reveal all a man's inner secret thoughts was cast into it.

The descent is steeper now, and follows the oblique strata lines of the fascinating rock terrain. Arolla pines dot the slope, many of them uprooted, their gnarled deep red-brown shapes transformed into ghostly sculptures by lightning bolts. The path can be quite slippery if wet. Further down with alpenrose and bilberry shrubs, the path curves to pass over the miraculous gushing spring (identifiable on the maps) that cascades down to the lake. Past some dark old timber huts and across a buttercup carpeted meadow you come out at R. La Varella (2042m) (2h from the forcella). It is the quieter of the two refuges, but should it be full, cross the wooden bridge over the lake cascades and a damp area thick with yellow marsh-marigold flowers and try R. Fanes. Booking is advisable. (Note that accommodation charges at R. Fanes include a compulsory breakfast.)

From this point you can link up with walk 10.

Stage Two: via Passo di Limo, Malga Fanes Grande (1h),
Passo Tadega (20mins)

There are many springs and thus plenty of water on this stage, particularly during snow melt periods or after rain. The track is n.11 all the way. From R. Fanes climb the gentle curves of the jeep track (south) or follow the marked steeper short cuts. About 25mins of gentians, buttercups and globe flowers will see you to Passo di Limo (2172m) and its small lake. A little further on is a white painted military building and a wooden cross on your right. The Valle di Fanes continues in descent straight ahead (east), and the mountains to its right are Monte Vallon Bianco and Furcia Rossa. Take the path right indicated as '11/VB/17' painted on a rock, and after rejoining the jeep track heading south now, in another 20mins or so, you'll reach the timber building of the dairy farm, Malga Fanes Grande (2104m) - 1h so far.

A wooden bridge crosses another cascading newborn stream and shortly various paths fork off left (east) up into the war-debris-strewn reaches of the surrounding mountains. This valley area sheltered important technical, medical and supply positions for the Austrians during the 1915-18 war. Keep to the right track variant. Up to your right (west) are some wondrously contorted rock strata formations that seem in continual movement. The track climbs up and down very gently through pasture land used for both horses and cows, and there is a marmot colony among the rocks left (east) under the Campestrin peak. The mountain sides have a light tree cover of Arolla pines, larches and the ever-present dwarf mountain pines.

A narrow path branches off right up into the realm of the Cunturines where the drawbridged castle of the legendary Fanes people once stood. Several years ago instead, a cave was discovered there containing a great number of skeletons of the "ursus spelaeus", a gigantic and solitary bear thought to have lived up to 14,000 years ago. It is planned to open the cave to the public when the experts have finished.

Straight after the Cunturines turn-off is the small rise of Passo Tadega (2153m), and the Fanis peaks come into view straight ahead (south), along with the far-off Marmolada, (around 20mins from the Malga).

Alternative (a) to Capanna Alpina (1h30mins) and San Cassiano (45mins)

This alternative gives you the chance to make the walk a round trip, returning to the village of San Cassiano.

It's 20mins down across scree flows to the path junction to Forcella del Lago for alternative (b). But you go straight ahead, and the dry white gravel torrent bed left suddenly springs into life! You cross it shortly and climb briefly into thickening low pines where you have a good chance of hearing nightingales singing. Around and up to a grassed outcrop known as Col Lòcia (2069m) (20mins) with an excellent view of the Sella Group before a steep zigzag descent southwest on loose stones, with a helpful handrail and protective cables. Past the turn-off left across a difficult passage to R. Scotoni (known as the "via dei camosci" = chamois path), and it's about 30mins down to a grassy clearing among various tall conifers. Under the towering black and orange walls of the Cunturines is a perfect rest or picnic spot near the gushing torrent. 20mins more down across loose rough white stones and rubble on the later stretch will bring you out at the confluence of the path and ski slope descent from R. Scotoni and Lagazuoi and the squirrel-inhabited forest picnic area and Capanna Alpina (1726m) (bar and restaurant) and parking area. You're now only about 15mins away on unsurfaced road via the sand and gravel quarry, from the main road Passo Falzarego-Passo di Valparola-San Cassiano. There is a bus stop (seasonal service), otherwise, on foot to San Cassiano (turn right and nortl west at the asphalted road) is about 30mins.

Alternative (b) via Forcella del Lago (1h45mins) to R. Lagazuoi (1h45mins) and descent to Passo Falzarego (1h30mins)

This variant is definitely only for fit people with a good head for heights as it involves a very steep descent in between two stiff ascents, but ends with a rewarding arrival at R. Lagazuoi at 2752m, one of the highest placed refuges in the Dolomites.

As in alternative (a), continue on from Passo Tadega 20mins down to the signposted turn-off left (Alta Via 1). Now there's a steady but long 350m ascent south to Forcella del Lago at 2486m. On a good day on the way up during rest stops, you can admire the Campestrin peak, left, then Monte Cavallo, and Fanis on the right. You may see ermine (mountain stoats) here. The forcella is a narrowish rocky opening between the Torre del Lago (right) and the Scotoni peak, and leads to a plunge down into a ravine on loose scree to where the green waters of Lago Lagazuoi await you (2182m). Now yet another tiring ascent - this time for 600m on clearly marked path n.20 traversing the Alpe di Lagazuoi. The refuge is usually visible right from the start of the ascent, but you never seem to actually reach it. There are several path junctions, but just keep following indications for R. Lagazuoi. Note that the water at the refuge is not suitable for drinking.

Connection with the Tofane and Val Travenanzes walk 5 is feasible from R. Lagazuoi.

Should you decide not to overnight here (booking is advisable) to enjoy the views and sunset, you can descend to the underlying Passo di Falzarego (2105m) either by cable-car or on foot in about 1h30mins including a visit to the war galleries with a torch, (see walk 5 for details), or via Forcella Travenanzes (paths n.401/402) plain walking. There should be plenty of chamois on this stony terrain. At the pass there are bus connections both east to Cortina and northwest to Val Badia.

Walk 4 to Monte Averau, Nuvolau and the Cinque Torri also starts out from Passo Falzarego.

PRACTICAL INFORMATION

R. FANES TEL:(0474)501097 Private, sleeps 70. (*)
R. LAGAZUOI TEL:(0436)867303. Private, sleeps 70. (*)
R. LA VARELLA TEL:(0474)501079 Private, sleeps 40. (*)
R. S. CROCE TEL:(0471)839632. Private, sleeps 30. (*)
TOURIST OFFICE SAN CASSIANO TEL:(0471)849422.
(*) possible extended opening.

* * *

WALK 13 (see sketch map D, page 93)

PUEZ-ODLE GROUP
via La Villa - R. Gardenazza (1h30mins) - Ciampani (2h) -
R. Puez (30mins) - Forcella Ciampai (30mins) -
[alt. to Colfosco 1h45mins] - Passo Crespeina (1h15mins) -
Passo Cir (20mins) - Passo Gardena (40mins).
TABACCO MAP NO.07 scale 1:25,000
TABACCO MAP NO.9 scale 1:50,000
(2 days suggested)

After the initial climb up through tall forest, this walk consists of a delightful crossing over the sparsely vegetated high level limestone plateau that makes up a large part of the Puez-Odle Nature Park. The dolomite base of coral origin has been overlaid with layers rich in ammonite and consequently in fossils, found in the few natural 'monuments' and bizarre eroded shapes of residual deposits that emerge in solitude from the plateau base.

Walking on the plateau itself is mostly on level or across undulating terrain, with only several steepish ups and downs on the final stages approaching Passo Gardena. There are no particularly difficult sections and it can be recommended for all walkers of average fitness.

Views are magnificent and non-stop in all directions. The walk should preferably be done with clear weather conditions, as orientation on this exposed high-level plateau can be confusing and even treacherous with low cloud or when mist or fog roll in unexpectedly. Several detours and alternate descents are given.

Stage One: to R. Gardenazza (1h30mins) and via Ciampani (2h) to R. Puez (30mins)
There are bus connections with the Val Badia township of La Villa (Stern) (1483m) from virtually all directions of the compass: from Cortina in the east via Passo Falzarego, from the south via Arabba (connection with Passo Pordoi) and Corvara, from the Bolzano-Bressanone valley and Val Gardena in the west via Passo Gardena and Colfosco, and from Brunico in Val Pusteria in the north.

Once you've arrived in La Villa walk downhill a little, south of the Tourist Office on the main road and take the first road right in the direction of the main church. There is red and white waymarking though no number

SKETCH MAP D

at this stage. It's 10mins up to the hamlet and a notice-board - path n.11 starts uphill left (keeping to the right of the church). Soon it follows a lane signposted "Plotn" - the name of the abandonned dark timber farm buildings you soon reach (possibility of drinking water). Now it's up (northwest) gently through a shady cool forest, soft underfoot. Where the ski slope cuts across the path, keep left, on a level. In 30mins you are joined by a path from Hotel Dolomiti, and soon enter the Puez-Odle Nature Park. Stop and look south for the snow-laden Marmolada.

Continue to another path junction at the foot of a steep slope and take the path on the right that zigzags steeply up, then obliquely left, over rock into a narrow valley. Now there's a steep slog up a gully with high rock sides, before you reach the picturesque light wood and pasture terrace where R. Gardenazza stands, at 2045m. It occupies a brilliant panoramic position, with the Sassongher peak nearby southwest, the Marmolada and part of the Civetta visible far south. West to the Cunturines, Fanes, Lagazuoi, Col di Lana, and the crescent-shaped Sasso della Croce northeast with Forcella di Medesc clearly visible and the adjoining Lavarela peak.

Access to R. Gardenazza is also possible from Pedraces in Val Badia - path n.5 in 3h.

The next stretch takes you up to the high level plateau and, despite frequent waymarking, orientation in conditions of fog or low cloud can be very difficult. It is extremely inadvisable to proceed with this next section if the weather is already bad or looks like deteriorating.

From R. Gardenazza take n.11 briefly south past the malga hut and after the last of the alpenrose and thin wood and the n.5 turn-off to Sassongher with a waterfall to the far left, path n.11 winds and climbs straight up the hillside (due west). You come out onto a brief flowered (including edelweiss and gentians) level, then bear left towards a rock face - an arrow points up left and shortly you arrive at the entrance to the wild but not deep, narrow-sided Val Gardenazza. It is steep at first with irregularly strewn rocks (path junction and n.15 goes off left) but levels out a little. This quiet and solitary stretch, in a constant northwest direction, will take around 1h. Chamois are frequently seen. Even as late as July there may be old snow patches to cross or detour. When you finally emerge onto the vast Gardenazza plateau at the path junction with n.1 from Pedraces, you have made it to 2663m (2h this far). This, the highest point on the altopiano is referred to variously as the Ciampani, or as Piz or Cima (both meaning peak) della Gardenàccia (with various spellings). Weather permitting, you can now sit down with your map and start

R. Gardenazza with Sassongher

identifying all those mountains - even as far away as Austria. There is a triangular wooden trigonometric point to the right.

The multitude of flowers growing on such a desolate windswept limestone plateau is miraculous. Up here they take root in the meagre soil deposits sometimes found in dolinas - the typical shallow depressions found in karstic areas and that are the result of solution.

For the last 30mins to R. Puez, the path (still n.11) proceeds in a southwesterly direction and waymarking has been prepared with great care to help walkers. You pass under the green-red-yellow-grey mass of the continuously eroding Muntejela, and see its cone-shaped sister Col dles Soneles to the south. The descent is gradual and the refuge's Italian flag, which serves as a fixed reference point is visible long before you see the building itself. R. Puez occupies a protected position slightly into the right (northish), at 2475m sheltered from strong winds, with the old building nearby. Above it are the grey, fast weathering stratas of Col de Puez (2725m) and a great flock of crows.

A link with walk 14 is feasible here, including the descent to Selva in Val Gardena via Vallunga.

Stage Two: to Forcella Ciampai (30mins), Passo Crespeina (1h15mins), Passo Cir (20mins) and descent to Passo Gardena (40mins)

Following path n.2/4 head towards the flag pole, and you see magnificent vertical cliff walls as Vallunga opens up before you southwest. In good weather you can see all the way down to Selva in Val Gardena and further back to the Alpe di Siusi and the Sciliar.

It's 15mins on to a path junction (with n.15 to Forcella Gardenazza). Coast around the edge of the plateau to reach Forcella Ciampai and descend a brief narrow rock gully before a sharp right to the narrow saddle of the signposted forcella.

Alternate descent to Colfosco (1h45mins)

Should weather or personal circumstances necessitate a descent to Colfosco in Val Badia, take path n.4 southeast down the stony slope and into the wide amphitheatre where Lago Ciampai (2173m) glitters when it's not dried up and waters a marmot colony. Then down past the n.4 turn-off to Sassongher, and a small shrine before the next path junction. Here, one alternative is to turn right (south) down the wide valley on loose stones via Capanna Edelweiss to the scarred and newly developed valley. Lower down, just after the dark timber barns and farm buildings, as you near the departure station for the Col Pradat chair lift, is a signposted walkers-only path down the rest of the way to Colfosco (1h45mins total). Otherwise, to save time, take the southeastern branch (left) coasting under the Sassongher peak to reach Capanna Pradat (2038m), a refreshment stop with a high rating panoramic loo and the chair lift down to Colfosco (1640m). This should save you at least 30mins.

From Forcella Ciampai, take path n.2 southwest. It climbs briefly then meanders across the great vast altopiano once again. Sheep graze around the rocks, and any number of picnic spots present themselves for your perusal. Down to Lago Crespeina (2374m) with its 'beaches'. Here on enchanted nights, flaming red mice evidently used to come flying through the air and plunge into the lake!

You zigzag up amongst loose rubble to Passo Crespeina (2529m). The Sassolungo massif is now just visible ahead of you (southwest). But there's yet a further 'up and down' before you get anywhere near Passo Gardena. The path ahead is clearly visible crawling up the next mountain side. But first, after you've climbed over the wooden stile to keep the livestock on the side they're supposed to be on, there's a zigzag down

Aided rock passage on R. Chiggiato-R. Baion stretch (Walk 29)

Lago di S.Caterina and Auronzo with Sesto Dolomites (Walk 29)

R. ai Brentei and Cima Tosa (left) and Crozzon di Brenta (right) (Walk 31)
During the first part of the descent from R. Pedrotti & Tosa
looking west (Walk 31)

some 100m, then n.12 branches off west down Val Chedul to emerge at Selva in Val Gardena (3-4h). You keep left (n.2) and start climbing again gradually across the rubble slope towards Passo Cir. Even here there are still more crags and outcrops hiding the view of your destination! Instead, there's a short descent on loose rubble, a meander between rocky crags and finally the gradual descent to the Baita Clark (2222m) refreshment stop.

Here, as an alternative, you can take the brief path variant (n.2) right coasting (west) (10mins) to the Dantercepies cable-car (2298m) (closes at 5.30pm) to descend to Selva in Val Gardena. On foot via R. Panorama it takes around 1h30mins. Another possibility is to head left (east) for Colfosco (unnumbered path) via R. Forcelles (allow 1h30mins).

Otherwise, follow the final stretch of n.2, winding across flowered slopes and south down to Passo Gardena. Here you can contemplate the awesome walls of the Sella massif closeby and the Sassolungo southwest, and choose your accommodation.

PRACTICAL INFORMATION

R. ALPINA-FRARA (PASSO GARDENA) TEL:(0471)795225.
Private, sleeps 30.
R. CIASOTTA EDELWEISS (COLFOSCO) TEL:(0471)836024.
Private. Accomm.
R. GARDENAZZA. Private, sleeps 40. Information c/o Albergo
Miramonti, Pedraces, TEL:(0471)849282.
R. OSPIZIO (PASSO GARDENA) TEL:(0471)795133.
Private, sleeps 50.
R. PUEZ TEL:(0471)795365. Alpine Club, Bolzano section.
Sleeps 70.
TOURIST OFFICE COLFOSCO TEL:(0471)836145.
TOURIST OFFICE LA VILLA TEL:(0471)847037.

* * *

WALK 14 (see sketch map D, page 93)

ALPE DELLA PLOSE / PUTIA / PUEZ-ODLE GROUP
via Plancios - Passo Rodella (1h15mins) - Forcella di Putia (2h) -
R. Genova (30mins) - Rio San Zenone (50mins) -
R. Malga Brogles (2h30mins) - Forcella Pana (1h45mins) -
R. Firenze (1h20mins) - Forcella Forces de Sielles -
R. Puez (3h30mins) - Vallunga - Selva (Val Gardena) (2h30mins).
TABACCO MAP NO.07 (only partially) or
NO.05 (from R. Genova onwards) scale 1:25,000
TABACCO MAP NO.9 scale 1:50,000
(4-5 days suggested)

This itinerary starts out at the farthest northwestern top corner of the Dolomite region, just behind (southeast of) the city of Bressanone. It takes you into the heart of the Puez-Odle (or Puez-Geisler) Nature Park by way of a wide range of terrains of great geological interest, with a number of spectacular ascents and descents. You pass nearby the majestic Sass de Putia, move around to the west to coast under the north wall of the rugged Odles Needles with their strangely-shaped slender rock points, before the final stages east above Val Gardena across part of the exposed and sterile white-grey Puez plateau, with its rare patches of green grass. The itinerary comes to an end with a southwest descent to Val Gardena via Vallunga - here you will find perfect alpine scenery, lush meadows in flower and hopefully some wild animals.

The route can be divided into smaller sections - points providing alternate access are given where relevant in the walk description.

Stage One: to Passo Rodella (1h15mins)
The starting point of Plancios (or Palmschoss) has been chosen as it can be reached by public transport. However, if you arrive from Val Badia - bus from S. Martino to Passo delle Erbe at 1987m then walk 3km - by all means start your walk from Passo Rodella (Stage Two).

From the valley centre of Bressanone (main rail arteries north and south) a summer bus service runs via S. Giorgio di Eores and Plancios (1697m) up to the Sport Hotel (1911m). On foot from here to Passo Rodella will take you just over a pleasant hour, across meadows and through pine woods. Follow the dirt track (no.8) with its ups and downs, in a southeasterly direction. There is a torrent to cross, then a pine wood and a clearing with chalets.

At the path junction follow the signposting around and down slightly to R. Schatzer (1984m). Do take time to enjoy the magnificent views over southeast to the isolated Sass de Putia with its spruce woods underneath, and the Odle group. Then continue on path n.8 over open meadows, before descending (track n.4) to R. Halsl on the road at Passo Rodella (1866m). (This name for the pass is not used on older maps and is in fact hardly a 'pass' in the strict sense. However it coincides with Passo di Eores).

Stage Two: to Forcella di Putia (2h) and R. Genova (30mins)
Turn left up the asphalted road and it's 10mins to where path n.4 forks off right (south) into the Puez-Odle Nature Park (direction Forcella di Putia). Walking starts on level ground through the woods, then gradually climbs out of the trees to cross a torrent bed. Over to your left on the western flank of the imposing fossil-rich Sass de Putia are thick coverings of dwarf rhododendrons and mountain pine. Only the outskirts of this Nature Park are wooded, as the heart comprises the exposed rocky reaches and peaks.

Among the boulders next to the stream is a good spot for a restorative pause. Next is a somewhat stiff but steady climb - first up over a series of crests and gullies on the right-hand side of the valley before the steeper ascent up the centre of the narrow gully to the forcella straight up ahead, in a southeasterly direction. You'll probably find late-lying snow on the last stretch. If you decide to do this walk in the opposite direction you'll be able to enjoy sliding down it, as you'll probably see others doing. The omnipresent well-fed Dolomite forcella crows will be circling overhead, in the full knowledge that walkers always need a rest and snack (and hopefully leave edible scraps too) at the top.

It is quite astonishing to arrive at the forcella (2357m) from this direction as the narrow arrival gully and loose rock scramble leads you to expect a precarious ledge or similar on top and an equally steep descent on the other side. Instead however, you find almost rolling grassland. There are sweeping views east and southwards over towards the ranges of the Fanes-Sennes-Braies Nature Park and the mountains of Cortina.

Should these views not suffice, better ones will be available if you attempt the 500m, 3h-path up to your left - it leads to the summit of Sass de Putia (2874m). It is a rather steep, often exposed path, and is considered to be either an easy climb or a hard walk. The final stretch is a 150m fixed metallic cord ascent on rock.

From the forcella, one track southeast leads down to Longiarù, in the valley of the same name. Your path, still n.4, is the right branch, an easy 30mins in a southerly direction. Coasting around the wide open basin of Munt de la Crusc, it crosses undulating grassy slopes. In summer there are plenty of wild flowers here, including varieties of bellflowers and alpine asters. After crossing a spur you come to Passo Poma and its cross at 2340m. Take a moment to look back at the Sass de Putia as the views are about to change.

R. Genova (or Schlüter Hütte after its founder) is a brief stroll just below to the right, and offers a worthy introduction to the first outposts of the Odle group to the left (south). It also occupies a commanding position with views down the delightful and still heavily-wooded Val di Funes. The refuge's original wood and stone building has remained virtually unchanged since its construction, begun in 1908. The pleasant dining-bar area is almost entirely in warm wooden panelling with various decorative elements of a local flavour. One speciality of this predominantly German-speaking refuge is Kaiserschmarm, that pancake-fruit mixture dessert guaranteed to fill two people's empty gaps!

Stage Three: to Rio San Zanone (50mins) and R. Malga Brogles (2h30mins)
Head down the panoramic steep rough jeep track (n.3) southwest towards Malga Gampen at 2063m, but don't go all the way down to the buildings. Continue on dirt road (n.33) coasting across pasture land then descending a little more through a wood. You come out at the bridge crossing the icy cold terraced cascades of Rio San Zenone at 1890m. The malga (dairy farm) of the same name is briefly upstream.

This point can alternately be reached in about 40mins from the downstream parking area at R. Zannes (1684m) at the head of the Val di Funes. In summer a bus service links it with Bressanone and Chiusa via S. Pietro and S. Maddalena. The area around R. Zannes is famous for its spring flowers which carpet the meadows. These include the protected pasqueflower and pink bird's eye primroses, snowbells and crocuses, as well as anemones later in the season. It is also known to be an old haunt of roe-deer, particularly in the winter months.

Rio San Zanone is the start of the magnificent itinerary which skirts the base of the Odles at an average height of 2000m, and known since

1905 as the 'A. Munkelweg', after the founder of the Dresden Alpine Club. It is frequently signposted as such, or as the 'Sentiero delle Odle' (Odles Pathway). The path number is now n.35 and straight after the stream takes a southwesterly direction and climbs gradually through the woods. There are a number of clearings between woods of larch and Arolla pine, with the occasional shepherd and grazing cows with their heavy neck bells ringing and echoing around the rock faces. After about 30mins there is a signposted track leading off right down to Malga Glatsch (10mins). You continue straight on and up a little more, with ample opportunities to admire the imposing line-up from the left Sass da l'Ega and Gran Furcheta before Sass Rigais.

You cross grassy openings, more woods, then cut across the dwarfing debris-strewn northern flanks of the Odles. It is a magnificent walk, and the typically pale rock can actually be quite blinding in strong sunlight. There are several points in which the track, curving around natural obstacles and alternating between rough boulders and wood may be unclear. This scree area is constantly encroaching on the wood, as it is subject to occasional rock slides from the walls fringing it, and tracks are re-routed for brief stretches. Keep an eye out for the red and white paint markings, to save wasting time.

Just below a lower reach of Sass Rigais the path climbs an eroding earth ridge to Forcella del Pradel (2017m) and a path junction. A branch (n.34) turns right, north over and down to the picturesque meadows of Prati di Casnago and the unpronounceable Malga Gschnagenhardt (1996m). You keep left on the lower branch and descend into an ample basin filled with a thick covering of springy low-growing mountain pines. After crossing a bleached rock stream bed and a short, mainly level stretch, there is another path junction.

Should you decide at this stage to skip R. Malga Brogles and go straight on over to the Alpe di Cisles and R. Firenze (Regensburger Hütte), take the second turn-off to the left (south) for Forcella Pana (signposted Pana Scharte). It is a stiff and steep climb through the last groups of trees and boulders before the immense scree slopes, where you'll join up with the path from R. Malga Brogles - see Stage Four.

Otherwise, continuing on the previous path, in another half hour or so you'll arrive at R. Malga Brogles at 2045m. Set on the edge of the wood it provides one of the best points for viewing the jagged range of the Odles, and can also be reached directly from S. Maddalena in Val di Funes in about 2h30mins on path n.28.

Stage Four: to Forcella Pana (1h45mins) and R. Firenze (1h20mins)
This stage presents some difficulty as the approach to the forcella is extremely steep and the loose scree covering and old snow patches can make the going laborious and slippery at times. Taken with time and appropriate care however it is particularly rewarding as yet another superb panorama awaits you at the forcella.

Path n.6 from R. Brogles sets out through light wood, before moving onto the enormous scree slope. It climbs steeply in a southeasterly direction before joining up with the path variant from Stage Three and entering the narrow gully leading to the forcella. Seen from below it is awe-inspiring! A fixed metallic cord helps you over some initial rock, then you climb over loose scree, with some timber terracing supporting the track. Take it slowly with plenty of rest stops, so that you still have the breath and energy to enjoy the wonderful view as you come out. The tortuous ascent is quickly forgotten as you emerge from a rocky wilderness onto lush grassy slopes in sight of chalets, chair lifts and Val Gardena and the Sella Group southeast. A dark stone plaque at the forcella proclaims this as one of the borders of the Puez-Odle Nature Park.

The next section will probably mean more people, as the area is easily reached by day-trippers, from Ortisei and Santa Cristina in Val Gardena who make use of the cable-cars up to the arrival stations of Seceda (close by, slightly west from Forcella Pana) and Col Raiser (further along the track, southeast towards R. Firenze) as starting points for shorter walks. Should you wish to end the walk here, the cable-cars could be useful for a quick descent to the famous wood carving centres of Val Gardena.

The next stretch is on the southern side of the Odles, and down below on the grassy slope is the (Malga) Troier Alm chalet (no accommodation). It is quite a delightful homestyle place, providing hot meals, an abundance of interesting pieces of woodcarving in the local tradition, and a live peacock!

Soon afterwards along the path is a small lake. Its invigorating icy water can provide a welcome dip on a hot day. There are usually plenty of colourful butterflies and coleoptera beetles around here, and several types of grouse higher up.

Carrying on path n.1 towards the Alpe di Cisles, in a southeasterly direction, you climb up briefly to cross a rather bare earth ridge (Nature Park signpost), then return to grass and flowery meadows. R. Firenze at 2039m, visible below you now with its flag flying, is just an easy descent away. As its alternate name Regensburgerhütte suggests, the refuge was originally built by the German Alpine Club of the town of the same name, in 1888. It now belongs to the Florence branch of the Italian Club. As a backdrop the refuge has the Fermeda peak, the Odle di Cisles and the Sass de Mesdì, the lower reaches of which are inhabited by marmots, and the higher parts by chamois.

R. Firenze can also be reached on foot on path n.1 in just over 2h from Santa Cristina in Val Gardena, or by way of the Col Raiser gondola-car.

Stage Five: to Forcella Forces de Sielles (1h45mins) and R. Puez (1h45mins)

This stage is long and demanding with several exposed points, and crosses desolate landscapes, so it is advisable to attempt it after a good night's rest.

In hot weather set off as early as possible, because once you're out of the wood there is no shade. Carry plenty of water as R. Puez is more than 3h away.

Leave R. Firenze in a northeasterly direction on path n.2-3 and head down briefly to cross a torrent onto the other side of the Cisles valley. The well-marked path then climbs briefly before a level stretch preceding the opening to the immense scree and rubble valley that leads up to Forcella Forces de Sielles. Track n.13 branches off left. You continue southeast now on n.2, dwarfed by the rocky crests of Montijela above right and the Pulpiti later up left. As the path moves up into the wider upper valley head, path n.3 breaks off left to the Forcella della Roa. You continue climbing straight ahead in zigzags up the steep scree slope, to the Forcella Forces de Sielles at 2505m. The forcella itself is approximately halfway to R. Puez, but it's rather precarious taking a break perched on the narrow saddle with the crows. Signposting indicates an ascent to Col de la Pieres up right (2750m).

Now you turn north (left) and climb the narrow crest. There are several exposed passages and fixed metal cable is provided as this rock tends to crumble easily. You soon climb out onto a muddy, grassy platform affording excellent views of the Odles and suitable for a rest stop. Continue on path n.2 (don't be tempted by the Alta Via N.2 signs north to Forcella della Roa) bearing east now with several more narrowish sections. You coast down a little, but are still high up on steep scree slopes with a series of strange rocky pinnacles high above. After a steep descent over loose rock, there is a grass and earth level *Pian dal Ciaval* (2463m), probably with sheep grazing. After crossing a torrent bed and passing turn-off n.4 down south to Vallunga and Selva, walking is easier.

R. Puez

The last 30mins or so are along the grassy terraces of the Alpe del Puez, and waymarking is clear and frequent (n.2-4). You follow the edge of this high altitude, grey treeless plateau south then east with several more ups and downs and small streams to cross. You soon circle the base of the sandy Col del Puez (2720m) and continue around to R. Puez in its commanding position in a small lightly grassed valley at 2475m.

The position itself is not particularly picturesque because the area is so bare and desolate, but in good weather the views range all around the plateau. The modern building has pleasant wood-pannelled dormitories, tiled bathrooms with hot running water and delicious home-made apfel strudel. Owing to its difficult isolated position this refuge has its supplies flown in by helicopter, instead of the usual mechanised aerial cableway.

At this point, an alternative extension northeast across the plateau and on to Val Badia, or descents to Colfosco or Passo Gardena are possible by referring to walk 13.

Stage Six: descent via Vallunga to Selva (2h30mins)
Follow signposting for n.1 proceeding straight down south into the Vallunga (long valley). This initial stretch is very steep with plenty of loose rocks and scree, so take special care. The path descends obliquely passing several large rock outcrops covered with thickets of anchoring vegetation such as dwarf mountain pines. After 450m of descent the path
104

crosses white boulders and a torrent bed, and the stream then accompanies you down west to the wide top part of Vallunga. The U-shape profile of the valley is a typical glacier formation.

The rest of this stage consists in a long pleasant stroll southwest, so you'll have time to appreciate the wild flowers, which should hopefully include rare protected specimens such as the Lady's-slipper orchid and the flesh red, dark-spotted martagon lily. Chamois are known to inhabit the grassy moorlands of Vallunga, and resident birds include the eagle-owl and members of the grouse family.

At about 1800m are the meadows known as the "Prà da Ri". According to the locals, this means 'meadow for laughing' as the gentry of Wolkenstein (Selva) were said to have held great fancy dress parties there once, complete with musicians and comedians.

The n.4 turn-off up right to the Alpe del Puez is soon passed, and you enter light forest with a stream criss-crossing the way. The track number is now 4-14, and the valley narrows a little. Once out of the Nature Park, and after the car parking area castle ruins are visible up to your right, clinging precariously to the rock face. Pass the military sport centre below on your left and keep going straight ahead on the narrow road which will soon take you right into the township of Selva in Val Gardena.

Here you will find a shopping centre, tourist office and bus services connecting with both Passo Sella (south) and Passo Gardena (east) and beyond, or back west down Val Gardena to the main Isarco valley and the railway line between Bressanone and Bolzano.

PRACTICAL INFORMATION

R. MALGA BROGLES ALM. Private, sleeps 35.
R. FIRENZE (REGENSBURGER HÜTTE) TEL:(0471)796307. Alpine Club, Florence section. Sleeps 106.
MALGA GAMPEN TEL:(0472)40110. Private, sleeps 30.
R. GENOVA (SCHLÜTER HÜTTE) TEL:(0472)40132. Alpine Club, Bressanone section. Sleeps 80.
MALGA GLATSCH TEL:(0472)40270. Private, sleeps 17.
R. HALSLHÜTTE (PASSO RODELLA) TEL:(0472)40082. Private, sleeps 15.
R. PUEZ TEL:(0471)795365. Alpine Club, Bolzano section. Sleeps 70.
R. SCHATZER TEL:(0472)51343. Private, sleeps 12.
SPORTHOTEL (PLANCIOS) TEL:(0472)51329.
TOURIST OFFICE FUNES TEL:(0472)40180.
TOURIST OFFICE SELVA VAL GARDENA TEL:(0471)75122.

WALK 15 (see sketch map E, page 107)

SELLA GROUP
via Passo Gardena - R. Cavazza al Pisciadù (2h) -
R. Boè (2h30mins) - R. Forcella Pordoi (45mins) -
Passo Pordoi (1h30mins).
TABACCO MAP NOS.05, 06, 07 scale 1:25,000
TABACCO MAP NO.2 scale 1:50,000
(1-2 days suggested).

This enormous massif stands isolated, bounded by 4 road passes, and its unique fortress shape can be recognised from afar. Its sheer flanks are forbidding, and it would appear to be reserved for mountaineers and "via ferrata" experts. Several valleys however slice deep into the block, so the average walker can reach its high level plateau and even spend a night at over 2800m. The walk is not recommended for absolute beginners, as Stages One and Two involve a very steep ascent and several aided rock passages. A part of Stage Three however can also be covered from Passo Pordoi via the cable-car, which is also useful for avoiding the final steep scree descent and is immensely popular with day-trippers.

Walkers at the start of the season (June) should check that the refuges are open before starting out, and should expect to find extensive snow cover and possible icy tracts. High season walking, on the other hand, will mean a lot more people, but guaranteed easier conditions (and total absence of ice) at least by mid-July. It goes without saying that refuge accommodation should be booked beforehand, and if possible, weekends avoided.

Storms and snow falls are not unknown phenomenon in summer and autumn, and although the intervals between the various refuges are not excessively long, forecasts or any signs of unsettled weather or deteriorating conditions should be taken seriously. It is inadvisable to attempt the ascent and crossing of this high level plateau in anything but good weather. Paths and rock passages which seem easy in good weather can be treacherous and slippery when wet, and you could easily lose your sense of direction and way. Storms can also provoke rock falls, and lightning could be attracted to people on the plateau.

This stone desert is totally devoid of trees, but you may see the occasional hardy wild flower such as the tiny white alpine mouse-ear and saxifrage. The presence of wildlife is suggested by several place names

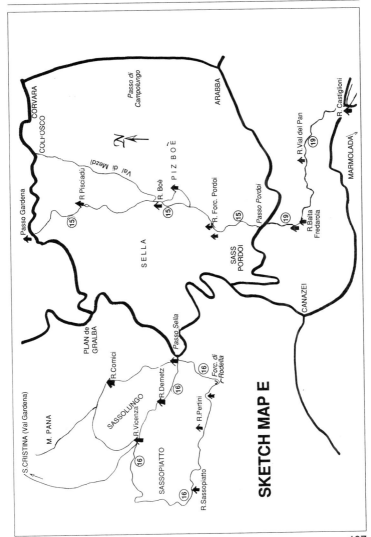

SKETCH MAP E

- Lago del Dragon, and Val di Lasties - the original Ladin name for which, "Stries" meant "witches", though it is now inhabited by large shy herds of chamois. Nowadays, don't expect to see more than some bird life, crows apart.

Stage One: to R. Pisciadù (2h)

Passo Gardena (2121m) can be reached by various buses from Val Badia (east), Val Gardena (west) or from Val di Fassa (south) via Passo Sella. If you're arriving directly from lowland areas, it's probably a good idea to spend your first night at Passo Gardena to give your body time to adjust to the altitude, instead of rushing straight up to the refuges at 2587m or 2871m.

Path n.666 (signposted) leaves the pass at its highest point, next to R. Alpina-Frara. It climbs straight up a grass and earth crest then bears left coasting on rocky terrain directly beneath the Sella's imposing northern flank, then climbs a little. After 30mins, you finally reach the opening to the wild Val Setus (right), and a path junction - here climbers for the famous "via ferrata Tridentina" keep on east around the mountain base a little longer, whereas you take a breather and prepare for the steep assault. As is immediately obvious the narrow Val Setus is more a ravine than a valley, and is full of mobile scree and rubble.

The path (n.666) turns up to the right (south) and starts climbing in tight zigzags. It is well and regularly marked by red and white paint on rocks. Don't be tempted by anything vaguely resembling a short cut though - it will undoubtedly be more slippery and may even be dangerous lying in the path of rock falls from above. As you climb, the sound of traffic winding up the road to the pass echoes up to you, and the road is in fact visible for some way when you look back. The overhead cables belong to R. Pisciadù's goods cableway. The path keeps mostly to the right-hand side of the gully, and as you approach its head, there will be tracts of old (well-trodden) snow to cross in all seasons. The path bears left and passes close to a rock outcrop, straight after which a signpost warns "Attenzione - caduta sassi" = "Watch out for falling rocks". The near vertical gully up sharp right regularly discharges rocks which come thundering dangerously down. Should you hear a not-so-distant rumbling sound, move up past the next signpost (only 10m or so away up the path) as quickly as possible to get out of the path of the falling material. There are frequent and deadly rock discharges as the iron cross on the rock face above testifies.

The path continues up left and the aided section begins with a thick

Signposting on the Sella Plateau

metal cable fixed firmly to the rock, and metal rungs. It is classified as an easy "via ferrata" and if done in ascent in normal conditions (it is extremely inadvisable in ice, snow or even rain) offers no difficulty. Without rushing, the aided stretch will take some 30mins, and you come out onto the rock terrace under the Sass da Lech. It's then only 10mins (left) to R. F. Cavazza al Pisciadù (2587m), a very pleasant, well-run refuge, recently modernised and enlarged. The township of Colfosco is visible down northeast, and on the mountain side is the pretty tarn Lago di Pisciadù which feeds the waterfall (hence the name) clearly seen from the road below.

Stage Two: to R. Boè (2h30mins)
Signposting for path n.666 points you down to the lake - bathing prohibited - which you then skirt on its left. The path climbs slowly south cutting across scree falls from the yellowish west flank of Cima Pisciadù. It soon turns left and there is a brief aided (fixed metal cable) rock passage (not exposed) which leads up into debris-filled Val di Tita. Snow patches abound, and as they slowly melt, there is a music of trickling water from beneath the surface. In a wet hollow (a spring is marked on the map), is the turn-off left up to the peak of Pisciadù (2985m). Keep right

on n.666. Though the path is not particularly difficult, you may find the going hard in ascent due to the altitude, so take your time. After following a narrow gully, you come out onto a rough platform where, with a brief detour right you can get a good airy view right down to R. Pisciadù and its lake.

Back to the waymarked path, and you'll soon reach the high point of 2900m, marked by a pole (1h20mins to here). You traverse a level top section next (south), with sweeping views over west to the vast Altipiano delle Meisules. All you can see now, any way you look is a stone desert. The terrain is barren, treeless, and not particularly attractive. The graceful rounded Sass Pordoi with its sheer sides is a welcome sight, virtually straight ahead (south, slightly west), the arrival station of the cable-car from Passo Pordoi perched on its peak. South and slightly east is Piz Boè with its repeater and hut clinging to it.

There is an easy 30min descent (south) now to a flattish area and path junction (n.657 Val Lasties). Nearby left, in the proximity of the elegant shape of the Torre Bérger, you get your first unnervingly dramatic glimpses plunging down into Val di Mesdì (east). For the final stretch there are 2 alternatives: right, signposted "corda metallica" (meaning an aided passage) which, while it avoids another ascent, follows a very narrow exposed ledge, and is recommended for experienced climbers only. The normal route climbs once again to 2900m, the highest point on the Antersas, naturally panoramic, and R. Boè is also visible now. Another 30mins or so down, then a curve right, will see you down at the refuge (2871m), an old rambling building with various extensions. On the slope to its east is the remnant of the small Boè glacier.

A less frequented but longer route to R. Boè is n.651 from Colfosco (1640m) south up the desolate Val di Mesdì. Allow 4h, but expect to find snow and possibly ice on the final 150m up to the refuge, if not before. This valley is a popular winter route for dauntless alpine skiers.

If the weather and visibility warrant it, a side trip to Piz Boè is feasible (path n.638). It is probably the easiest peak above 3000m to reach in the whole of the Dolomites, and is recommended for its far-ranging views. The path is however very steep and tiring, covering crumbly terrain, but all effort is adequately repaid. Capanna Fassa (3152m) perched on the mountain side is a refreshment stop rather than a regular refuge, and can only offer accommodation in

R. Forcella Pordoi

emergencies. Allow at least 1h for the ascent. There is an alternate descent (still n.638) but it bypasses R. Boè and rejoins path n.627 not far from R. Forcella Pordoi (see Stage Three).

Stage Three: via R. Forcella Pordoi (45mins) to Passo Pordoi (1h30mins)
From R. Boè path n.627 crosses well-trodden snow patches heading south across the rock upland. It cuts across the rubble and scree flows from Piz Boè, including some curiously red boulders. Follow the marker poles and coast on a level, before a curve down right across a series of rock ledges to a depression, most probably containing snow. There are several path variants here, due to winter ski routes, but they all end up at the same place - the path junction where n.638 links up (from Capanna Fassa on Piz Boè). The last part of the path coasts right (west) towards Sass Pordoi and R. Forcella Pordoi (2829m). This neat hut even provides limited accommodation.

On a good day, even if you don't intend to use the cable-car, it's worth climbing the final 100m (20mins) up to Sass Pordoi and R. Maria (no accommodation) for the views at 2950m.

From Forcella Pordoi, the 600m descent on foot to Passo Pordoi goes straight down that giddy gully opening left - "Pordoi" is painted on the rock next to the refuge's cableway machinery. There is virtually always snow at the top (possibly ice), and extra care is needed early in the season. There is a long stretch of metal cord secured to the rock (right), but after the brief initial part, you're better off going straight down on the easy scree. On the way down you have the cable-car dangling above right, while the magnificent Marmolada and its glacier are straight ahead (south). It's 30mins in (slowish) descent to the brief grassy terrace visible where the scree ends. At this point where you rejoin the path (n.627) it curves left around the rock outcrop among large boulders, then widens and winds easily down across grass and dark earth.

From the pass, buses connect with Val di Fassa (southwest), Passo Sella (northwest) and Arabba (east).

If you would like to see more of the Marmolada, continue on foot south via the Vial del Pan to Lago di Fedaia - see walk 19.

PRACTICAL INFORMATION

CASA ALPINA (PASSO PORDOI) TEL:(0462)61279. Private, hotel accomm. (*)

R. ALPINA-FRARA (PASSO GARDENA) TEL:(0471)795225. Private, sleeps 30.

R. BOE TEL:(0471)847303. Alpine Club, Trent section. Sleeps 60.

R. F. CAVAZZA AL PISCIADU TEL:(0471)836292. Alpine Club, Bologna section. Sleeps 100.

R. FORCELLA PORDOI. Private, sleeps 4.

R. OSPIZIO (PASSO GARDENA) TEL:(0471)795133. Private, sleeps 50.

TOURIST OFFICE ARABBA TEL:(0436)79130/79300.

TOURIST OFFICE COLFOSCO TEL:(0471)836145.

TOURIST OFFICE SELVA VAL GARDENA TEL:(0471)75122.

(*) possible extended opening.

* * *

WALK 16 (see sketch map E, page 107)

SASSOPIATTO / SASSOLUNGO
via Passo Sella - Forcella di Rodella (30mins) -
R. S. Pertini (45mins) - R. Sassopiatto (45mins) -
R. Vicenza (2h) - [alt. Passo Sella -
R. E. Comici (1h) - R. Vicenza (1h30mins)] -
R. Demetz (1h30mins) - Passo Sella (15-45mins).
TABACCO MAP NO.S 05 & 06 scale 1:25,000
TABACCO MAP NO.2 scale 1:50,000
(1 day possible but 2 suggested)

The magnificent Sassolungo group ("Langkofel" in German and literally "Long Stone" in English) stands isolated in extreme dramatic beauty. It is said that when the mountain was created, it buried the cruel king Laiadro who had refused a mother a medicinal herb needed for her dying son. On particularly windy days they say the desperate cry of the king can be heard, prisoner of the mountain.

The Sassolungo is easily reached by car and bus from all directions and consequently is not one of the quietest and naturally wild areas in the Dolomites. Despite this, it is still well worth visiting, and offers high altitude panoramic walking with classical Dolomite mountains and scenery, as well as ample opportunities for mountaineering.

The group, including the Sassopiatto ("Flat Stone"), the flattish 'squashed' southwestern part, is shaped like a horse-shoe, open at the northwest end, and it contains three small glaciers. Its highest peak is just over 3,000m.

The first part of the following itinerary runs along the 'F. August Weg', a walking route named after the last king of Saxony, a Dolomite enthusiast and in whose memory the Siusi section of the Alpine Club constructed this pathway in 1910, following traces of old pastoral routes. It coasts along between 2200-2300m under the south side of the Sassolungo and Sassopiatto.

This itinerary could be covered in a single day. However, in view of the possibility of crowds on the stretches of track within strolling distance of a road at peak times (mid-morning and mid-afternoon) at the height of the summer, it is proposed here as a 2-day walk with an overnight stop at R. Vicenza (Langkofelhütte). This hut is high in the heart of the massif, worlds away from the valley resorts, and this choice will furthermore, give you the added advantage early next morning of being alone on the track before the arrival of the daytrippers from the valley. To make a complete round trip of the group, including the north-eastern flank, the alternate route via R. E. Comici can be followed in either direction, from or to Passo Sella, and extended with a final descent to Val Gardena, famous for its delightful woodcarving.

Stage One: to Forcella di Rodella (30mins), R. S. Pertini (45mins) and R. Sassopiatto (45mins)

Various bus lines from Val di Fassa, Val Gardena and Val Badia serve the famous Passo Sella. It can also be reached in about 1h30mins on foot from Plan Gardena or 2h from either Campitello or Canazei down in Val di Fassa. It is superbly situated, although best appreciated if you manage to be there before the car hordes arrive, sitting among undulating grazing lands with ever-diminishing rhododendron shrubs between the dramatic mass of the magnificent Sella group, the flat-topped Sass Pordoi to its east and Sassolungo and Sassopiatto. The pass, strictly speaking, is a narrow stretch of road with snack bars, restaurants and souvenir stalls at 2214m. Slightly lower down towards the Val Gardena side is the wide grassy saddle and main parking area where R. Passo Sella (2176m) stands - the lovely old 4-floor stone building with its dark timber interior.

Starting from here, with the gondola-car station on your right, cut up (south) over a grassy slope (keeping the road to the pass itself and R. Valentini on your left) and head for the dirt track n.594/4 (no thoroughfare to unauthorised traffic) which bears right (southwest) and up towards Col Rodella. It's a 30min stroll among alpine pastures and glossy grazing cows - a contrast to the stark grey-white rock above. Go past a private refuge and up to Forcella di Rodella at 2308m. And stroll you must, so as not to miss savouring the sweeping views southeast to the gleaming glacier on the unmistakable immense form of the Marmolada.

As you arrive at the wide bare earth saddle of Forcella di Rodella, in addition to Col Rodella up to the left (south) with its two refuges and the arrival station of the cable-car from Campitello, another superb panorama spreads itself out before you - from southwest to west (left to right) - the Catinaccio range then right and the Sciliar and Alpe di Siusi.

The F. August Weg (n.594/4) turns right (west) here, passes the private historic refuge bearing the name of the king and his photograph, and coasts beneath the Grohmann peak. The brown earth track curves left and around but keeps at a constant high level leaving you free to appreciate the views. About halfway around is the new smart timber refuge (meals only ie. no accommodation) named after the late, well-loved Italian President, Sandro Pertini, a great lover of Val Gardena. The track continues with slight ups and downs, under the steep sides of the Torre Innerkofler then the Dente di Mezzodì. There are brief descents over white loose rock then a grassy platform before you pass above dairy farm buildings on your left and come up to the commanding position on a grassy crest occupied by the R. Sassopiatto (Plattkofelhütte) at 2256m. After the Alpe di Siusi to the west you now look north over towards the Austrian mountain ranges.

Stage Two: to R. Vicenza (2h)
The next stretch is quieter and, as well as plenty of wild flowers, you may see falcons circling and swooping for small rodents. Should you hear the sweet notes of a nightingale's song instead, remember that it is probably the princess of Sassolungo. The power to turn into a nightingale and back to human form at will, was her reward for saving a nightingale from the clutches of a sparrow-hawk. Unfortunately she was carried away with her sweet singing and an innocent young hunter fell in love with her. When he consequently died from a broken heart because the bird stopped visiting and singing to him, she stayed as a nightingale as punishment.

As you leave R. Sassopiatto you'll see the signpost pointing up right to climb 'via ferrata' (aided climb) on the Sassopiatto mountain - it climbs down inside the Sassolungo to the refuge. Your path (n.527) instead follows a rough ditch-like earth track for a short stretch in descent then across stone and muddy earth and branches right (north) becoming a narrow path across grassy slopes. A good few watershed courses are crossed and pasture becomes more lush and there are lightly wooded areas. There are several tracks leading up from various huts down left. You circle around the western base of the Sassopiatto to a brief flat area and a fence and stile at Piz da Uridl (about 50mins to here).

Briefly left along the eroded earth crest and you descend to 2000m (various short cuts possible). There is drinking water at the trough at the base of the slope. Large boulders and tall Arolla pines characterise the next brief stretch, then it's back onto rock - this time extensive stretches of white scree. The track is well signposted and on a level or in ascent eastwards, so don't be tempted to follow the variants leading off left to join the main track (n.525) down to Val Gardena. Curving right you begin climbing to enter the wide internal valley of the Sassolungo and, after a delightful stream crossing are joined by track n.525 coming up from S. Cristina. The wide white stone and scree jeep track now proceeds

Looking up inside the Sassolungo / Sassopiatto massif with R. Vicenza

upward in easy zigzags with a final sweeping curve around right to 2258m and R. Vicenza al Sassolungo.

This refuge dates back to 1894, and was rebuilt in 1903 after being destroyed by an avalanche. It is set right in the heart of the group at the foot of the Punta Dantersass at the confluence of the two valleys (leading up right to Sassopiatto and left to Forcella del Sassolungo). It is dwarfed by the immense towering walls around it. Sunsets bring superb deep pink colouring to the wall of the Sassolungo facing the refuge. Despite its stark silent surrounds (apart from the omnipresent scavaging crows) the refuge has a very comfortable dormitory and provides typical home-style cooking. This usually includes Knödel ("Canederli" in Italian) which are light dumplings flavoured with liver or smoked pork (known as "Kaiserfleisch") and served in a consommé or sauce with Parmesan cheese. Another Tyrolese delight found here, particularly recommended if you're starving, is the Kaiserschmarm, a sweetish concoction of pancakes with pieces of fresh and dried fruit, served with blackcurrant jam and liberally sprinkled with icing sugar. Must be tried!

One alternate access route to R. Vicenza from Santa Cristina in Val Gardena takes about 2h30mins, and follows path n.525 via Pian del Confin and a jeep track. Others are referred to in the following section.

Alternate access from Passo Sella via R. E. Comici (1h) - R. Vicenza (1h30mins)

The alternate access (n.526/528) from Passo Sella goes right (north) from the gondola-car departure station and crosses the area known as "Città dei Sassi" ("Rock City"), so-called due to the enormous irregular rock masses and boulders lying there, the result of some ancient landslide. There are no particular difficulties on this section, so you'll have ample time to identify all those mountains, including the Puez-Odle Group peaks to the northeast as well as the imposing Sella massif with the flat-topped southern part Sass Pordoi. After R. Comici (2153m) with its chair lift connecting with the Piz Sella cable-car station and Plan de Gralba (road), you essentially keep left (northwest). N.526a maintains a higher level after it branches off from the main n.526 which rejoins it around the corner at Col de Mesdì, while n.528 descends to Monte Pana and Santa Cristina in Val Gardena. The only remaining ascent then is on the final stage, as you bear south to enter the Sassolungo and have 200m or so to climb.

Stage Three: to R. T. Demetz (1h30mins) and descent to Passo Sella (15-45mins)

This 400m ascent is not particularly difficult but can be tiring. As you leave R. Vicenza there are good views north toward the undulating Austrian alps. At the signpost right outside the hut, follow the pointer for path n.525. It will take you up left of the base of the Punta Dantersass to climb southeast into a spacious cirque. There's an unreal silence in this barren scree and snow wilderness, particularly if you're there early enough to precede the daytrippers who take the gondola-car up from Passo Sella and descend this way.

Waymarking may occasionally be unclear as snow and subsequent movements of the scree as well as erosion from the rock faces above may change the course slightly. If walking when the season is well under way, the best hint is to follow the most down-trodden variant. Early spring walkers should consult their map frequently for the desired direction as late-lying snow will inevitably cover waymarking and the path itself. The general direction though, once you've entered the Sassolungo valley, is straight up (southeast) towards the narrow forcella visible high up ahead. The track follows the valley floor and you'll get a glimpse of the névé, the permanent snow laying on the small glacier up right, as well as superb views of the craggy Cinque Dita (Five Fingers), the rocky pinnacles right of the forcella. The path crosses the stream and climbs steeply on the right side of the valley. Rough terrain with loose earth and stones among large uneven boulders characterises the climb to the brief level area and Forcella del Sassolungo at 2681m. Snow lies here almost all year round.

Compulsory rest stop here to admire the views of the Marmolada massif (southeast), among others.

Now the decision about the 500m descent - whether to take the gondola-car down (cheaper rates for the down trip) in that swaying yellow bubble or to scramble down the rough scree path clearly visible under the cableway. Path n.525 drops down steeply in zigzags which widen out into an open gully then continue over grassy slopes all the way to Passo Sella. Should you prefer to do this in ascent, allow at least 1h20mins.

At this point, should you wish to complete a round trip of the Sassolungo, proceed with the alternative at the end of Stage Two to circle the northeastern face, then descend to Val Gardena.

PRACTICAL INFORMATION

R. E. COMICI - no accommodation
R. FRIEDRICH - AUGUST TEL.(0462)764919 - accommodation
R. PERTINI TEL.(0462)750045 - accommodation
R. T. DEMETZ TEL:(0471)795050. Private, sleeps 40.
R. ALBERGO PASSO SELLA TEL:(0471)795136. Alpine Club, Bolzano Section. Sleeps 80.
R. SASSOPIATTO (PLATTKOFELHÜTTE) TEL.(0462)750342 Private, sleeps 40.
R. VICENZA AL SASSOLUNGO (LANGKOFELHÜTTE) TEL:(0471)792323. Alpine Club, Vicenza Section. Sleeps 40.
TOURIST OFFICE S. CRISTINA TEL:(0471)793046.
TOURIST OFFICE SELVA VAL GARDENA TEL:(0471)795122.

* * *

WALK 17 (see sketch map F, page 120)

SCILIAR / CATINACCIO / RODA DI VAEL
via Siusi - Bagni di Razzes (45mins) - Malga Prossliner
Schwaige (1h20mins) - R. Bolzano (2h15mins) -
R. Alpe di Tires (1h45mins) - Passo del Molignon (45mins) -
R. Passo Principe (1h30mins) - R. Vajolet (40mins) -
Passo delle Coronelle (1h30mins) - R. A. Fronza (1h) -
R. Roda di Vael (1h30mins) - Vigo di Fassa (2h30mins).
TABACCO MAPS NO.05 & NO.06 (both partially) scale 1:25,000
TABACCO MAP NO.2 scale 1:50,000
(3-4 days suggested)

This is undoubtedly one of the most enjoyable and beautiful itineraries in the Dolomites and should definitely be taken at an easy pace, not rushed. Starting from the township of Siusi (Seis) the route climbs to where the Alpe di Siusi (Seiser Alpe) open out into lush rolling alpine pastures. Evidence has been found of prehistoric settlement throughout the area, including an elegant Bronze Age sword from Castelvecchio (now in Bolzano's Museo Civico). Since the 16th century, the 56sq.kms have been subject to strict regulations to ensure protection for grazing (mostly sheep and horses nowadays) and intensive hay-making. Vehicular access is also strictly limited.

The rich top layer of clay which serves to hold water, makes for abundant springs and swampy areas and, of course, fertility, also helped by the presence of the deteriorating volcanic layers of tuff and lava. The extraordinary plant life on these upland pastures has evidently undergone damage in recent years due to the use of artificial fertilisers as well as tourism. The area is by no means bare though, with a range of wild flowers from crocuses, alpine snowbells and anemones to the purple monk's-hood, gentians, alpine poppies, red lilies, columbines and the low-growing armeria or thrift, known as the 'witch of the Sciliar'. The most interesting examples are to be found on the next stage, as the route proceeds up to the high Sciliar rock plateau. It is of ancient coral reef origin, typical of the western Dolomites. As the massif seems to have stayed above the levels of glacier flow, surviving flowers that are thus considered endemic include Moretti's campanula (bellflower) that grows in the crannies on bare rock faces, and the unusual spiky devil's claw.

The route then continues south to cross immense scree slopes and

119

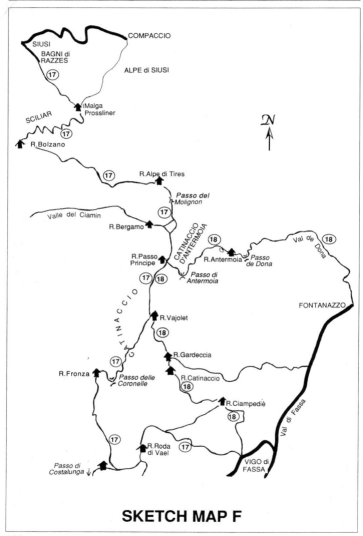

SKETCH MAP F

an unworldly lunar landscape before dropping down inside the main shell of the Catinaccio. Then, after a climb out to the western side, the panoramic track coasts south. The last stage is the descent to the pastoral peace of the picturesque Fassa valley.

The area is steeped in legends, as the (friendly-looking) witches on broom sticks on the tourist brochures suggest. The legend of the Catinaccio massif itself has to be the most delightful in the Dolomites. The story, containing Germanic and Rhaetian-Ladin elements, is related to the German name "Rosengarten", ie. rose garden. The Italian name in fact (originally used only for a small part of the massif) derives from 'bowl', referring to its shape. The story tells of dwarves who once lived inside the Rosengarten, with their kindly king Laurino, and countless treasures. On the outside slopes were wonderful gardens of red roses that flowered all year long. Disaster struck when a party of locals attacked to rescue their kidnapped princess and capture the dwarf king. This involved a battle with magic rings and belts to render the wearers invisible.

Laurino later escaped to return home and cast a spell on his beloved roses turning them to stone, as it was their presence that had led the enemy to the entrance to his kingdom. Never again, at neither night nor daytime would his roses be seen in their glory. But he forgot to cover in-between times, and so it is that every evening after sunset, on the rocky flanks of the Rosengarten/Catinaccio King Laurino's red roses appear in their glowing splendour, for just a few moments prior to nightfall. This phenomenon is known as "Alpenglühen" in German ("alpenglow"), and more evocatively "Enrosadira" in the local Ladin language, and can luckily be enjoyed all over the Dolomites.

Stage One: via Bagni di Razzes (45mins), Malga Prossliner Schwaige (1h20mins), to R. Bolzano (2h15mins)

Buses connect Bolzano (Bozen) (bus terminal is across the park from the railway station) with Siusi (45mins), and there are also services to Val Gardena and beyond. Before you start out from Siusi (1000m) however, stock up on the delicious crunchy rounds of local rye bread with fennel seeds, known as "Völser Schüttelbrot".

There are various ways out of the village. One is slightly uphill from the Tourist Office on the right, by way of Via Ibsen (Strasse). Turn right (easterly direction) along it until it meets up with Via Ratzes (Weg), go right (south). If in doubt ask for "Bagni di Razzes" in Italian or "Bad Ratzes" in German. It soon crosses the cold rushing torrent Rio Freddo and starts to climb quite steeply, though still as a road all the way to the tranquil (and somewhat costly) spa hotel set in thick dark fir-woods at 1212m.

Now it's a proper walking track as this is the farthest cars can go, being one of the outer limits of the Sciliar (Schlern) Nature Park. Just behind the hotel cross a brief meadow then the path (n.1a) is signposted and turns right to cross Rio Freddo and start the climb. The path is clearly marked through woods inhabited by birds such as crossbill finches feeding on conifer seeds, tits, the black woodpecker and several types of owls. It then follows the torrent with its couple of cascades all the way up. In about 30mins another track forks off right to R. Malghetta Sciliar (Schlernbodenhütte), and you go briefly left and re-cross the torrent by way of a bridge.

Climbing up the left bank is likely to be very cool and shady in the early morning, a relief as the going is steep here. At last you climb out to pastoral peace and a wooden cross at Malga Prossliner (1739m) (meals only - no acommodation). Rest a while and enjoy the view of the north end of the Sciliar plateau with Punta Santner far right. Below that broken-away point or 'tooth', above the township of Siusi, stands the castle (Castelvecchio - Havenstein -), erstwhile home of the medieval troubadour Oswald von Wolkenstein. (See walk 18 for the well-known legend that links him with Lago Antermoia).

Should you prefer a short ramble across the flowery meadows (particularly in July before the grass has been cut) dotted with hay chalets, an alternative for getting this far (and cutting out the climb) leaves from the Alpe di Siusi itself. Buses run up to the resort villages, and from the car park at Compaccio (Kompatsch) (1844m) on path n.10 to Malga Prossliner will take you just under an hour. You can also branch off before Malga Prossliner, on n.5 to Malga Saltner (1826m), then join up with n.1 to R. Bolzano (Schlernhaus). This last possibility requires a total of 3h from start to finish.

From the Malga, the track traverses grassy slopes and descends slightly to the torrent, which it then crosses (don't be tempted by signposting left to Malga Saltner as it lengthens the distance). Orientation is a little confusing on this stretch, as the track meanders a little, sometimes confused with muddy animal tracks, so watch out for waymarking. There is also a turn-off (northwest) to the Schlernboden Hütte. Shortly uphill you join the 'main road' n.1 (from Malga Saltner). As well as other walkers on this well-known route known as the 'Touristensteig', you will encounter affable local shepherds and hay-cutters (depending on the season) wearing their characteristic dark-blue aprons embroidered with flower motifs and often the name of their malga. Don't expect to hear them yodel though.

Now begins the hard 500m+ slog west up the mountain-side - the sun can be fierce in mid-summer as this entire stretch is exposed, so take your time and plenty of drinking water. The track is loose stone and there are wide bends through low springy mountain pines. The final stretch alternates grass and rock where glossy black alpine salamanders may be seen, particularly after rain. There may also be the odd snow patch as you come up to the edge of the Sciliar Altipiano and cross to R. Bolzano at 2457m.

The sturdy and comfortable stone building, constructed in 1885, stands just near Monte Pez ie. the 2564m 'hillock' to the north, which is worth the 20min or so wander up for an even more sweeping view. In fact, on a clear day you should be able to see from the Catinaccio and Latemar south, over to the Brenta Group southwest, behind Bolzano west to the Venoste peaks, northeast to the Puez-Odle Group, west to the Sassolungo and Sella, and even as far as the Marmolada and Cortina and Zoldo mountains. This is believed to be the site of prehistoric ritual animal sacrifices as well as witches' Sabbaths (until the cruel 16th century witch hunts started).

Alternate access from Fiè (4h30mins)
One very worthwhile alternate route to R. Bolzano is path n.1 from the village of Fiè (Völs) (bus from Bolzano), at 880m on the western side of the Sciliar. The track leaves from the lake (Laghetto di Fiè), going southeast and touches on Malga Tuff, Peter Frag (wooden crucifix), then a narrow rock corridor when the path crosses a very interesting 700m long timber 'bridge' with the river rushing away below. It is an ancient stock route still in use today for taking the flocks up to summer grazing grounds. Malga Seggiola is passed, before the final climb up to R. Bolzano.

Stage Two: to R. Alpe di Tires (1h45mins), R. Passo Principe (2h15mins) and R. Vajolet (40mins)
Your next destination is the private refuge Alpe di Tires (Schutzhaus Tierser Alpl), southeast from R. Bolzano. It's an easy walk, mostly level at first. Follow signposting for n.3-4, right along the top of the Sciliar rock platform. As it nears the Terrarossa peaks it bears down to the right over

a rocky spur. From here the rest of the path is visible including the refuge in the distance to the east with the Sella Group as its backdrop. Continue coasting along the base of the long wall. Below right is the Buco dell'Orso ("Bear Hole"!) and you come to a junction with the steep path n.3a that comes up from Tires. Further on you arrive at R. Alpe di Tires (2440m), set just below the pass of the same name.

A rest and refreshments in the sun will give you time to admire the Terrarossa Denti (literally 'Red Earth Teeth') and evidence of ancient volcanic activity on the coral reef directly behind this relatively new refuge and its small chapel. The snow hare is said to inhabit these high reaches. Sassolungo and Sassopiatto can be seen to the northeast. Due to the absence of roads in the underlying wide valley, there are footpaths linking it with R. Sassopiatto (about 2h) over the valley, where you can connect up with walk 16. Back on the western side, access from the township of Tires on the southwest side of the Sciliar takes about 3h30mins.

Walk up to the pass and follow signposting for path n.554 south across grass then obliquely up the rocks for a short stretch of easy climbing. Take particular care in wet conditions. Waymarking on this stage consists mainly of red and white paint splashes on rocks. After 2 small forcellas you zigzag steeply to a ridge. Cloud permitting the nearby Passo del Molignon will be visible from here straight ahead with the immense Valbona peak directly behind it.

You drop briefly and skirt around a silent debris-filled amphitheatre to the rocky opening of the pass at 2600m. It's a good 45mins this far. Now the path zigzags down the dramatic and very steep scree slope, probably with late-lying snow. Descend about 300m as far as the turn-off right down to R. Bergamo (Grasleitenhütte). (Set at 2129m, this Alpine Club Refuge is relatively quiet, being off the beaten track and is on an alternate access to the itinerary - the ascent from the village of Tires or Lavina Bianca on paths 3/3a takes about 3h30mins and follows the picturesque Valle del Ciamin).

Your path (still n.554) is clearly visible now, cutting across the extensive slope of scree and debris. Crossing this completely bare, silent amphitheatre (Conca del Principe) is quite dramatic, and mere walkers are dwarfed under the immense crumbling rock wall. Including the steep ascent up the gully on the other side between the Valbona peak right (2824m) and the Antermoia peak towering left (3004m), it takes another 1h30mins from Passo del Molignon to Passo del Principe (2600m).

You now leave the Sciliar Nature Park and enter the realms of the Catinaccio. The tiny private refuge R. Passo Principe

(Grasleitenpasshütte) comes into sight as you reach the pass. It nestles under a rock overhang in bare surrounds usually amidst late-lying snow on the southern side gazing down inside the Catinaccio, and in mid-summer is usually drenched in blazing sun. As well as a "via ferrata" to the top of the Antermoia peak (3004m), path n.584 climbs from here (east) to explore the pass, lake and refuge of the same name - see walk 18.

After the initial steep parts down loose rubble and scree, path n.584 is a stroll south down the right hand side of this silent sunny valley which leads down into Val di Fassa. The procession of the main peaks starting on the left (east) begins further down with Cima Scalieret then Cima Pope. Your attention is drawn to the right though, where the Torri (Towers) del Vajolet rise sheerly to just over 2800m. The large stone buildings of R. Vajolet and the newly-rebuilt timber R. Preuss are soon visible below at 2243m. R. Vajolet is more a rambling old hotel than an alpine refuge, and somewhat chaotic at the height of summer with day-trippers. Booking is strongly recommended. No complaints about the position though! R. Preuss only offers refreshments. Directly to the west is a seemingly vertical gully (leading to R. Re Alberto, R. Passo Santner and a via ferrata) with Punta Emma on its left and the long sheer Vajolet spires and towers on its right. Then, looking south down the valley towards Val di Fassa you should be able to see the Monzoni group with Punta Vallaccia.

> Access from the Val di Fassa is possible from Vigo di Fassa by way of the Ciampediè cable-car (or 1h45mins on foot) then a further 1h45mins on foot via R. Gardeccia. Otherwise, from Pera di Fassa a minibus taxi service runs part of the way to R. Gardeccia (limited traffic access), from where it's another 1h on foot.

Stage Three: to R. A. Fronza (2h30mins) then to
R. Roda di Vael (1h30mins)
Follow the main track south from the rock platform where the refuges stand, and take the first turn-off to the right - signposted n.541 (to the Coronelle and Cigolade passes). There is another short descent then the climb starts obliquely with occasional patches of grass, up the rocky flank at the base of the Cresta dei Diavoli (Devils' Crest) a procession of multiform small rock spires and needles.

After about 45mins a path junction is reached with the path coming up from R. Gardeccia and the one over to Passo Cigolade. Yours is n.550, the wider track going right and up into a pleasant rubble-filled amphitheatre. The narrow (about 1-metre) opening of Passo delle Coronelle at 2630m is easily reached (another 45mins from the last junction mentioned). Take a rest in this rock wilderness and time to admire the valley behind you with the Antermoia peak north, the Larsec precipices opposite (northeast) and hopefully the Marmolada to the southeast.

The next stretch is very steep and care is needed as the terrain is loose and crumbly down the narrow gully. Snow will be found early in the season. After some 300m or so in descent, the gully opens out and the path bears right across flatter ground, a sort of detritic ledge with interesting stratification. Now you will have time to admire the magnificent views to Bolzano, Val d'Ega and the Val di Tires. For the final stretch waymarking is the usual red and white painted stripes but on rock slabs. N.542 goes off north to Passo Santner, but you clamber down a short rock gully (extra care is needed in wet conditions) for a final drop to R. A. Fronza alle Coronelle (2239m). The arrival station of the second stage of the gondola-car from Nova Levante via Malga Frommer is just below the refuge and can mean crowds, however a stop should at least be made on the sun terrace to take in the wide-ranging views.

From here a descent on foot to Nova Levante in the valley takes about 2h-2h30mins, and you can connect with buses running northwest to Bolzano and southeast to Val di Fassa and beyond.

The next 5kms coast between 2200-2300m and constitute the 'Sentiero del Masaré'. Path n.549 heads south, and you keep to the highermost track - variants detour off to R. Paolina and Passo Nigra at a grassy knoll. All you have to do is keep strolling, virtually straight ahead and admire the imposing Latemar massif across the valley southwest, reflected in the famous multi-coloured waters of the Lago di Carezza.

The route passes under the western flank of the Vael group, including the Coronelle and the 400m smooth sheer reddish Roda di Vael. After passing above R. Paolina (two more paths lead off downwards) there is a large bronze eagle monument and stone plaque to Christomannos, a Viennese who was responsible for making this part of the Dolomites accessible to tourism. As the far-off Pale di San Martino come into view (southeast), the path bears gradually east then north and there are fewer people now, as the last stretch over grass brings the path to a finish at the rocky outcrop with the recently-renovated and whitewashed R. Roda di Vael (Rodwandhütte) (2283m). These days it is a very peaceful place to spend the night, and is positioned in front of the Mugoni peaks and Passo and Cresta Cigolade. Now inhabited by marmots, these mountains were once the dwelling place of witches. On full moon nights they used to go and sit atop the Mugoni and have parties, amusing themselves hurling flaming wheels down the other side onto the Cigolade, which means 'burnt'.

The refuge can also be reached from Passo di Costalunga in 1h30mins on path n.548.

Stage Four: descent to Vigo di Fassa: (2h30mins)
The concluding stage entails a descent of just over 900m down to the Val di Fassa. The path is n.545 at first, and it leaves the refuge in a northerly direction, allowing good views of the surrounding mountains. It curves around onto a level area at the head of the Vaiolon valley, before proceeding east and downwards. There are thinly wooded areas, and several corner-cutting path variants - take care not to stray off too far as there are other minor tracks down right. After about 30mins walking, soon after a small building on the right (2000m), path n.545 bears off left (northeast) to R. Ciampediè (about 1h). It is a fairly level track connecting with the cable-car down to Vigo, should you feel like treating yourself to a mechanised descent, and links with walk 18.

Otherwise keep heading downwards (new path n.547). For the most part across pasture areas, it goes from one side of the valley to the other, crossing the torrent a good few times. Waymarking is clear and frequent. After recent stone and rubble terracing work on the torrent, and the third crossing, you walk on a dirt road. There is a non-vehicle short cut across meadows, another brief stretch of dirt track, and you're back to civilisation - Vigo di Fassa (1393m) with shops and buses to destinations such as Canazei up valley northeast, and the towns of Trent (southwest) and Bolzano (west) with railway connections.

PRACTICAL INFORMATION
R. ALPE DI TIRES (SCHUTZHAUS TIERSER ALPL)
TEL:(0471)727958. Private, sleeps 68.
HOTEL BAD RATZES TEL:(0471)706131.
R. BERGAMO (GRASLEITENHÜTTE) TEL:(0471)642103. Alpine Club, Bergamo section. Sleeps 90.
R. BOLZANO (SCHLERNHAUS) TEL:(0471)612024 Alpine Club, Bolzano section. Sleeps 124.

Bolzano section. Sleeps 124.
R. A. FRONZA ALLE CORONELLE TEL:(0471)612033 Alpine Club,
Verona section. Sleeps 63.
R. PASSO PRINCIPE (GRASLEITENPASSHÜTTE)
TEL:(0462)764244. Private, sleeps 13.
R. RODA DI VAEL (RODWANDHÜTTE) TEL:(0462)764450. Alpine
Club, Trent section. Sleeps 60.
R. VAJOLET TEL:(0462)763292 Alpine Club, Trent section.
 Sleeps 115.
TOURIST OFFICE ALPE DI SIUSI TEL:(0471)727904.
TOURIST OFFICE FIE TEL:(0471)725047.
TOURIST OFFICE NOVA LEVANTE TEL:(0471)613126.
TOURIST OFFICE SIUSI TEL:(0471)707024.
TOURIST OFFICE VIGO DI FASSA TEL:(0462)602272.

* * *

WALK 18 (see sketch map F, page 120)

CATINACCIO D'ANTERMOIA
via Vigo di Fassa - R. Ciampediè (5mins-1h30mins) -
R. Vajolet (1h45mins) - R. Passo Principe (1h) -
Passo d'Antermoia (45mins) -
R. Antermoia (1h) - Val de Dona - Fontanazzo (3h).
TABACCO MAP NO.06 scale 1:25,000
TABACCO MAP NO.2 scale 1:50,000
(2 days suggested)

The Antermoia is virtually the central part of the Catinaccio Group, and
likewise is very popular with walkers and climbers. Weekends in mid-
summer are best avoided, unless you book your accommodation in
advance. Some huts may not however accept phone bookings. There
are a number of private refuges with no phone, meaning that you have
a greater chance of finding somewhere to sleep, as they work on a 'first
come first served' basis. Though this walk could, at a stretch, be done in
one day, it would be a pity not to overnight at one of the high-level refuges.
    Once you've climbed up inside this basin-shaped mountain group,

---

From Forcella Vallaccia looking down towards Biv. Zeni (Walk 21)

From Passo delle Vette Grandi, looking down onto R. Dal Piaz
(Walk 26)   Photo by G.Longo

Glimpse of the Schiara from the approach path   (Walk 28)

the second stage takes you over to the east into a stone desert valley ending with the lake - Lago d'Antermoia. Legend tells how it was formed when a jet of black water spurted up from the ground in place of the nymph Antermoia, bride-to-be of a local youth Oswald who had inadvertently caused her disappearance by finding out her name. The consequent pain he suffered broke the spell his mother had put on his hands when he was still a child, earning him the nickname of "Man de Fjer" (hand of iron). Having lost his chance for love, he became a famous minstrel, but his travels were aimless wanderings, as had been foreseen by the fortune-teller whose advice his well-meaning mother had acted on.

Another tragic story is told about the origin of the Rosengarten, the German name for the Catinaccio - see walk 17.

Stage One: via R. Ciampediè (5mins-1h30mins), R. Vajolet (1h45mins) to R. Passo Principe (1h)

Vigo di Fassa (1393m) can be reached by coach from Trent (and the railway) in the south, Falcade (east), Bolzano and the railway line (west) as well as various northern destinations.

The easiest way to get to R. Ciampediè on the other hand is to take the cable-car from Vigo di Fassa. Purists or low budget walkers can walk up on path n.544 which starts out near the cable-car departure station as a dirt track and winds up tortuously, traversing eroded, rather uninteresting terrain passing under the cables then looping around right then back left - allow 1h30mins.

R. Ciampediè (1997m) is virtually adjacent to the cable-car arrival station and, strangely enough, the water is deemed unsuitable for drinking purposes. A link is also possible (path n.545) here from R. Roda di Vael - see walk 17, Stage Four - allow 1h45mins.

Follow signposting for R. Gardeccia and Vajolet. Five minutes down the track on the left (west) is R. Negritella (1986m), then the wide path winds through a tall delicious wood and it's a 45min stroll to R. Catinaccio and R. Gardeccia (1950m). This is another entry-exit point for Val di Fassa (coming out a little north of Pera). The regulations governing vehicle access seem to change frequently and unpredictably, but the track is essentially limited to authorised traffic, and only at fixed times of the day. A private mini-bus taxi service operates on this stretch, but cannot always guarantee "delivery" all the way to R. Gardeccia.

Just a little further on from R. Gardeccia is R. Stella Alpina, after which there is a small 'bazaar' and stalls selling everything from kitsch souvenirs to basic groceries and fruit and vegetables. Go straight ahead

Lago d'Antermoia

on the white jeep track north into the Catinaccio's inner valley (path n.546), which can be extremely hot going on a cloudless mid-morning in summer. It's another 1h to newly-restored R. Preuss (no accommodation) and the rambling old R. Vajolet (2243m). This is justifiably a very popular spot, and the panorama warrants it, with the magnificent Torri del Vajolet towering overhead left (west).

(A worthwhile side trip at this point is an ascent to R. Re Alberto [Gartlhütte] signposted left - very steep - allow 1h15mins minimum one-way.)

The itinerary continues due north to 2599m and Passo Principe (Grasleitenpass) with its small private refuge nestling under the rock overhang left (1h from R. Vajolet). Supplies for this refuge are carried up by rucksack and trail bike. The mountain at the valley head is the Antermoia (3002m), and just north in the small cirque (often containing snow patches) bordered by the Cime di Valbona (west) you can gaze down into the scree-filled amphitheatre Conca del Principe and make out, on the other side, the tight zigzags of the path in almost vertical descent from Passo del Molignon (2598m) due north - see walk 17.

An alternative exit from here is feasible on path n.554/3a north then west via R. Bergamo (Grasleitenhütte) (2134m) then the pretty Valle di Ciamin to Lavina Bianca and Tires (bus connections to Bolzano). Allow about 3h.

Stage Two: via Passo d'Antermoia (45mins) to R. Antermoia (1h)
Path n.584 climbs straight up east skirting the Antermoia. It's steepish going, climbing loose scree (which accounts for the dotted lines on the maps), but the route is well-trodden and even with the occasional old snow patch it's no problem following the path. The first crest you reach (40mins) affords excellent views of the Torri del Vajolet - one of severe rock and the other (left) upturned and curved like petals of a petrified flower. On a clear day you can see all the way to the distant Ortles (west), and the Adamello and Brenta Dolomites (southwest).

It's 5mins more around (left) to the Passo d'Antermoia (2770m). Signposting is rather faded but the path keeps mainly to the right-hand side of the valley at first (the path on the left connects to the "via ferrata" that crosses the Antermoia) then winds a little in zigzags and there are steeper parts with old snow. It's well waymarked as you go down to the wide desolate stone desert valley which looks like a location for shooting a western.

After a gradual curve to the right walking on level ground, (there is often late-lying snow here too), you arrive at the glittering waters of the Lago d'Antermoia with the Croda del Lago towering overhead north (just under 1h from the last pass). The snow-capped point of the Marmolada is straight ahead (east), and the flag of the refuge over the next rise as well. The lake is very tempting, but treat it with respect as the water is pumped out for use at the refuge (after purification treatment). You coast round the lake on its left-hand side and over the brief crest come out at R. Antermoia (2497mm). (1h45mins total from Passo Principe).

Stage Three: descent via Val de Dona to Fontanazzo (3h)
This is a rather long descent, but traverses particularly pleasant zones so it is not advisable to rush. The path is now n.580, and after you've crossed the stream outside the refuge building, coast left around the mountain side and 15mins will see you at Passo de Dona (2516m), a small hut and the arrival point of the refuge's goods cableway. The panorama now opens up to take in the nearby Sasso Piatto and Lungo (northeast), then

further east to the unmistakable fortress-like Sella massif with Sass Pordoi its southern part. You now zigzag down an easy path partly under the cableway, towards the promising emerald green pastures of the Val de Dona visible below (east), dotted with small timber huts.

Some 40mins and you'll reach the signposted path junction: n.578 continues north to the Valle di Duron (connecting with Sasso Lungo or Campitello), while n.580 (signposted Fontanazzo and Mazzin) bears right, down amongst herds of grazing horses and cows with their young. You're at about 2200m here, and a nearby spring ensures perfect pastoral conditions in this divinely fertile valley. A little way down n.580 turns off for the Val di Udai coming out at Mazzin in Val di Fassa - several years ago, during unusually heavy rains there were serious landslides in the valley and the path was damaged. It is still passable, but not as pleasant or recommended as the Valle de Dona.

Path n.577 leads gradually down the green carpet past log cabins, mostly abandoned now. There is dark volcanic rock up left, and the path becomes rougher with loose stones lower down. As it moves into the pine woods the going becomes a little softer underfoot, but steeper rocky stretches reappear. Roe-deer inhabit the lovely thick silent pine forest. On the very last stretch you can cut across fields with the village in sight. Give yourself a good 3h total from R. Antermoia down to Fontanazzo (1395m). You should come out on the main road near the Municipio building. Head right downhill towards the old-style Albergo/Ristorante Antermoja, where buses stop for services in both directions.

PRACTICAL INFORMATION

R. ANTERMOIA TEL:(0462)602272. Alpine Club, Trent section. Sleeps 44.
R. CATINACCIO. Private, sleeps 24.
R. CIAMPEDIE TEL:(0462)764432. Alpine Club, Trent section. Sleeps 25.
R. GARDECCIA TEL:(0462)63152. Private, sleeps 36.
R. NEGRITELLA TEL.(0462)766971. Private, sleeps 33.
R. PASSO PRINCIPE (GRASLEITENPASSHÜTTE)
TEL:(0462)764244. Private, sleeps 13.
R. STELLA ALPINA TEL:(0462)763270. Private, sleeps 30.
TOURIST OFFICE MAZZIN TEL:(0462)767196.
TOURIST OFFICE VIGO DI FASSA TEL:(0462)764093.

*   *   *

WALK 19 (see sketch map E, page 107)

'VIAL DEL PAN'
via Passo Pordoi - R. Baita Fredarola - R. Vial del Pan (1h15mins) -
R. Castiglioni (1h15mins) (Lago di Fedaia).
TABACCO MAP NO.S 015 & 06 scale 1:25,000
TABACCO MAP NO.2 scale 1:50,000
(1 day)

This ancient route, known as the "Vial del Pan", is for the most part an easy stroll except for the last steepish descent, and is immensely popular nowadays. It takes a couple of hours and coasts along at an average of 2400m on the earth and grass slopes of the Padon chain. Its chief attraction lies in the unobstructed and unequalled panoramas it offers of the glacier on the magnificent Marmolada.

The "Vial del Pan" was once the sole route for communication between the Cordevole valley (that runs down from Arabba all the way to Belluno) and Val Gardena. When there were no roads in the thickly wooded valleys, an above-the-tree-line itinerary was the only feasible route. "Pane" in Italian means "bread", and the name "Vial del Pan" is usually attributed to the grain smuggling practised to evade the Venetian Republic's strict controls, or simply to transport grain. The path was 'restored' by the Germans around 1900, and alternately named 'Bindlweg' after the mountain climber who inspired the work.

However a more romantic explanation for the route's origin comes from legend: a countess from Vigo di Fassa was said to have travelled this route for her frequent visits on a white horse to her vast dominions, which extended from Val di Fassa along Val Pettorina as far as the Castle at Rocca Pietore (east of Malga Ciapela and the Marmolada).

Another point of interest is the military mausoleum at Passo Pordoi. Just a short walk downhill on the Sella Group side of the pass (towards Arabba), it contains the remains of 8,000 German and Austrian soldiers from the First World War and 800 from the Second.

Stage One: to R. Vial del Pan (1h15mins)
Passo Pordoi (2239m) is a wide pass that shows signs of having been glacially modelled, and is now surrounded by pasture land. It is well served in summer by buses from Canazei in the west and Passo Sella further north, and somewhat less frequently from Arabba in the opposite

direction, so you may have to hitch a lift on this stretch.

From Albergo Rifugio Savoia, take path n.601 going south. It passes a small chapel then skirts the base of Sass Beccé, climbing to a small saddle. Stop a while to observe the almost tame marmots romping around the rocky outcrops on your right. You probably won't want to stop for long though as the area presents a depressing and somewhat uninteresting aspect in summer, as there are extensive scars due to winter ski-run preparation and lift installations and facilities that seem to be continually developed and expanded. The path continues a little further south on a wide earth track under R. Sass Beccé (2423m) and chair lift cables, and is often windy. Then it's up to the grassy crest and R. Baita Fredarola (2388m) with its panoramic terrace with views over the other side west to the Catinaccio group, Crepa Neigra, Sasso Vernale south and of course the Marmolada massif.

N.601 continues in an easterly direction on the south versant of Sas Ciapel now, the gravel jeep track giving way to an earth path. The walking is easy, coasting up and down slightly, with plenty of grazing sheep to keep you company (not to mention the other walkers at the height of summer) and of course that glimmering glacier ahead on your right. In about 1h15mins from Passo Pordoi you'll reach the halfway point R. Vial del Pan (2431m), perched on the grassy slopes. Despite its classification of "refuge", it does not offer accommodation and, making the most of the treeless surrounds, even charges for use of the toilet! There are ample grassy knolls and levels areas where you can stop to picnic, instead of lunching with the masses should you so desire.

Stage Two: to R. Castiglioni (Marmolada) at Lago di Fedaia (1h15mins)
Soon after the refuge, up left are a couple of gaps in the dark crest, affording excellent panoramas back onto the Sella group with the Piz Boé pyramid. Sloping back down, you skirt the base and proceed on in a wide curve briefly south. Now above left are two strange black volcanic pinnacles, the Forfesc, 2579m, once said to be the haunt of a certain old prince when in a black mood. He was known by the intriguing name of Vögl delle Velme, formerly of the wealthy ancient kingdom of the Aurona, and had returned from his wanderings as a beggar, having renounced all riches.

The path continues towards the panorama point under the Belvedere, on a grassy ridge at 2349m, directly overlooking Lago di Fedaia. The left fork leads around and up to Porta Vescovo (2516m), the arrival point of the cable-car from Arabba. Your path to the right descends obliquely and very steeply over grassed areas with the occasional tree, then winds and zigzags before coming to some easy rocky passages. Then it's down to the road, coming out right opposite R. Castiglioni (Marmolada) at 2042m. It is set behind the dam wall on the shores of the artificial Lago di Fedaia (from the Ladin word 'feda' meaning 'sheep').

The original lake, a dark green glacial tarn, is the small one at Passo Fedaia at the eastern end. The area is justifiably well-known and well-visited, but quietens down considerably in the evening. However accommodation should be reserved. The privately-run R. Castiglioni, a stately old dark timber building, used to belong to the Alpine Club, and has retained its warm atmosphere, with pleasant terraces, comfortable dormitories with eiderdowns, excellent food and hot showers available on request. There are other refuges and guest-houses in the area.

The Marmolada massif, or 'Queen of the Dolomites' is actually principally composed of limestone, not dolomite. It was once the dividing line between Italy and Austria, with the border drawn right along its highest crest, and saw plenty of front line action on its icy reaches in World War I. The Austrians carried out the incredible feat of excavating an entire 'City of Ice' in the glacier, with fortifications and a good 12 kilometres of tunnels. Two pieces of heavy artillery were even dragged up there and positioned at 3259m on both Punta Rocca and Penia!

It is said that the glacier was formed one night in early August to punish a young peasant girl. Instead of attending the valley festivities for the 'Holy Virgin of the Snows', she had stayed back to rake in the hay and get it all under cover as the weather was turning cold. She herself was buried by the unusually heavy snowfall that followed, and which hardened to become the eternal glacier.

It's well worth taking the 600m or so trip up the chair lift from the southernmost end of the dam wall to Pian dei Fiacconi (2626m) just at the lower edge of the glacier - there's a refuge there too. Otherwise take a bus down to Malga Ciapela - the walk is not particularly recommended as the route follows the road and traffic can be heavy - and there is the cable-car station for the three-section ride up to Piz Serauta (2950m), then Punta Rocca (3250m).

Unfortunately, speculation and development for skiing purposes are still continuing, seemingly with no regard for the natural environment. At the time of writing, plans were in the pipeline for yet another chair lift or cable-car to connect Lago di Fedaia ie. the Marmolada, with Porta Vescovo and hence with Arabba and beyond. There are already far too many scars up the side of the Marmolada itself from the preparation of ski pistes, and the already apparently barren surrounds would be threatened even further. It is not the first threat of destruction in a quest for riches.

In fact, it was underneath the black tuffaceous Padon chain opposite the Marmolada that the fabulous Aurona treasure was said to lie hidden. Early stories told of an underground realm of gold and precious stones and the subjects doomed never to see the light of day in return for never-ending riches. An old man went blind when he accidentally glimpsed sunlight through a hole in the roof of a passage. The spell was eventually broken when a local king heard the lament of the imprisoned princess and managed to rescue her thus opening up the kingdom. Later on yet another king, from the legendary kingdom of Fanes (see walk 10), struck a deal - in vain luckily: he was to betray his warrior daughter Dolasilla and the kingdom in return for labour to excavate the entrance to the fabled underground city of gold.

Yet another curious legend is set in this area and concerns the ailing maiden Albolina, diagnosed as having 'night sickness'. She was cured with light therapy - and had to be subjected to the rosy rays of the sun at dawn entering her eyes directly. This condition sounds suspiciously similar to the recently diagnosed 'winter sickness' or S.A.D. (Seasonal Affective Disorder) which can be alleviated with early morning highly intensive light therapy.

PRACTICAL INFORMATION

HOTEL CASA ALPINA (PASSO PORDOI) TEL:(0462)601279. (*)
R. CASTIGLIONI (MARMOLADA) TEL:(0462)601117. Private, sleeps 90.
R. DOLOMIA (LAGO DI FEDAIA) TEL:(0462)601221. Private, sleeps 50.
R. PASSO FEDAIA TEL:(0437)722007. Private, sleeps 25.
R. PIAN DEI FIACCONI TEL:(0462)601412. Private, sleeps 25.
R. SASS BECCE TEL:(0462)602084. Private, sleeps 8.
R. SEGGOVIA (LAGO DI FEDAIA) TEL:(0462)601181. Private, sleeps 20.
TOURIST OFFICE ARABBA TEL:(0436)79130/79300.
TOURIST OFFICE CANAZEI TEL:(0462)601113.
(*) possible extended opening.

✳   ✳   ✳

WALK 20 (see sketch map G, page 138)

MARMOLADA
via Malga Ciapela - R. Falier (2h15mins) -
Passo di Ombrettola (2h30mins) - Passo delle Cirelle (1h) -
R. Fuchiade (1h15mins) - Passo San Pellegrino (45mins).
TABACCO MAPS NO.015 & 06 scale 1:25,000
TABACCO MAP NO.2 scale 1:50,000
(2 days suggested)

Despite its proximity to the world-famous Marmolada and the crowds it attracts, this route abounds in unusual alpine wildlife. Even though it covers a remarkable variety of terrain types, it is a walkers' route, and no climbing experience is required. Stamina however is a prerequisite for Stage Two in particular, but effort is well rewarded with exceptional panoramas from the high passes. Furthermore, the walk is a good follow-up to the 'Vial del Pan' (walk 19) which runs in front of the 'Queen of the Dolomites', the Marmolada, whereas this one follows the back south wall, helping you to understand the mountain structure better. You may in fact wish to digress first by taking the cable-car from Malga Ciapela up to the breathtaking upper reaches.

Stage One: to R. Falier (2h15mins)
Coach services from both north and south will deposit you at Malga Ciapela, the year-round resort centre. The nearest Tourist Information Office is at Rocca Pietore, 5.6kms down the road to the east.

Don't leave the centre before stocking up on the fresh local rye bread with fennel seeds and Tirolerspeck, delicate smoked pork sliced paper thin. You'll then need path n.610 just downhill from the shopping centre. It is a road at this stage, and branches off right (southwest) up beside the Torrente Pettorina to the camping ground. Continue straight on, right through the camping ground to wind up through the wood with the Scalon stream cascading up ahead. There are several farm buildings, then as the surfaced road comes to an end, you reach a path junction for Forcella Pianezza (link up with the Falcade valley to the south), Forca Rossa (southwest connecting with Passo San Pellegrino), and R. Falier (n.610) - keep following this one. Very soon a "scorciatoia" (short cut) is signposted to the right up through the wood - by all means follow this variant, but it's a lot steeper. The main route stays on an easy wide white

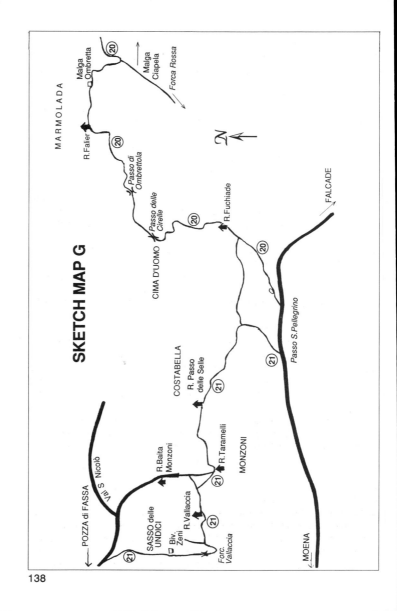

SKETCH MAP G

MARMOLADA

Malga Ombretta

Malga Ciapela

Forca Rossa

R.Falier

Passo di Ombrettola

Passo delle Cirelle

CIMA D'UOMO

R.Fuchiade

FALCADE

N

COSTABELLA

R. Passo delle Selle

Passo S.Pellegrino

POZZA di FASSA

Val S.Nicolò

R.Baita Monzoni

R.Taramelli

MONZONI

SASSO delle UNDICI

Biv. Zeni

R.Vallaccia

Forc. Vallaccia

MOENA

gravel track until n.610 turns right off it and narrows into a path. It manages to wind its way up and across in a northwesterly direction into the seemingly impassable wooded gully by way of a comfortable passage cut into the rock face.

Having climbed to 1900m, you now have the flat expanse of silent Valle Ombretta which opens out before you. It is idyllic grazing land and the Malga Ombretta keeps sheep and goats - a mad herd you'll almost definitely meet on the way up. Bordering it on the right is the immense south flank of the Marmolada. It's an excellent place for a picnic, and fresh water is available from a hiccuping pump fountain at the Malga. 1h45mins so far.

Continue on west after the malga and when you see the huge white 'H' (rescue helicopter landing place) down left on the plain, keep your eyes skinned for marmots. This has to be the largest marmot colony in the Dolomites that is so easily accessible to walkers. There is a very large settlement and with just a little patience you'll be able to watch them romping and digging, and even eating if you leave a piece of bread on a stone near a burrow entrance. They are very shy and one of the group always remains on guard to emit his high-pitched warning cry that causes a flurry of rears (especially well-padded in autumn as they prepare for hibernation) to disappear down the burrows.

It's only 30mins from the malga to R. Falier. It stands at 2080m on a rocky outcrop looking back down this delightful valley, and there are, naturally, great views of faraway mountains to the east, including (from right to left) the Civetta, Pelmo and Croda da Lago. If there is no cloud cover, these should all light up towards sunset time. Due to its strategic position - the Austrians had constructed a complete 'ice city' on the other side of the Marmolada - this refuge was of great military importance during World War I. Today instead, it is one of the few refuges left in the Dolomites where food supplies are still backpacked up. The dining area inside is plastered with photos and diagrams of the famous south flank with the numerous climbing routes pencilled in.

Stage Two: to Passo di Ombrettola (2h30mins) and crossing to Passo delle Cirelle (1h)
Leave the refuge around the back by way of path n.612 passing under the large rock with the memorial plaque to Captain Andreoletti who had command of this area during WW1. He and his men are undoubtedly to be thanked for the path leading southwest up the pass. It is a superb walk, particularly on a sunny day with good visibility. Shortly after its start, the

path crosses two gushing streams and there are more marmots to be seen around here. Up through an area of mountain pine scrub and bear briefly right over grass and rock where you're likely to see the prehistoric jet black glossy alpine salamander.

Another exciting feature of this valley is its superb herd of ibex - those wild alpine goats with grooved hollow horns that curve backwards. They are sometimes visible even from the refuge with the aid of a good pair of binoculars. If at rest there will be an adult male standing imposingly on a rock near his herd. They can be photographed quite easily if near the track, but it is probably not a good idea to disturb them unnecessarily.

Don't neglect to look back toward the Marmolada as you'll see the gleaming metallic wall of the second arrival station of the cable-car from Malga Ciapela, perched in a seemingly precarious position on the edge of the sheer rock wall at 3250m.

The track is good and well-marked, but climbs quite steeply in parts. Once you're above the tree line it becomes much narrower and turns right into a final cirque leading up to the pass. This last stretch is tricky at times due to the loose scree. Care should be taken on uncertain spots during the steep climb.

As you pant up you'll pass ruins of huts, then on top there are fortifications as well as another small plaque and rock tunnel, all from the First World War. This spot, Passo di Ombrettola at 2868m, helps you put the Dolomite groups and peaks in perspective - looking down the other side start on your right (north) with the Marmolada (behind Sasso Vernale) then further north is Sass Pordoi and the Sella Group, then Sassolungo and the Catinaccio further west.

Cross over the circular war trench, bear left and either follow the official n.612 which drops slightly into the wide bowl of the valley head to climb up again at the end to the pass, or keep to the higher path to your left. This latter is a little less clear and certain but coasts around, saving you more metres of descent and re-ascent and giving you the occasional glimpse of wild plunging detritus slopes or swirling clouds through to the south. There will be old snow patches on the scree even late in the season.

Below you, right (north), coming up the valley floor of Val de le Cirelle from R. Contrin is path n.607 which you join just under the pass. You curve around the valley head over to another cirque and, at 2686m is Passo delle Cirelle. The name "Cirelle" comes from a local name meaning "gravel", and indeed there is not much else in the valley down south. The pass itself is a modest opening between the Cima dell'Uomo group (with a glacier behind it on the other side) on your right and the Punta Zigole left.

Stage Three: descent to R. Fuchiade (1h45mins) and
Passo San Pellegrino (45mins)

Now, on path n.607, prepare yourselves to descend Valle di Tasca - this name comes from the local Ladin word meaning "basin", descriptively apt as it is enclosed by surrounding peaks. This has to be the best scree slope in the Dolomites. The gravel is just the right size and consistency to make this a memorable, effortless and extremely enjoyable descent. Just launch yourself heels in first, imagine you were skiing and spare a smile and greeting for those who are labouring upwards. The general direction is right, then curve down left, but keep an eye on the path itself so you don't go too far off course. As you come out at the end of the scree valley on the left, there is a flat grassy area then a wartime mule-track winding down towards the stream (Rio di Zigole) on your left. Cross the cattle pasture towards the picnickers and there is R. Fuchiade at 1972m. The name of the refuge means "place where scything is done".

From here there are various possibilities: you can cross over to Valfredda and either descend to Falcade or link up with the Val del Biois walk (see walk 23, Stage Three). Otherwise, continue on n.607 which, down from the grandeurs of the high altitudes takes you on a stroll amidst typical alpine meadows and timbered barns and small barns for storing hay along a rough then surfaced road. Should you intend to link up with walk 21, (over west to the Monzoni group and Val di Fassa), keep your eyes skinned for a rough vehicle track off right after a cluster of huts. It cuts across the hillside below Cima d'Uomo under chair lifts and across ski slopes towards Capanna Paradiso (arrival of the chair lift from Passo San Pellegrino), saving you the descent to the pass.

N.607 in the meantime, continues winding down past wooden chalets and through a final wooded area to come out at Albergo Miralago (2040m) with its small lake, then at the busy main road at Passo San Pellegrino (1918m). The area has been rather too heavily developed for winter sports and Col Margherita on the other side of the road is particularly unseemly with its slopes gashed by bulldozers to make way for ski slopes and chair lifts. Furthermore, note that no refuge-type accommodation is presently available at the pass itself - although hotels abound - and it will be so until the relevant owner municipality decides to renovate the historic old timber refuge on the site of the original 14th century refuge-hospice for pilgrims. At the time of writing R. Passo San

Pellegrino provided no accommodation, only bar service. Coach lines serve the pass in both directions, that is west to Moena in Val di Fassa and east to Falcade in Val del Biois.

PRACTICAL INFORMATION
R. FALIER TEL:(0437)722005 Alpine Club, Venice Section. Sleeps 40.
R. FUCHIADE TEL.(0426)574281. Private, sleeps 10.
TOURIST OFFICE ROCCA PIETORE TEL:(0437)721319.
TOURIST OFFICE FALCADE TEL:(0437)599241.
TOURIST OFFICE MOENA TEL:(0462)573122.

✳   ✳   ✳

WALK 21 (see sketch map G, page 138)

MONZONI / VALLACCIA
via Passo San Pellegrino - R. Passo delle Selle (2h) -
R. Taramelli (1h) - R. Vallaccia (1h) - Forcella Vallaccia (45mins)
[alt. via Sasso delle Undici (1h15mins)] -
Bivacco D. Zeni (1h15mins) - Pozza di Fassa (2h15mins).
TABACCO MAP NO.06 scale 1:25,000
TABACCO MAP NO.2 scale 1:50,000
(2 days suggested)

The Monzoni-Vallaccia Group (between Val di Fassa and Passo San Pellegrino) is an outrunner of the Marmolada. It is wild and differs from the rest of the Dolomites geologically in its regularly formed volcanic crest and rich variety of mineral deposits. The plutonic (from cooled magma, ie. volcanic) rock monzonite in fact was first found here, hence its name. There is a "Museo Geologico" at Predazzo in Val di Fassa.

The Monzoni group is easily accessible from the valley floor and is crossed by several "via ferrata" routes. Note that Stage Three of this itinerary involves some exposed pathways and a very steep descent down rough scree, and some stretches could be dangerous during conditions of rain or low cloud (ie. poor visibility). It is thus not recommended as a first walk, though the walk can be cut short after Stage One and an alternate exit route is given.

R. Passo delle Selle

Stage One: to R. Passo delle Selle (2h) and descent to R. Taramelli (1h)
Start out from the wide open saddle of the winter ski area at Passo San Pellegrino (1918m) that connects the towns of Moena in Val di Fassa with Falcade in Val del Biois. Either take the chair lift just below Hotel Costabella or start out on foot on path n.604 in a northerly direction, up across the grassy ski slopes to the arrival point of the chair lift at about 2000m, where there is a small chalet-bar Paradiso (45mins this far). The track bears up left and the modest Passo delle Selle (means 'saddles') is already visible. You climb gently across grassy knolls and dolinas then up loose rock to the narrow pass (2529m) where the delightful refuge perches, balanced and securely anchored on all sides by metal cables.

Two via ferrate itineraries set out from here following the crests in both directions - namely Costabella and the Cima d'Uomo group (northeast), and the Monzoni chain (southwest). The refuge itself is tiny but very hospitable. Guests bed down on the floor in the loft, directly over the dining room area. Views all around and sunset and sunrise are superb, across south to the Pale di San Martino, for example. As will be immediately obvious from the ruins of buildings and extensive fortifications just below the hut, as well as a touching barbed wire cross and simple

143

memorial, this strategic saddle saw a considerable amount of action in World War I.

Path n.604 is an easy 500m descent crossing a lightly grassed rocky basin and past more ruins, some built into the rock, in their commanding position looking down Val delle Selle. The rather atypical square shape of R. Taramelli far down below (west) can be seen. At the edge of the basin you veer right and curve down a rather steep corridor with rocky terrain and a small lake on the left (2258m). Waymarking is clear.

There are the unusual formations of the Pale di Carpella pinnacled rock wall opposite the lake. About half way down you are joined by a gushing torrent cascading over jet black stones. The last stretch can be slippery when wet, down a dark coloured earth slope with scattered dwarf pines, and you wind around to the rock platform and tall pine trees - the setting for the well-run R. Taramelli at 2046m. Named after an eminent geologist, it has been constructed with blocks of the local igneous rock monzonite, and often serves as a base for geological excursions in the Monzoni group.

Walkers wishing to descend directly to Val di Fassa at this point can follow track n.603 north. It will take about 2h via Valle dei Monzoni and the road in Val S. Nicolò to the township of Pozza in Val di Fassa.

Stage Two: ascent to R. Vallaccia (1h) then Forcella Vallaccia (45mins), alternative via Sasso delle Undici (1h15mins)
If you don't take time out for a geological side trip into the Monzoni Group, continue down the track (n.603) leading below R. Taramelli. After a brief stretch there is a signed path junction for R. Vallaccia and n.624 left (west). It traverses a peaceful wooded area with dwarf rhododendrons, then passes huts and cows grazing. It soon joins up with the track branch (n.624) from Malga Monzoni - which can also be reached from Pozza di Fassa by car following Val San Nicolò then right (south) along Valle dei Monzoni via R. Baita Monzoni - or on foot in a good 3h.

Continue west climbing Val Gardeccia. There is a wide curve on the last (puff) stretch as the terrain becomes more rocky. R. Vallaccia (2275m), a new timber and stone construction run by a local family occupies an isolated position. At the time of writing it was not shown on any maps. Note that no water suitable for drinking purposes is available here.

Your path proceeds behind the refuge left and up west - don't be tempted to follow the one marked "Sas Morin". You pass a thriving colony of marmots where you can observe the young ones greyish and slim and the adults light reddish brown and plump, particularly late in the season when they fatten up in preparation for the winter hibernation. Path numbering is not always obvious, but red and white paint splashes are reasonably frequent. As the terrain becomes more rocky and there are large boulders in the head of the valley, keep an eye out for a path junction (about 25mins up from R. Vallaccia), near a watering trough for the tranquil cattle, at about 2300m.

At this point an interesting optional side-trip is to the top of Sasso delle Undici at 2503m, with the possibility of a direct return (without backtracking) to Forcella Vallaccia (see following section). Note that the tracks in this area do not correspond exactly with those marked on the maps, but on-the-spot signposting is reliable.

For those who prefer the more direct route to Forcella Vallaccia, proceed left up the fork signposted "Pozza". The path continues briefly left up the rock then sharp right along a narrow exposed stretch to the forcella (2468m). Take this last part slowly and carefully, as the ground is crumbly in places. This last stretch (from the trough and path junction) should take about 20mins.

Ascent to Sasso delle Undici (40mins) then to Forcella Vallaccia (30mins)
During the ascent (right) to Sasso delle Undici, take care not to lose sight of the waymarkings (unnumbered). It is not at all difficult, but climbs constantly around the mountain side, through the grazing herds, then up north to a grassy slope. Should you miss the waymarking, use your map and compass to get your bearings and head straight for the top. There is a Madonna with a tall cross on your right looking over at the Marmolada (northeast). On your left from the crest is a dramatic sheer drop into a void - do watch your footing as there's no guard rail here! From the underlying path junction to here is about 40mins. Great picnic spot.

Now, head for Forcella Vallaccia southish along the top crest, bearing left. Take extra care on the exposed stretches. It is a little precarious, and there are frequent gaps in the crest giving you plunging views down the scree valley right. Don't be tempted to try any of these descents, as there are no tracks and the valley below is extremely steep and even the 'official' path is difficult. There are occasional faint red and white markings dotted along the crest top, but you essentially follow the ridge, with brief loops down left to avoid impassable stretches. The final passage prior to Forcella Vallaccia is a grassy flowered slope, but rather exposed and not recommended if heights don't agree with you. You come out onto the narrow rocky saddle of the forcella where you may meet climbers about to set out on one of the "vie ferrate" on the adjacent peaks. From the peak of Sasso delle Undici to here should take about 30mins.

Stage Three: descent via Bivacco D. Zeni (1h15mins) to Pozza di Fassa (2h15mins)

At Forcella Vallaccia take a moment or two to get your breath back and contemplate this narrow entrance to the wild Vallaccia valley dropping down before you due north. It is enclosed by the Vallaccia peak on your left and the sheer rock wall of Sasso delle Undici right. Most dramatic. You can make out the orange metallic form of the bivouac hut (Bivacco D. Zeni) down there. Now the fun starts - the 300m descent can be dangerously slippery at first as there are loose stones on an earth base, but it soon becomes reasonable scree. It is not the ideal consistency for a trouble-free scree run. However, dig your heels in and 'walk' down letting the rubble take you sliding with it a little at a time and you won't lose your balance. After the initial narrow neck, you enter the gorge as it opens a little and is a little less steep, but you continue down on scree as far as the flattish base. Now the rock wall on the right hand side is even more imposing in its sheerness, and there are old snow mounds even late in the summer. Cross the watercourse, then for the last 50m or so the path crosses rolling grassy hillocks carpeted with rhododendrons and other wild flowers, a welcome sight after all that rock and scree. Timing on this stage will obviously depend on the speed of your descent, but on average allow 1h15mins to Biv. D. Zeni. The orange metallic hut at 2100m has a rugged setting. It contains 4 bunks but is principally reserved for mountaineers.

You still have 600 more steep metres to go down north, but path n.615 is clearly marked. Just below the bivouac hut is a steep passage, slippery if wet, including an aided passage under an enormous boulder with steel cable anchored to the rock face. The path climbs down sometimes alongside a rushing stream into a rubble and vegetation-filled valley. You proceed down through tall woods inhabited by red squirrels and roe-deer. There are several detours made necessary due to small landslides and rubble incursions. Path n.615 exits onto the tarmac road just below the guest-house Soldanella and the camping ground at 1415m (1h45mins this far). Turn left and walk the remaining 2.5kms down into the popular small town of Pozza di Fassa at 1310m.

Many long distance coach lines pass this way, with bus stops down on the main road.

PRACTICAL INFORMATION

BIVACCO D. ZENI. Alpine Club, Trent Section. Sleeps 4.

R. PASSO DELLE SELLE TEL.(0347)4039331. Private. Sleeps 15. or c/o Information c/o Albergo Miralago, Passo San Pellegrino (0462)573088/573791.

R. TARAMELLI TEL.(0368)3577617. Alpine Club, Trent Section. Sleeps 15.

R. VALLACCIA. Private, sleeps 24. Information c/o (0462)764922. Sleeps 24.

TOURIST OFFICE POZZA DI FASSA TEL:(0462)501564.

* * *

WALK 22 (see sketch map H, page 148)

LATEMAR

via Pampeago - R. Torre di Pisa (3h15mins) -
Forcella dei Campanili (1h15mins) - Bivacco Latemar (45mins) -
Malga Valsorda (1h30mins) - Val Sorda -
Forno (1h45mins) (Moena).
TABACCO MAP NO.014 scale 1:25,000
TABACCO MAP NO.7 & NO.2 scale 1:50,000
(2 days suggested)

The northern part of the Latemar Group is its most dramatic face, with a series of rugged rock spires, and is best viewed either from the path coasting the eastern flank of the Catinaccio - see walk 17 - or from the road that connects Passo Costalunga with Val d'Ega and Bolzano. In the proximity of this road, and nestling in the thick tall pine forest at the northern base of the Latemar, reflecting it in its famous multi-coloured crystal-clear waters, is the Lago di Carezza. Legend has it that a wicked wizard created a rainbow in the hope of winning the heart of a beautiful nymph who would sit singing on the lake's edge. When his plan failed however, his anger was such that, as well as uprooting trees and unleashing ferocious storms on the mountain, he smashed the rainbow into smithereens and threw it into the lake where its colours melted into the water.

The Latemar's vast inner rubble-filled basin is hidden from outside view, and the mountain is less visited than the other Dolomites. Strictly speaking it does not in fact consist of dolomite but simple calcite (calcium

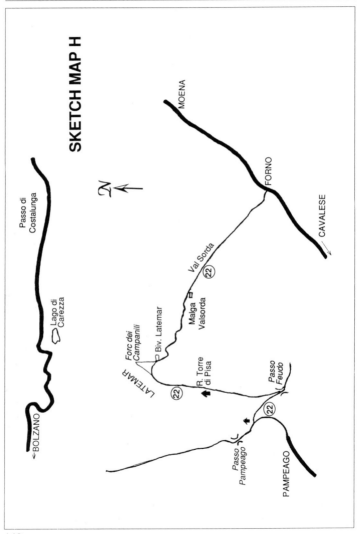

SKETCH MAP H

carbonate) and the rock is extremely friable and crumbly. You will find a variety of coloured rocks, including intrusions of dark solidified lava, as the Latemar was part of a volcano more than 200 million years ago, (before the Alps were raised) with its centre where Predazzo is nowadays. Its northern flank in particular was heavily mined, and rare, early visitors would have been hunters and shepherds.

Apart from Stage One (easily adapted as a 1-day return trip), the itinerary is of intermediate difficulty, and includes a very long descent (1500m) with a couple of crumbly rock passages (slippery if wet). The unmanned hut Bivacco Latemar could be conveniently used as a rest stop or overnight point as well.

As described here, access by public transport is more convenient from the Val di Fiemme, the southwest continuation of Val di Fassa, (an important winter cross-country skiing centre). It is however, also possible to link into the itinerary from the northwest: either on one of the paths starting out in the proximity of Lago di Carezza, or by making use of the bus line (Sundays excluded) that connects Bolzano with Ponte Nova, Novale (Obereggen area) and over via Passo Occlini and Passo Lavazè to Cavalese, and getting off at a convenient point - consult your map as there are several possible paths.

Stage One: to R. Torre di Pisa (3h15mins)

From the town of Cavalese (1057m) in Val di Fiemme, a summer bus service (Sundays excluded) runs via Tesero up the Val di Stava (the site of the tragic 1985 mudslide) to Pampeago (1757m). This small ski resort consists of a modest cluster of hotels. Either take the chair lift or follow the dirt track curving to your right facing uphill. It's a pleasant stroll. Continue past the turn-off right to Malga Latemar (dairy farm and trattoria) and after some 25mins on foot, the road is closed to unauthorised traffic. The winding track climbs gently through thinning woods and pasture and you can see a cross and a small hut high up on the Latemar's unlikely looking grass crest northwest - your destination R. Torre di Pisa. The track curves north again to where the chair lift arrives at 2000m (just under 1h this far) slightly before Passo Pampeago. Of the 2 refuges here, only Pension Zischgalm will provide accommodation, but it's much preferable to proceed to R. Torre di Pisa.

Clear signposting indicates path n.504 climbing the grassy slope bearing right (southeast). There is a steeper path cutting straight up, but it hardly saves time and is much more tiring. Keep an eye out for vipers on this stretch. The best advice is to tread heavily to scare them away.

149

R. Torre di Pisa

Thirty minutes will see you to Passo Feudo (2121m) where n.504 descends via Val Gardone to Predazzo. At the small shrine take the path left (n.516) climbing north along the crest. Waymarking for the most part here consists of short wooden posts with red and white stripes, though the brown earth path is obvious. As far as flowers go, there is an unusual abundance of tiny chocolate-coloured black vanilla orchids and slightly less attractive but likewise protected, largish pale yellow spotted gentians.

The path climbs steadily and you come into a hollow with boulders where other paths from points north of Passo Pampeago join up. There are much steeper sections now, on dark crumbly terrain. You are soon treated to a first glimpse of the Latemar's weathered white rock towers. You bear left and around under the first of two anti-avalanche barriers, then sharp right to climb obliquely over a rock outcrop. It is very slippery with loose earth and stones, and the rest of the ascent is similar - corresponding to the dotted lines on the maps. The refuge is visible all the time but hardly seems to get any nearer. After a final easy clamber over rock and under the goods lift cables, you reach the refuge at 2671m (2h15mins total from Pension Zischgalm).

When you've got your breath back after the 900m ascent, go over to the low rock crest behind the refuge for your first look down into the

Latemar's immense horseshoe-shaped amphitheatre. Now for the other mountains that come into view: south is the Lagorai chain, further east the Pale di San Martino, the Civetta and the Pelmo behind it (left), the point of the Marmolada with its eternal snow, and Sass Pordoi and the Sella Group northeast. You can hand feed the birds here.

Perched on the southern rim of the Latemar, this modest homely building, R. Torre di Pisa, was the work of a family from Predazzo, the present day hosts. There is no running water in the refuge, as the supply comes from the rain water they collect, but on request you can get a basinful for a quick wash. It is classified as not suitable for drinking though.

Stage Two: via Forcella dei Campanili (1h15mins) to Bivacco Latemar (45mins)

It is inadvisable to proceed with the next stage with low cloud cover or if mist threatens to roll in, as orientation could be difficult.

Path n.516 heads off north and up to a brief exposed stretch along the crest, but nothing difficult. The weathered rock shapes including the leaning (tower) Torre di Pisa which gave the refuge its name, are very close now. Following the red and white waymarking, watch your step as you descend into a small but spectacular narrow, tall-sided gully where you clamber over rubble, fallen boulders and old snow, and there are yet more precarious rock towers and unusual formations. The path climbs out to the right, then descends curving left into the vast expanse of the Lastei di Valsorda, (good echoes). It coasts across undulating rock with scattered bright flower patches of yellow (poppies and dandelions) and pink (moss campion), to a junction where n.18 turns off left (to Forcella dei Camosci). Continue straight on, and soon, after an old wooden signpost propped up on the ground, n.516b branches off down right (don't take the unnumbered one further right) for Biv. Latemar (45mins so far).

If you are pressed for time, turn down (east) here to start the descent straight away, and take about 30mins off the total walk time. Otherwise, if weather and visibility warrant it, a highly recommended detour is to continue straight on n.516 north, coasting then climbing briefly to the farthest opening - Forcella dei Campanili (meaning 'spires') (2685m) - this will take another 30mins. As well as the views of the Catinaccio chain and the pretty coloured Lago di Carezza in the thick forest far below, you will find yourself right up close to the Latemar's brilliant rugged rock needles and spires on your left and the spectacular rock wall right. This spot is quite sensational and not to be missed.

Proceed with the descent, either returning to the previously mentioned path junction with n.516b, (slightly more frequented), or look for waymarking for 516a just under the forcella in descent - it rejoins n.516b at Biv. Latemar. Both paths descend across karstic terrain, white soluble rock characterised by water-cut channels, crevices and even deep holes. In the presence of late-lying snow, early season walkers should test snow depth before proceeding as such deep holes could be hidden. Waymarking is relatively recent, and there are several "!!"s painted on rocks to draw attention to particularly deep and potentially dangerous crevices. Surface water is absent as it drains straight underground coming out much further down in the form of springs.

You should reach the Bivacco Latemar building (2365m) with its red and white painted roof and helicopter landing pad in another 45mins from Forcella dei Campanili. (A little less if you omitted the detour.) The hut is unmanned, but very well equipped and always open, thanks to the Alpine Club in Predazzo. There are bunk beds, mattresses and blankets for 10 people, as well as a stove and wood and some emergency food supplies (but bring your own if you plan on using the hut). Fresh water comes from the spring less than 5mins below the building (signposted "acqua"). The hut is set in a delightful grassed semi-circular terrace directly under the sheer rock flank of the Torri del Latemar. Ahead (east) are the Pale di San Martino, and the Fradusta glacier with its glimmering snow cover is visible.

Bears used to live on the Latemar, but extensive hunting in the 18th-19th century in particular put an end to them. Nowadays, apart from the grazing sheep whose tinkling bells and plaintive baahs echo around the rock walls, you may see marmots, especially on these high levels.

Stage Three: down Val Sorda to Malga Valsorda (1h30mins)
then Forno (1h45mins)
Follow the path (clearly marked) down past the spring, and right along the grassy ridge where concentrations of edelweiss grow. You curve right and down the narrowing path with a short section of fixed cable. This descent (300m in all to the floor of Val Sorda) consists in alternating passages on easy rock (some aided) and crumbly mixed earth and stone terrain. There are a few slippery stretches, and a brief 'chimney' (aided) on the last stretch. Some extra care is necessary to avoid disloding too much material and losing your foothold! The good news is that it traverses an immense rock garden and there are also veins and patches of brightly

The leaning tower of Pisa (Torre di Pisa) on the Latemar

coloured rock - green, blue and red amongst others. As you come out onto the flowered grassy slopes a host of orange then dark red martagon lilies greet you. The high sombre walls of Monte Cavignon and its underlying scree are on your right (south). Bearing left you enter the soft peaceful woods at last, with tall mixed pine and larch.

About 1h15mins from the Bivacco are signs in Italian requesting walkers on the way up to carry firewood with them. Now another 15mins past grazing cows, alongside the dried up torrent bed, and shortly after a small plaque in memory of a death due to an avalanche the path veers left to cross the watercourse to reach the rise where Malga Valsorda stands (1684m). The hut could be used as shelter in an emergency, but is very basic, with a dirt floor and just 1 bed and a wooden bench. It is decidedly not a seasonal refuge as most maps show! From this position there is a good view back up the valley of the rock wall at the head of the valley you have just descended.

Keeping to the left side of the valley (though a path does continue down on the right side leaving out the malga) you cross a couple of watercourses, past a drinking trough, cleared pasture area (possibility of vipers), and at the next log cabin turn down right and re-cross the torrent, which is flowing now.

From this point and all the way down to the village of Forno the path (n.516) follows an ancient man-made channel lined with stones, a bit like a bob-run. In winter water thrown into it freezes, enabling timber cut in summer to be slid down the 'chute' to sawmills in the valley. There are many bridges, ingeniously constructed with timbers laid lengthwise, and judging from the good state of repair of the lower sections, some parts are still in use. A very interesting and enjoyable walk. Lower down the valley narrows and while the torrent cascades on one side, the channel passes through wild and romantic steep-sided rock gullies. The large grouse-like and somewhat clumsy capercaillie inhabit the conifer forest.

Some 1h45mins are sufficient for reaching the tranquil village of Forno (1168m) with its fountains and old dark timber houses. You must continue right down to the main road (which bypasses the village proper) to the bar and bus stop for connections south to Cavalese and Trent, or north to Vigo di Fassa and beyond.

PRACTICAL INFORMATION

BIVACCO LATEMAR (A. SIEFF). Alpine Club, Predazzo section. Sleeps 10.
R. TORRE DI PISA. TEL:(0462)501564. Private, sleeps 18. (*)
R. PENSION ZISCHGALM TEL:(0462)83600. Private, sleeps 20.
TOURIST OFFICE MOENA TEL:(0462)573122.
TOURIST OFFICE NOVA LEVANTE - CAREZZA (WELSCHNOFEN - KARERSEE) TEL:(0471)613126/613360.
TOURIST OFFICE CAVALESE TEL:(0462)340298.
(*) possible extended opening.

* * *

WALK 23 (see sketch map I, page 156)

'ALTA VIA DEI PASTORI'
via (Falcade) Molino - R. Bottari (50mins) -
R. Malga Caviazza (1h30mins) - Lago di Cavia (1h) -
R. Fior di Roccia (40mins) - Baita Floralpina (30mins) -
Forca Rossa (2h10mins) - Passo di Col Beccher (20mins) -
Baita dei Cacciatori (1h45mins) - Baita Col Mont (50mins) -
Forcella Pianezza (1h10mins) - Baita di Pianezza (45mins) -
Vallada (1h)
TABACCO MAP NO.015 scale 1:25,000
TABACCO MAP NO.2 scale 1:50,000
(3 days suggested)

In the summer months in these mountains the shepherds, and often their families, take the cattle, sheep or goats up to graze on the lush alpine pastures. A seasonally-used farmhouse is known as a "malga", "casera" or "baita". Some now provide meals and accommodation or fresh dairy products for tourists. Another characteristic activity of the area is the scything of grass on the mountain side for hay. It is taken down to the lower villages and dried by hanging out on racks under the eaves in the old graceful timber "tabià" houses.

This itinerary, the name of which means the "High Way of the Shepherds", was put together in the '70s to link up such places around the Valle del Biois and to reactivate old paths. Starting out at the western end of the valley it runs in a clockwise direction at an average height of 1800-2000m, crossing varying terrains, from pastures to woods and rocky mountain sides. Some infrequently used paths from the original itinerary are in a state of disrepair so have been excluded here.

Stage One: via R. Bottari (50mins) to R. Malga Caviazza (1h30mins) and Lago di Cavia (1h) then descent to R. Fior di Roccia (40mins) and Baita Floralpina (30mins)
Falcade (1145m) has bus connections with Belluno (trains) and further south, Bolzano (trains) to the northwest, as well as Alleghe and northern destinations. Stock up on tasty local seasoned cheese or the speciality of ricotta known as "schiz", a soft fresh cheese, then set out on the road from the town centre in the direction of Passo San Pellegrino. Fork left (signposted R. Bottari) to reach the village of Molino (10mins). Before you

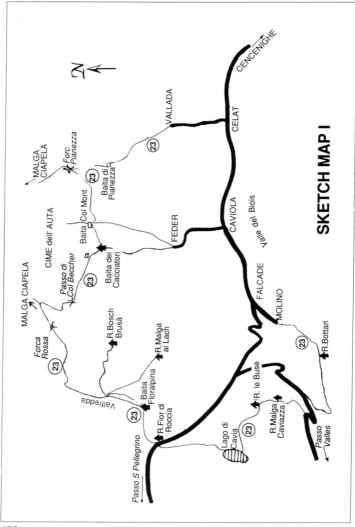

SKETCH MAP I

actually reach the village shops take the dirt road left over the stream and just after the camping ground head up right (southwest) into the woods (signposted R. Bottari with blue and white waymarking used for the "Alta Via Pastori"). A great variety of wild flowers and conifers will accompany you up the winding 50min ascent to 1575m where R. Bottari stands in a clearing. Owned by the CAI Oderzo (Treviso) section it is a converted farm building (old equipment has been preserved) and looks due north over to Valfredda and the Auta peaks. The track passes in front of the cow stalls then through woods and across 4 streams, (a few will probably be dry), and a picturesque grazing area with Malga Valles Bassa (meals and dairy products on sale) up to your left against the mountain (detour to visit it).

At the dirt road, turn right and proceed down across the stream and up to the bitumen road. Now left for 1.5kms and two bends to where another unsurfaced road branches off to the right (signposted Malga Caviazza). A brief wooded stretch with dwarf rhododendrons and bilberry shrubs, and you're in alpine shepherd and cow country (jingling bells and smells included). R. Malga Caviazza (1887m) offers accommodation and meals to walkers as well as cows, and airy views of the Focobon peaks and the distant Civetta (east). It's another 10mins to 1895m and R. Le Buse (private and no accommodation) and the arrival station for the chair lift from Molino (alt. access).

Trying to ignore the scars from the ski slopes gouged out of the hillside on your left, take path n.695 around past Casera Le Buse and there's a lovely winding stretch up through rocks and various flowering shrubs to the artificial Lago di Cavia (2102m) belonging to the Electricity Commission (ENEL), at Zingari Alti (50mins). The track follows the lower wall of the dam (not lower down as shown on the maps) past the hut. At the far end, just a little way up, keep an eye out for the turn-off right due north (not straight ahead as for Passo San Pellegrino). It's another 40mins over the crest of the hill and down the snaking mule-track then through mixed wood to the road at the area known as Zingari Bassi. Buses pass here in ascent to Passo San Pellegrino or in descent to Falcade. Here you can overnight (but no hot meals available) at R. Fior di Roccia. Across the road from it are ancient stones marking the border between the Veneto Republic, Principality of Trento and the Bishopric of Bressanone, with the dates 1474-1778-1845 clearly visible. Just after the lake on the right is the blue and white signposting and after another 30mins, in part on the bitumen side road, you'll reach Baita Floralpina, a modernised pension-like baita (you must book beforehand in high season to stay here).

*Stage Two: via Forca Rossa (2h10mins), Passo di Col Beccher (20mins)
and Baita dei Cacciatori (1h45mins)*

A side trip to Malga ai Lach (1815m) is possible from here (path n.694 in
1h15mins), otherwise follow the signs for Cas. Valfredda (path n.693) in
idyllic Valfredda with its modest chalets and huts set in an active hay-
making area. Stay on the main valley track until it narrows at the last
houses (these are the "asoni" - some 25mins this far) and cross the rustic
wooden bridge on the right (1908m). At the junction just above the
stream, curve left under Sasso Palazza (possibility of roe-deer sighting)
to a boulder and a junction: n.631 leads east over to Malga Bosch Brusà.

It is rather tiring as a side-trip, but recommended as an *alternative
access route,* with several scenic points. The starting point is
Meneghina (1368m), above Caviola (buses). Through flowered
meadows, follow the signposted road northwest for R. Barezze
(1380m), a refreshment stop, then continue up the path (n.631) under
tall conifers to Malga Bosche Brusà (1867m) (1h30mins). This small
hospitable summer dairy farm-cum-refuge serves homestyle meals
and sells dairy products, though accommodation is somewhat
primitive. (An "Alta Via dei Pastori" sign gives "Forca Rossa - 2h" but
it's at least 2h30mins from here.) The path climbs more steeply
northwestish through marmot territory to a grassy saddle (45mins) at
2176m with excellent views of the Focobon peaks (south), the San
Martina altopiano, Col Margherita with its ski-lifts (southwest), Passo
delle Selle and its refuge (west), the zigzag path descending the
scree from Passo delle Cirelle (northwest), and even the Forca
Rossa (north). It's now only 20mins down the 200m to the previously-
mentioned path junction.

Keep left (north) on n.694 and start the gradual 600m climb to Forca
Rossa (about 1h45mins more). After crossing smallish gushing streams
(last chance to fill your water bottle) you soon fork right (left to the crucifix
leads over to Passo delle Cirelle - see walk 20) and continue over rocks
and grass. Just under the pass there are marmots around, then the usual
scavenging crows on top. If there are no low-lying clouds at Forca Rossa
(2486m), as well as the views of the San Martino Group (south), you'll be
able to see the resort centre Malga Ciapela down in the valley (northeast),
and Dolomites ranging from the Lagazuoi, its refuge and cable-car
station (northeast), the Tofane, Sorapíss, and even the Pelmo in the gap
between the Auta peaks (the nearest ones on your right, east), then the

unmistakable 'organ pipe' formation of the Civetta (east). This is the highest point on the Alta Via, and could be blocked by snow early in the season.

After a well-earned rest, it's down the easy zigzags of the wartime mule-track and take the right fork (no.689) to Passo di Col Beccher (20mins, 2312m). From here on, you're walking beneath the Cime dell'Auta and will have ample opportunities for admiring edelweiss. The track narrows somewhat and crosses the occasional scree patch, before a rather steep 200m descent finishing in the woods at Baita Papa G. Paolo 1 (1850m), a private hut. 15 more mins down, (1h45mins in all from Passo di Col Beccher), is the homely and hospitable Baita dei Cacciatori, at 1751m, a private refuge which, despite its name (cacciatori = hunters) welcomes walkers and climbers and closes up when the hunting season starts in late September. It replaces a goat-herder's hut built nearby in the 1920s. (Access from Colmean above Caviola, path n.689 in 2h). Roe-deer are often seen in this area.

Stage Three: via Baita Col Mont (50mins) and
Forcella Pianezza (1h10mins) and descent to Baita di Pianezza (45mins)
and Vallada (1h)
In an easy 50mins, following the blue and white signposting east along n.697, you'll cross many cascading streams, flowering meadows and ascend gradually to Baita Col Mont (1954m). This hut is the property of the Falcade Council and can be used as a bivouac if necessary (access from Feder 2h). Track n.687 (not numbered on signposting) leads straight up north to Col Negher (2286m) and over to Malga Ciapela, and yours - n.688 - is the furthest right (not numbered either), soon joined by another path from the valley (artistic wooden signposting here).

East then northeast over more meadows with orange lilies, through scrubby wooded areas with dwarf pines, some scree stretches and you wind up and around north and reach the track junction directly below Forcella Pianezza (2044m, 1h10mins) (also connecting with Malga Ciapela). Time and weather permitting, pop up for the view, but it's not advisable to continue on the Alta Via at this point as the track is unsafe and not particularly worthwhile. Head straight down (south) n.684 through the woods to the spring and Baita di Pianezza (1725m, 45mins). Though not marked on all maps it is a delightful chalet in a grassy clearing and can be used as a bivouac. This area is regularly scythed for hay-making. Continue down (still n.684) past the artistic wooden crucifix and into the forest where you will probably see signs saying *"Pericolo taglio legname"*

'Tabia' near Vallada

meaning "Danger timber cutting". The descent is steep but easy, and squirrels are plentiful.

The path joins up with a forestry track and in 45mins you come out on the road at a Forestry Commission hut and nursery (vivaio) (1275m). Turn left and follow the road until the first old dark timber *tabia* house, then go off the road to the right and down an old shady pathway bounded by stone walls, turning right then left across a wooden bridge and fields to some clusters of farm buildings and the village of Vallada (1130m) in 15mins. There is a bus service here to Falcade, but a more frequent one that includes Cencenighe, can be picked up down on the main road (15mins) outside Albergo Val Biois at Celat (952m). A side-trip to the 12th century church of San Simon (1142m) is interesting.

PRACTICAL INFORMATION

BAITA COL MONT. Falcade Council, bivouac hut, limited accomm.
BAITA DEI CACCIATORI TEL:(0437)592145 Private, sleeps 12.
BAITA DI PIANEZZA. Bivouac hut, sleeps 4.
BAITA FLORALPINA TEL:(0437)599150/599319 Private, sleeps 40.
R. BOTTARI (CASERA DELLA COSTAZZA) TEL:(0437)599200
Alpine Club, Oderzo Section. Sleeps 25.

R. FIOR DI ROCCIA TEL:(0437)599120 Private, sleeps 32.
No hot meals.
R. MALGA AI LACH TEL:(0437)599280 Private, sleeps 22.
MALGA BOSCH BRUSA. Private, sleeps 8.
R. MALGA CAVIAZZA. Private, sleeps 20.
TOURIST OFFICE FALCADE TEL:(0437)599241.

✳   ✳   ✳

WALK 24 (see sketch map J, page162)

PALE DI SAN MARTINO
via Fiera di Primiero - R. Cant del Gal (1h30mins) -
R. Treviso (1h45mins) - Passo Canali (2h) - Fradusta Glacier -
Passo Pradidali Basso (1h30mins) - R. Pedrotti alla Rosetta (1h) -
R. Baita Segantini (2h30mins) -
R. Mulaz-G.Volpi (2h20mins) - Molino (Falcade) (3h30mins).
TABACCO MAP NO.022 scale 1:25,000
TABACCO MAP NO.4 scale 1:50,000
(3-4 days suggested)

A fascinating itinerary, this one takes you climbing north through thick woods and over rock leading to the Fradusta glacier crossing - perhaps the only other one in the Dolomites apart from the Marmolada that is within such easy reach of the average walker. The route proceeds northwest over the Pale di San Martino limestone plateau, with the possibility of an alternate descent (west) to San Martino di Castrozza in Val Cismon. Otherwise you coast northwest under the Cimon della Pala and glimpse yet another small glacier above Baita Segantini, before crossing over to the northern side of the group and descending to Falcade in Val del Biois.

Stage One: to R. Cant del Gal (1h30mins) and R. Treviso (1h45mins)
Fiera di Primiero (711m), formerly Primör under the Austrian Hapsburg Empire (15th-20th centuries) is now a bustling market town ("Fiera" means "Fair" and tourist resort, and is served by several intercity coach lines. You can cut out the first 1h30min ascent by availing yourself of the summer bus that operates from the town up to R. Cant del Gal (1160m)

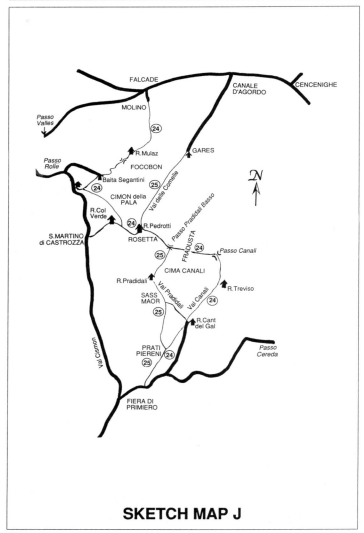

SKETCH MAP J

at the mouth of Val Canali. By car, take the road for Passo Cereda and turn off left at the Castelpietra intersection. Otherwise, if you leave Fiera on foot, walk out of it on the road for Passo Cereda. You pass the sawmill and a picnic area on the right next to the torrent, the Tonadico turn-off (left) and soon uphill is an electricity substation. Opposite, on the left-hand side of the road is a small shrine and the start of n.719 (20mins so far). Recently asphalted, this narrow road soon becomes a walking track, climbing pretty stiffly through hazel and beech woods then fields. There's a lovely mossy stretch with rough old paving enclosed by stone walls. After 40mins you come out to the Prati Piereni chalets and meadows which are usually carpeted with crocuses. (1h so far). Now take the right road and it's only another 30mins on mostly level ground around to cross a rushing torrent and pass the Baita La Ritonda (and the beginning of Val Pradidali) to R. Cant del Gal. It stands at 1160m with a parking area, at the edge of the wood in Val Canali, just inside the border of the Paneveggio-Pale di San Martino Nature Park.

Set out northeast on track n.707 up the Canali valley floor. It starts out as a wide vehicle track through a conifer zone, and is a straightforward route, clearly signposted. The stream is on your right at first. Further up it becomes a little rougher, and after the path junction (left turn-off n.711 to Biv. Minazio) crosses the Canali Torrent (right) and continues a little longer on a level then enters a conifer wood for a longish stretch before a series of tight zigzags in ascent. The refuge stands in a commanding position at 1631m on a wide rocky outcrop under the Pala del Rifugio (2394m) looking west over to mountains including the Lastei and Canali peaks.

In view of the long tiring haul that makes up the next stage (some 4h30mins walking time), it is advisable to make this refuge your overnight stop and fill your water bottles.

Stage Two: to Passo Canali (2h), Passo Pradidali Basso (1h30mins) then R. Pedrotti alla Rosetta (1h)
Path n.707 passes the refuge's small chapel and heads north. Waymarking is frequent as you climb up through woods which thin out to give way to grassy rock. Wildlife is plentiful, particularly roe-deer in the wooded parts and a variety of birds including the capercaillie, black grouse, and also the rock partridge which inhabits the rocky reaches. You wind up and up, across a scree gully around the Sant'Anna rock spur (at approx. 1900m), and proceed under the peaks at the head of the Canali valley (in order on your right are Cima Vani Alti, Cima del Coro and Cima Alberghetto).

A very steep path branches up right to Passo dell'Orsa (meaning female bear, suggesting that they too once inhabited this area). You proceed straight on (bearing northwest now) toward the wide Passo Canali at 2469m. 2h so far.

The path is now n.708. The next stretch can be very cold and windy, and though some stretches are exposed there is no particular difficulty. With good visibility you will be rewarded by sweeping views all around. At first, on this high altitude area there is a series of large characteristic "buse" (literally "holes") formed by ancient glacial movement. The path crosses zones of loose stones and large rocks, and climbs again to 2716m, before another drop to cross the lower reaches of the Fradusta Glacier in gradual descent. The path will undoubtedly be well-trodden and easy to follow but the snow may be soft and slippery so a ski stock or alpenstock could be helpful here.

Up until 10,000 years ago, ie. the end of the last ice age, the whole plateau was covered in a thick layer of ice. It is certainly still a spectacular sight, this impressive stretch of snow and ice. There are some crevasses as you come off the lower edge, and water from melted snow flowing off the glacier is quickly absorbed by the porous limestone. It's straightforward walking around to the nearby Passo Pradidali Basso (2658m). (1h30mins from Passo Canali).

Halt for a pause to take stock of the Pale di San Martino peaks ahead of you northwest now.

An alternative at this stage is to turn left (southwest) down path n. 709 (there may be late-lying snow at the head of this valley) into a scree-filled cirque and valley to R. Pradidali at 2278m - 1h.

Otherwise, weather permitting, as orientation can be extremely difficult on this high plateau in conditions of low cloud and mist, proceed on path n.709 northwest across the karstic stone desert of the Pale di San Martino. On this next stretch waymarking is frequent (and regularly maintained and checked) but where painted indicators are unreliable due to effects such as snow and weathering, small mounds of stones or cairns ("ometti" in Italian = little men) have been heaped up, reminiscent of the prayer stone heaps in the Himalayas. The track from the pass bears left and crosses rock - it is not aided and can be tricky, so proceed with care. Around the corner it's easy walking across the gentle ups and downs and characteristic dolina shallow depressions of the Altopiano. R. Pedrotti alla Rosetta soon comes into sight in the distance west between the

Stone marker (cairn) on the San Martino plateau looking north

Rosetta peak on its left and Cimon della Pala (3184m) and Vezzana peak right. Strangely enough, walking times indicated on some signposts are often misleading.

This refuge (2581m) dates back to 1899, but was destroyed during the World War I. Rebuilt in 1921, enlarged in 1934, burnt down by the Germans in 1943 as retaliation, it was rebuilt again and inaugurated by Alpine Club members in 1952. It is another very popular refuge, (part of the Dolomites 'High Way' walk Alta Via n.2) so it's advisable to book in advance. You have a very good chance of enjoying a typically pink Dolomites sunset here.

As in other refuges in the area, the tap water here has been classified as unsuitable for drinking purposes (see note in Introduction under 'Refuges and Bivouac Huts'), so be prepared to buy mineral water if your water bottle is empty.

For people with time to spare on a clear day, the 30min stroll southwest up to the summit of the Rosetta at 2743m is highly recommended. From the refuge, follow the path towards the cable-car station, then head up the vast incline to the 'pulpit' at the top for superb views down over the township of San Martino and around northeast to the Zoldo and Ampezzo Dolomites and northwest to the the Fassa groups.

Access from and Descent to San Martino di Castrozza

R. Pedrotti alla Rosetta can also be reached from San Martino di Castrozza (1466m) on foot on path n.701 in 3h via R. Col Verde (1965m) (halfway timewise), or by taking the chair lift then cable-car. (See Stage Three for a description of the second section in the opposite direction.)

The same routes can obviously be used for an alternative descent, should you wish to finish the walk at this point.

The patron saint of the town is portrayed in the city's emblem with Saint Martin cutting his cloak in two in midwinter to share it with a beggar. It is an important resort in both summer and winter, and dates back to at least the 12th century. A Benedictine monastery and its Hospice were founded there at the time of the Crusades when Christians needed accommodation on the way to the Holy Land. When the Hapsburg domination came to an end the Austrians fled, burning down everything in sight and only the church survived.

Experienced walkers, on the other hand, who desire a less-frequented path, can follow Stage Three of walk 25 northeast down Val delle Comelle to the village of Gares then Canale d'Agordo.

Stage Three: to Baita Segantini (2h30mins) and ascent to R. Mulaz-G. Volpi (2h20mins)

Continuing the itinerary from R. Pedrotti alla Rosetta, follow the well-trodden track towards the arrival station for the cable-car, and just after Passo di Rosetta (2572m) turn sharp right, virtually straight downwards on n.701. The first stretch crosses over rock and passes under the cable-car lines twice. It is quite steep and the few rocky, exposed stretches are equipped with lengths of metallic cable and bars fixed to the rock face. This stretch is actually marked on some maps as "via ferrata", though it is easily tackled under normal weather conditions. This itinerary is preferable to the cable-car trip down to R. Col Verde, as it means you can save yourself a good 100m of descent by taking the path variant forking off right (about 1h this far) towards the Crode Rosse instead of actually dropping down to the level of the Refuge at 1965m.

If you begin your walk from San Martino, allow 1h30mins on foot (or the time to travel up by chair lift) as far as R. Col Verde.

The path number changes to n.712 and is known as the "Sentiero dei Finanzieri" (Revenue Officer's Path). Continue around past the path junction with n.706 turning up right to the Bivacco Fiamme Gialle. The path coasts around northwest with only slight ups and downs (save your energy for the last stretch today). You bear left and climb a little onto a grassy slope which will soon lead over and down the eroded red and brown hues of the earth of the Crode Rosse and fossilised ripple marks can be seen. Waymarking is not always that easy to find and care must be taken on this stretch as the earth is crumbly and is subject to mini-landslides. You're now under the immense mountain Cimon della Pala, whose upper reaches are known to be inhabited by the golden eagle. After crossing two wide rubble gullies and torrent beds, the path comes out on the road at Malga Fosse di Sopra, 1935m, (refreshments available) to avoid the steep hillside. The path (still n.712) keeps to the right (east) of the road and moves away again, under an area with barriers to prevent snow avalanching onto the road during winter. You curve around to the right with Passo Rolle, the first pass in the Dolomites to become an actual road, down left (west) then cross grassy slopes. The chair lift from Passo Rolle comes into sight ahead (north). This area is noted for the presence of the (protected) least primrose - a small flower that resembles a shorter version of the British red campion. You join the vehicle road and summer tourist masses at Baita Segantini (2170m) (no accommodation). Total walking time from R. Pedrotti alla Rosetta - 2h30mins.

To join the walk at this stage, catch a bus from San Martino di Castrozza north up to Passo Rolle then allow 45mins to walk to Baita Segantini, (or the brief time to travel via chair lift).

Despite the influx of 4-wheeled traffic, this spot is still worth visiting as it is situated right in front of another small glacier - the Travignolo Glacier high up (southeast) on Cima Vezzana which you first saw from the southern side from Passo Pradidali Basso in Stage Two.

After having refilled your water bottles, leave Baita Segantini by the road signposted n.721 and follow it down for 20mins as far as the turn-off right (northeast) to R. Mulaz n.710 - whereas the road continues in descent north along picturesque Val di Venegiotta. There should be plenty of protected dwarf alpenrose on the left-hand side of the road. The path begins the 600m climb (allow 1h45mins) amongst large boulders and loose rubble with clear waymarking. Winding up the steep scree-covered slope is hot work on a sunny summer afternoon. About halfway up, the terrain opens up into an ample amphitheatre, and the path follows the tiring northern side up over more detritus. There are wonderful views up right (south) of the northernmost chain of the Pale di San Martino Group and rock needles. Soon up at Passo del Mulaz (2619m) the vision opens up to include views over in Falcade's Val del Biois.

It's only 15mins more briefly northeast down a morainic stretch to

167

welcoming R. Mulaz at 2571m. At the head of the Focobon valley, under the Mulaz peak (2904m) the site is dominated by the imposing Focobon peak (3054m) with its glacier, along with the Campido and Lastei mountains. During a hot dry summer the refuge will most probably be short of water. Abundant snow however can just as easily mean the refuge will open late in the season as the valley faces north.

Stage Four: descent to Molino (Falcade) (3h30mins)
It's a long haul in a northerly direction down to the Val del Biois and Falcade, but is an easy walk. The time normally given for the ascent is 4h, but allow at least 3h30mins in the opposite direction unless you have knees of steel.

From the platform where the refuge is set, you start out on a common track with "Alta Via 2" which soon branches up left (n.751). Proceed downwards on n.722, winding on the grassy base of Sasso Arduini, to cross the top end of a gully, and continue down over the frontal moraine of the Focobon Glacier. Soon the path climbs over the rocky outcrop of Col dei Pidocchi (lice mount!) and follows a desolate valley. You bear left and steeply down, past a turn-off right (n.752) to Forcella della Stia. Next is a rocky amphitheatre with another path junction and ruins of a hut (1895m, Casera Focobon). This is about halfway, so take a break to look back up at the Lastei rock spires and the Campido peak, south behind where the glacier is. Your path n.722 forks down right following the Torrente Focobon, crosses the valley floor, and has a steep narrow passage. Now there are more wooded areas and rubble and you keep on the right-hand side of the torrent, before the valley opens out for the camping ground. Just before it, is the turn-off left (southwest) for R. Bottari and the "Alta Via dei Pastori" - see walk 23. Otherwise, walk straight on across the bridge and either turn left on the bitumen road to the village of Molino (shops) or take the right turn leading down to the main road and centre of Falcade (15mins). Here there are coach services west to Val di Fassa and east to Cencenighe and beyond.

PRACTICAL INFORMATION
R. CANT DEL GAL TEL:(0439)62997. Private, sleeps 23.
R. MULAZ-G.VOLPI TEL:(0437)599420 Alpine Club, Venice Section. Sleeps 70.
R. PEDROTTI ALLA ROSETTA TEL:(0439)68308 Alpine Club, Trent Section. Sleeps 120.
R. TREVISO (CANALI) TEL(0439)62311 Alpine Club,

Treviso Section. Sleeps 40.
TOURIST OFFICE FIERA DI PRIMIERO TEL:(0439)62407/62985.
TOURIST OFFICE SAN MARTINO DI CASTROZZA
TEL:(0439)768867.
TOURIST OFFICE FALCADE TEL:(0437)599241.

✳   ✳   ✳

WALK 25 (see sketch map J, page 162)

PALE DI SAN MARTINO
via Fiera di Primiero - Prati Piereni (1h) - R. Pradidali (3h20mins) -
Passo Pradidali Basso (1h30mins) - R. Pedrotti alla Rosetta (1h) -
Val delle Comelle - R. Comelle (3h30mins) -Gares -
Canale d'Agordo (1h30mins).
TABACCO MAP NO.022 scale 1:25,000
TABACCO MAP NO.4 scale 1:50,000
(2-3 days suggested)

Starting at the lively market town and tourist centre of Fiera di Primiero
(711m), this itinerary crosses some quite spectacular terrain ranging
from meadows and woods to the stark and desolate Pale di San Martino
rock plateau. While it is not a mountaineering route in the strict sense, the
descent from the plateau in Stage Three does include a long descent on
rough terrain with rock climbing stretches of some difficulty. Previous
experience is preferable. However, an alternate descent west to San
Martino di Castrozza is included, and there is also the possibility of linking
up with walk 24.

Stage One: to Prati Piereni (1h) and R. Pradidali (3h20mins)
If you catch the summer bus that runs from Fiera di Primiero up to R. Cant
del Gal 1160m) at the confluence of Val Canali and Val Pradidali, you'll
then need path n.709 northwest. In 1h30mins on an easy, well-trodden
path up the right-hand side of Val Pradidali, past Malga Pradidali you'll
reach the path junction with the main route at the area known as
Pedemonte.

Otherwise, the more direct walk from Fiera as far as Prati Piereni (1h),
is described in Stage One of walk 24.

At the Prati Piereni meadows spread with chalets and crocuses, you'll have entered the Paneveggio-Pale di San Martino Nature Park. Follow signposting for n.719 north for 20mins along a surfaced road. Traffic is rare, and you wind up through mixed wood to a bar blocking further car access. Then it's 1h more through wood with the occasional scree and boulder stretch, and sweet-smelling mountain pine patches in Val Pradidali - this name comes from the Italian "prati gialli" meaning "yellow meadows". Further on before the ascent, the Sass Maor peak is up left (west). At an area known as Pedemonte ('foot of the mountain') under the rocks, you join up with n.709 from R. Cant del Gal (1h20mins so far).

Now you have a 2h (600m) climb in wide zigzags past mini-meadows set amongst rock faces that nurture a myriad of unusual and protected wild flowers. These include members of the bellflower and speedwell family, the pink cinquefoil as well as the more common saxifrage. Soon three of the supports for the refuge's cableway are visible - take heart, R. Pradidali is not far behind them, just over the top where the valley opens out into an amphitheatre. This magnificent all-rock setting, above the tree line, is bordered by a series of imposing walls and peaks: the mountains that start on your right (east) while you're still labouring up the valley are the Canali group peaks - good for sunset colours. Torre Pradidali is directly north behind the refuge, the Cima di Ball is due west with Sass Maor further downhill (southwest from the refuge). R. Pradidali at 2278m is a very important and popular base for "via ferrata" climbers and mountaineers, so be sure you phone to book beforehand. The Dresden Alpine Club was responsible for the first construction here in 1896, later enlarged in 1912.

Note: a placard warns that the refuge water is not fit for drinking ie. "acqua non potabile". (See note in Introduction under 'Refuges and Bivouac Huts'). You can always buy mineral water.

Stage Two: to Passo Pradidali Basso (1h30mins) and
R. Pedrotti alla Rosetta (1h)
Early risers will be rewarded by some wonderful sunrise rock colours both at the refuge and on the way to the pass. Check the signposting and head up the silent stone valley north on path n.709, keeping the small lake on your right. You climb some easy rock faces (not exposed) with footholds, alternating with extraordinary flat morainic cirques. Old snow patches are common. Waymarking is clear and frequent, but don't be misled by the faint indications for Passo Pradidali Alto (slightly west of

Passo Pradidali Basso) as the relevant access path goes virtually due north from the lake. Yours on the other hand, proceeds in an easterly direction briefly, to where n.711 continues east to Passo delle Lede, and (n.709) bears north again up another valley. Some 100m below the pass itself, it turns sharp left (northwest) climbing steeply over rock to Passo Pradidali Basso (2658m). There may be deep snow drifts on this approach side of the pass, so proceed with care if walking early in the season (check your map but the general direction is essentially upwards). At the top take a rest stop to get your bearings - the panorama takes in the glittering extension to your right (east) of the Fradusta glacier, then south back down Val Pradidali are the Canali peaks, and looking northwest over the San Martino plateau, you have the Vezzana peak (3192m), the highest of the San Martino group, and an enchanting line-up on a clear day.

The next stretch over the barren plateau of the Pale di San Martino is still on path n.709. As orientation on this unworldly terrain can be treacherously confusing in low cloud or mist, it is strongly inadvisable to proceed if in doubt. For a more detailed description of this section see the final part of Stage Two, walk 24. After rounding a slightly exposed rock corner, it's easy walking west across the undulating rock plateau. You follow little mounds of loose stones (cairns) and regular red and white paint waymarking. You can soon make out R. Pedrotti alla Rosetta with the low Rosetta peak and the cable-car (from San Martino di Castrozza) arrival station to its left (southwest), and Cimon della Pala (3184m) and the Vezzana peak right (north).

This refuge (2581m) is very popular and advance booking is recommended for overnight stays. As at R. Pradidali, the tap water here has also been deemed unsuitable for drinking.

As well as access from San Martino by taking the chair lift to R. Col Verde (meals only) then cable-car to the top, the refuge can be reached in the same direction, in about 3h entirely on foot.

Should you decide not to attempt the Val delle Comelle descent, alternatives are: a) continue with Stage Three of walk 24 to Baita Segantini then R. Mulaz and Falcade, or b) return to Val Cismon via either the cable-car then chair lift, or on foot - see walk 24 for more details.

Stage Three: descent to R. Comelle - Gares (3h30mins)
and Canale d'Agordo (1h30mins)

This stage descends Val delle Comelle in a northeasterly direction towards the village of Gares. It is one of the lesser-frequented parts of the San Martino group and is wild and desolate. The rock caverns there used to be inhabited by the legendary Comèlles - female creatures with two favourite pastimes: playing on the ice fields of the Fradusta glacier, and playing with the reason of man. They would spirit his mind away and the victim would go mad.

The seemingly barren rocky stretches, surprisingly enough, are dotted with hardy flowers such as the protected yellow rhaetian poppy. The path follows a series of steep rocky descents which alternate with easier flatter river-like plains. The track is classified as an 'alpine' itinerary as there are some elementary rock descents, but they are not exposed and are aided with fixed steel cables. However do not attempt it in bad weather, as rain could make it very slippery and the gorge lower down could be dangerous if swollen with water.

Start out from R. Pedrotti alla Rosetta on path n.703 and follow its gentle descent northeast to the edge of the plateau, then steeply down the narrow scree gorge to Pian dei Cantoni (2312m) (45mins so far). There's a junction and n.703 climbs steeply up left (and over to Passo delle Farangole and consequently R. Mulaz). You continue down n.704 which follows the valley floor then goes down a loose rubble descent into a scree-filled depression. Keep to the right-hand side and climb down the first of several aided stretches - there are 5 in all, with fixed metallic cables. Check that they are still well-anchored before trusting your weight to them as some of the metal pegs occasionally work loose, probably due to snow movements. There's a sort of rocky ledge, a rubble climb (aided) then further down, a longish stretch over rock with more cables. There are some enormous old snow masses to cross. They have been weathered into artistic sculptures by rain and wind and the snow-melt stream flowing underneath.

You come down into the wide river corridor plain of Pian delle Comelle (1818m) and start to see vegetation and wild flowers once more. At the end it narrows and you enter the dramatic "Orrido" (Italian for "ravine"). Bleached boulders and sheer cliff sides dwarf you as the rushing crystal clear stream cascades alongside. The path is a series of 'surprises' aided by 4 ladders in all. At one point the path seems to disappear into a black hole (with a metal ladder), and after yet more scrambling, it ends up with a series of metallic ladders then a wooden bridge crossing, just back from the top of the Gares waterfall, at 1509m. It's not a good idea to attempt to get closer to the fall here, as the terrain is not reliable, and there are good views from the bottom. Over the stream right (east) there's another aided stretch along a wide ledge with springy vegetation underfoot and sweet-smelling mountain pines. The descent through woods with slippery tree roots brings you out at the base of the crashing waterfall. From here it's another 20mins further down to R. Comelle (1345m) (meals only, no accommodation) and 'civilisation'. An alternative straight to Gares village (1380m) is by following signposting from the base of the waterfall, across the wooden bridge at the stream and north through the woods (about 20mins shorter). Otherwise continue on from R. Comelle either by road or the signposted track which branches off right across meadows just downhill from the refuge, (it joins up with the road about halfway down). It's 1h30mins and 8km to the village of Canale d'Agordo (970m). It is a site of pilgrimage, being the birth place of Pope John Paul I, Albino Luciani (1912). Here you will also find well-kept flowering gardens and coach services west to Falcade and east to Cencenighe and beyond.

PRACTICAL INFORMATION
R. CANT DEL GAL TEL:(0439)62997. Private, sleeps 23.
R. PEDROTTI ALLA ROSETTA TEL:(0439)68308 Alpine Club, Trent Section. Sleeps 120.
R. PRADIDALI TEL:(0439)64180 Alpine Club, Treviso Section. Sleeps 72.
TOURIST OFFICE FIERA DI PRIMIERO TEL:(0439)62407/62985.
TOURIST OFFICE SAN MARTINO DI CASTROZZA TEL:(0439)768867.

WALK 26 (see sketch map K, page 175)

ALPI FELTRINE
via (Fiera di Primiero) Imer - R. Fonteghi (2h) - R. Boz (2h30mins) -
Passo Finestra - Piazza del Diavolo - Passo Pietena -
R. Dal Piaz (6h) - Croce d'Aune (1h45mins) (Pedavena).
TABACCO MAP NO.023 scale 1:25,000
TABACCO MAP NO.4 scale 1:50,000
(3 days suggested)

The Alpi Feltrine which lie briefly to the south of the famous Pale di San Martino, is a lesser-visited area of the Dolomites, even though it constitutes the final stage of Alta Via 2. The modest (in terms of height) and rugged mountain chain (Vette Feltrine) is traversed lengthwise (northeast to southwest) in Stage Two. There are simply magnificent views in clear weather, in addition to the wide open glacially-formed bowl and amphitheatre landscape crossed. The walk does, however, have several exposed stretches and is therefore not suggested as a first itinerary for inexperienced walkers.

Stage One: to R. Fonteghi (2h) then R. Boz (2h30mins)
The village of Imer at 620m, is on the main road just 4.5kms south of Fiera di Primiero and is well-serviced by buses. If you're travelling by car and just doing a day-trip to R. Boz, then you can drive as far as R. Fonteghi. Otherwise, if you intend to walk this itinerary in its entirety, you'll be better off leaving the car here in the valley at Imer, and returning by public transport from Pedavena or Feltre.

From the main road through Imer, head south to cross the Torrente Cismon and join with track n.726 from Mezzano (a road at this stage), in the direction of Val Noana. Unless you do this on a Sunday, traffic should be light. There are alternative routes, but they tend to be asphalted as well and take you up and down over hills wasting time where the road is more economic in terms of energy at this stage. The road itself up the narrow rock-walled valley is picturesque, and there is a series of rock tunnels or "gallerie" (use a torch as a warning headlight for oncoming drivers), most of which can be detoured around by way of the old track around the side. After a couple of steep switchbacks in the road then a flattish stretch that runs above the south shore of Lago di Noana, you'll reach R. Fonteghi in about 2h total. This homely friendly refuge is set at

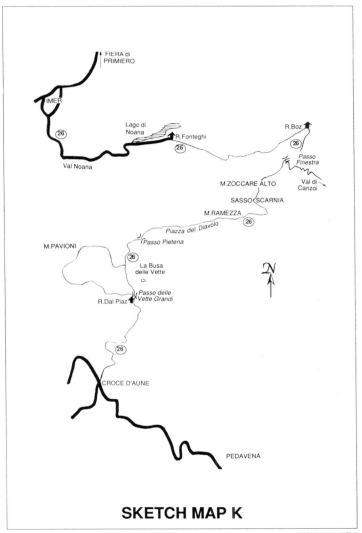

SKETCH MAP K

1100m at the end of the sealed road.

Track n.727 around the right of the refuge in an easterly direction, means another 30mins of dirt road through woods with abundant wild strawberries. You come to a clearing used as a car park - from here on authorised forestry commission or refuge vehicles only are allowed. The R. Boz signpost says 1h30mins, but allow at least 2h. It's easy walking but steep in parts, through grazing land and woods, and frequent corner-cutting is possible. Where the jeep track finishes is the loading point for the refuge's cableway. Keep to the right of the small stream - there are red arrows going right, though the path is narrow and appears insignificant. Follow the cable lines northeast through light wood and grassland and the refuge will soon come into sight. It's a good 30mins more, with a steep pull up the hill on the last leg to the top where the refuge is panoramically placed at 1718m (not 1618m according to older maps).

The clanging cow bells belong to the dairy farm across the valley which supplies R. Boz with fresh milk and cheeses. This home-style refuge is run by friendly local people who serve tasty food, including local specialities such as "toséla" - local fresh cheese that has been fried very lightly in butter and oven-baked briefly with the addition of fresh cream. It is usually served with polenta, a type of hot corn purée.

Stage Two: via Passo Finestra, Piazza del Diavolo and
Passo Pietena to R. Dal Piaz (6h)
This is a very long stretch and you should carry plenty of water with you as there are no intermediate supply points. Most of the day will be spent crossing crests and ridges on the south side of the Vette Feltrine chain, and should the weather be unsettled or shows signs of deteriorating, it is not advisable to start out, as the exposed sections could be dangerous. Furthermore, low cloud cover will not enhance visibility - a pity as it's panoramic all the way.

From R. Boz you head uphill right (south) on n.801. An easy gentle ascent amidst abundant wild flowers and light woods with dwarf rhododendrons takes you to 1766m and Passo Finestra (literally 'window pass'), where in fact the view opens out onto Val di Canzoi on the other (east) side. Turn sharp right (southwest) and coast the south side of the crest at first, in very slight descent. Be careful not to go too far down, as waymarking is not so clear. Path n.805 actually branches off here (southeast) to descend rather rapidly and steeply and come out just below Albergo Boz and Lago della Stua on the secondary vehicle road connecting with Feltre - useful as an alternative exit point.

Keep high up. The next 1h30mins or so (dotted lines on the map) will need your fullest attention, as there are several exposed ledges. The path bears right and narrows, climbing to 1929m on Monte Zoccare Alto. You soon enter the Piazza del Diavolo (Devil) Nature Reserve, where is is forbidden to leave the marked track without permission and walkers must not disturb the natural environment in any way.

Continuing just under the crest on rocky terrain with dwarf pines, the path is exposed in places and there is overhanging rock - mind your rucksack doesn't catch here. The trickiest passages are aided (steel cable set into the rock). There's a series of steps cut into exposed rock up to Sasso Scarnia (views north towards the Pale di San Martino) with yet another aided stretch. Then you bear left and down (southeast) into a wildish area of large irregular boulders and interesting rock formations. A path from Forcella Scarnia comes in from the left, and there's another area of low-lying mountain pines to be crossed by a narrow path. Then you're back on the old military mule-track. There's a bit more roughish scree terrain then another small saddle to cross beneath Monte Ramezza. After just one final exposed stretch crossing a crest, the worst is behind you and it's easier going, so you'll have time to appreciate the magnificent views on both sides, in the absence of cloud or mist.

Plenty of wild flowers, particularly in early July, as you're in the Nature Reserve now. You'll soon cross the uncanny Piazza del Diavolo itself, where you are dwarfed by gigantic stone masses. It used to be the favourite haunt of witches, but can now be crossed safely thanks to a local priest from Vignui (a village to the southeast). He was an expert in magic and, not able to accept the fact that the witches should have chosen to abide in his parish, hunted them out by erecting a huge cross there.

There's also a very interesting cave nearby (a natural ice cave) - "La Giazera di Ramezza" (from dialect, meaning the "Ramezza icery") at about 1800m. The local inhabitants from Feltre and Pedavena used to climb up there for their ice supplies.

At the last pass - Passo Pietena (2094m) - there are superb examples of glacier-sculpted stones. It is at the northernmost edge of an immense crater-like hollow called "La Busa delle Vette o delle Meraviglie" (from the local dialect and meaning "the Hole of the Peaks or Wonders"). In actual fact it is a cirque formed by ice, and there are others like it in the Vette Feltrine. Ancient glaciers sculpted odd rock shapes from the strangely coloured rocks you'll see in this area, and many fossils have been found. The cirque houses the dairy farm buildings of Malga Vette Grandi and cattle fill the air with the echo of their clanging bells. You descend into the valley (there's a spring too) with its grazing grounds, coast the western flanks of Monte Pavione then climb gently up the opposite side. R. Dal Piaz (named after an eminent geologist) is just over the Passo delle Vette Grandi (1994m) and looks out southeast over the valley of Feltre.

At this point a side trip to nearby Monte Pavione (2335m) is recommended. One path (n.817) turns straight up a ridge (west) from Passo delle Vette Grandi. Following the line of crests (a little exposed at times) with several longish up and down sections, it takes a very panoramic 1h30mins. The final stretch affords magnificent views north to the towering Val Canali peaks of the San Martino Group and the valley township of Fiera di Primiero, and northwest to the Lagorai mountains. A longer route (2h) is signposted from R. Dal Piaz and it coasts west through grazing areas before a final ascent to Monte Pavione.

Stage Three: descent to Croce d'Aune (1h45mins)
Path n.801 is a delightful walk winding south downhill with plenty of marked short cuts to eliminate the meanderings of the old military road. The initial grassy hillside offers panoramas east towards Monte Pizzocco and the Schiara from points between openings in the jagged rock crest. July walkers are guaranteed carpets of wildflowers including deep blue trumpet gentians, yellow bear's-ear primulas, alpenrose and heather, and, further down, slopes of pheasant's-eye narcissus. About halfway down, the well-marked path veers right and descends steeply into silent fir and beech woods where it becomes rough and stony. It brings you out at a water trough on the edge of the sleepy hamlet and summer resort of Croce d'Aune (1015m). Continue down briefly to the main road. (In ascent to R. Dal Piaz this stage takes 2h30mins.) A bus service runs from here southeast to Pedavena and its brewery and gardens (on foot approx.1h) and hence to the fascinating historic township of Feltre. Here there's a railway station (connections with Trent to the west and Venice southeast), as well as coach lines in most directions.

PRACTICAL INFORMATION

R. FONTEGHI TEL:(0439)67043. Private, sleeps 20.
R. B. BOZ TEL:(0439)64448 Alpine Club, Feltre Section. Sleeps 42.
R. DAL PIAZ TEL:(0439)9065 Alpine Club, Feltre Section. Sleeps 34.
TOURIST OFFICE FELTRE TEL:(0439)2540/2839.
TOURIST OFFICE FIERA DI PRIMIERO TEL:(0439)62407/62985.
TOURIST OFFICE IMER TEL:(0439)67023.

✳   ✳   ✳

WALK 27 (see sketch map L, page 180)

CIVETTA / MOIAZZA
via Pecol - Casera di Pioda (1h45mins) -
R. Sonino al Coldai (1h15mins) - R. Tissi (2h) - R. Vazzoler (2h) -
alt. a) Van delle Sasse (3h) - Forcella delle Sasse (30mins) -
Sentiero Tivan - R. Sonino al Coldai - (3h30mins) -
Casera di Pioda (30mins) - Pian di Pezze (45mins) - Alleghe (1h).
alt. b) R. Carestiato (3h30mins) - Passo Duran (40mins).
TABACCO MAP NO.015 scale 1:25,000
TABACCO MAP NO.4 scale 1:50,000 (except very first bit)
(2-3 days suggested)

This Civetta itinerary starts out from Val Zoldana as it offers easier access, though a final descent on its western side to Alleghe in Val Cordevole is included.

The Civetta, which strangely enough means "owl" in Italian, is shaped like an enormous trident. This round trip gives the walker the chance to appreciate the almost unbelievable metamorphoses this Dolomite stronghold undergoes when circumnavigated. While the initial stages are both easy and popular, Stage Three, the 'over the top' crossing between the Civetta and Moiazza is very long and tiring with several difficult stretches and should only be attempted by walkers with some prior experience, and in good atmospheric conditions. Several worthwhile alternatives are given.

Should you wish to do this itinerary after walk 2 from the nearby Pelmo, then leave the latter at either Passo Staulanza (thence n.568/561 via Casera Vescovà to Casera di Pioda) or via path n.474 descending to Palafavera, (thence n.564 to Casera di Pioda).

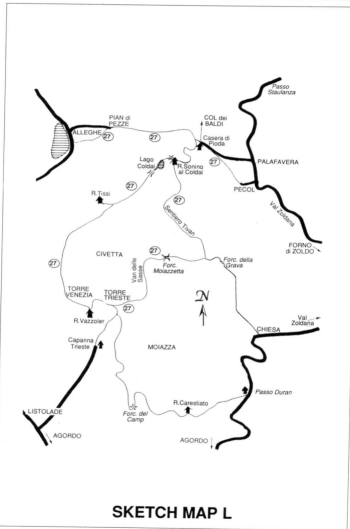

SKETCH MAP L

Stage One: via Casera di Pioda (1h45mins) to R. Coldai (1h15mins)

Val Zoldana can be reached by the bus service running up from Longarone south in the Piave valley, via Forno di Zoldo. As the name suggests, (forno = furnace, oven) the area was once an important iron-making centre employing a significant number of local blacksmiths. Its chief exports were iron nails, in great demand for house and shipbuilding as well as shoes.

If you're travelling by car, by all means drive via Palafavera to Casera di Pioda where there's a car parking area.

On foot, the starting point is the village of Pecol (1380m) north of Forno. From the main road in Val Zoldana (facing up valley), turn left into Pecol Vecchio, and after the last houses, keeping uphill of the stream, follow path n.556 in a northwesterly direction. You cross meadows, go under a chair lift, then through mixed wood climbing quite steeply at times. The path joins up with the narrow secondary road from Palafavera, which can be quite busy in August. A brief easy stretch and you arrive at the dairy farm Casera di Pioda (1892m), where dairy produce (not necessarily at bargain prices), refreshments and drinking water are available. Walking time this far is 1h45mins. Note that the position of the Casera on the 25,000 map is shown as being higher than it actually is.

Alternate accesses from Alleghe:
a) via the gondola-car as far as Pian di Pezze (1470m) (you can also drive this far), then chair lift to Col dei Baldi from where you coast around (n.561) southeast then south to Casera di Pioda - allow 20mins for the final stretch on foot.
b) see Stage Four in reverse, and allow 3h30mins.

Leave the Casera with its noisy herds of cows and head uphill (south) on the wide signposted track (n.556), now for walkers only. It follows an easy wartime mule-track and winds and climbs over scattered grass patches and rock. In just over an hour and a couple of rock crests, you reach the top point of the refuge's mechanised cableway, then go briefly southwest around the corner to clean, spacious, R. Sonino al Coldai (2135m) itself. It stands in front of the Cima di Coldai, a northern extension of the Civetta, and is separated from it by the forcella of the same name. The refuge, like all respectable ones worth their name, has a sun terrace facing southeast, and is a good point for viewing the Pelmo, slightly northeast and unmistakable. If it fits in with your plans, an overnight stay here is most pleasant, but be sure to sit right next to the large panoramic windows in the dining area for sunset. Booking is advisable.

Stage Two: to R. Tissi (2h) then to R. Vazzoler (2h)
From R. Coldai the well-used path climbs briefly (due west) through a wide neck to Forcella Coldai (2191m). You now pass over to the northwestern side of the Civetta and just below in a shallow round amphitheatre is the glittering dark green water of the tarn, Lago Coldai (2143m). The occasional concert of classical music is held on its shores on the long midsummer evenings. From here you get your first close-up of the Civetta's majestic west wall. Path n.560 (well waymarked) circles the lake then heads southwest towards R. Tissi. Several points along the way afford dizzy views down to the township of Alleghe and its lake, northwest to the Marmolada (south wall) and further right the Sella massif. It's a series of ups and downs as you skirt this "wall of walls", regularly likened to set of gigantic organ pipes. After the lake there is a gradual climb to the small Forcella Col Negro (2210m). Afternoon walkers will most probably be treated to the rifle-like sounds of the frequent rock discharges from the exposed rock face - a reminder that these mountains are in continual devolution, crumbling bit by bit into scree. Bird cries echo eerily along the wall.

Further along, after about 1h30mins walking (from R. Coldai), is an enormous boulder next to the path, with painted waymarking indicating the 30mins (150m) ascent to Col Rean where R. Tissi is perched. This can be cut out of the itinerary, but only in case of particularly bad weather or lack of time, as it is definitely one of the best placed and hospitable refuges in the Dolomites, with its famous terrace and carefully artistic interior woodworking, the legacy of previous owners. Furthermore, it would be a pity to miss the purple sunset on the Civetta, which rises some 1,200m from its scree base at this point, to its summit of 3220m virtually straight in front of the refuge. Just behind the refuge is a lookout with the well-anchored cableway that brings supplies up from Alleghe - quite a mechanical achievement in itself, and must be seen to be believed.

When you can drag yourself away from this unique spot, head straight back down the path you came up to get here, and down at the large boulder turn right, at painted signposting for R. Vazzoler. It's a stroll, across grassland and past more enormous boulders, fallen children of the Civetta. The path goes due south now and as you near the last outpost of this giant, the Torre Venezia, there's a very good chance you'll see, or at least hear, rock climbers at work. After you've passed some timber huts amidst the trees, there's a final stretch along a dusty white gravel jeep track (used by the neighbouring dairy farm) to the larch wood sheltering the refuge. To the northeast, very close, is yet another important tower for climbers, Torre Trieste - so out with the binoculars! The sheltered position of R. Vazzoler (1714m) in the afternoon offers an unequalled view southeast of the Moiazza, pink at sunset time. It is a comfortable, rambling wooden building and has an alpine garden, containing named and labelled species. It is advisable to reserve your accommodation beforehand.

An alternate exit route from here is to descend (path n.555) to Capanna Trieste (1135m) (car access) then Listolade in Val Cordevole (2h total), where there are bus connections north to Alleghe and beyond, or south to Belluno.

Otherwise an alternative to the long and tiring, but very exciting and rewarding 'over the top' crossing is to continue via R. Carestiato as far as the road pass, Passo Duran. This description can be found following Stage Four.

Stage Three - Alt. a: via Van delle Sasse (3h),
Forcella delle Sasse (30mins) and via Sentiero Tivan to
R. Coldai (3h30mins)
Though Alpine Club signposting gives a total time of 6h from R. Vazzoler to R. Coldai and some guides even suggest 5h, 7h is a better estimate, not including time for rest stops. This stage is long and tiring with several difficult points on steep scree and exposed rock, particularly on the final stretch. It's a good idea to start out early in the morning to avoid the blazing sun on the climb and crossing of the Van delle Sasse section. Carry plenty of water as there are no intermediate stopover points.

Leave the refuge on the white dirt jeep track (n.555 same direction as descent to Capanna Trieste and Listolade) heading north then east downhill. About 15mins down, just after a watercourse crossing, is a black and white signpost for Biv. Torrani - take the narrow path branching off left. The climb starts immediately (east), through springy mountain pines with sweetly perfumed alpine pinks. It's 30mins more to another turn-off right (marked "Nevere"- faded paint on a rock - to Biv. Moiazza and a mountaineering route). Keep left and up. The path (n.558) is virtually void of waymarking and numbering, but is clear and easy to follow and there are no alternatives to confuse you. Towering on your left, impossible to ignore, the Torre Trieste and Torre Venezia are quite a sight illuminated by early morning sun. Back behind you, (southwest) the high peak of Monte Agner flanked by the Pale di San Martino may emerge from beneath clouds. The rock on this ascent shows evidence of intense water erosion, and there are entire walls with parallel vertical channelling caused by running water. A brief grassy hollow reveals a host of edelweiss, before an enormous silent rock amphitheatre backed by a seemingly impassable rock wall which rears up ahead due north. Old orange paint splashes now indicate the way up, and where these give out, small cairns take over as waymarkers. You ascend steeply (and slowly) to 2400m and after you've gone left round a low rock wall, you enter the desolate realm of the cirque called Van delle Sasse - "van" refers to its having been glacially formed and "sasse" to the stones. The area is completely enclosed by mountains, and the few walkers are dwarfed by the imposing rock walls that surround it. Essentially, the mountains north and west belong to the Civetta, and those east and south to the Moiazza. A signed path junction points climbers heading for R. Torrani left, and you right for Forcella Moiazzetta (also referred to as Forcella delle Sasse). (Total 3h this far.)

The silence is broken by the occasional marmot cry of alarm. Follow the faint waymarking carefully some 15mins across the undulating grass, scattered wild flowers and rock plateau to the foot of the final ascent for the forcella. It's an easy scramble up the rock face, but keep an eye out for path markers which are few and far between here. Allow another 15mins up to Forcella Moiazzetta (or delle Sasse) (2476m) that separates the Civetta and Moiazza Groups.

After a breather, brace yourself for the 500m descent. Beginning with an initial narrow stretch hugging the rock face, you then climb down (east) over rock and scree through a small upper cirque then down more steeply. Extra care is needed as it is easy to slip and stumble or lose your foothold on the rough mobile scree and rubble. There are spectacular orange and black rock flanks and enormous slabs and irregular collapsed sheets that have come away. There is some waymarking but the direction is generally clear - ie. down, so you can't go wrong. Head for the path traces below. Descent time obviously depends on individual confidence and speed, but 1h should be sufficient to the path junction (about 2200m) - painted on a rock in the centre of the valley, but with the indications facing downwards. Orange paint marks on a couple of rocks indicate where the path to Biv. Grisetti turns off south. You turn decisively left (north) and the path is now n.557 though numbering is virtually inexistent. The exceptional sweeping panorama now takes in the Cortina

At Forcella Moiazzetta

mountains including the Tofane (north), bearing east to the line-up of the Sorapíss, Marmarole and Antelao, then the Pelmo massif and around southeast to the Bosconero.

Alternate exit:

Should the weather look like turning bad as you descend the scree from Forcella Moiazzetta, then think seriously about making a fast exit to Val Zoldana, as the remaining path to R. Coldai is still long and definitely not recommended in adverse weather conditions. Proceed from the aforementioned path junction - n.558 goes virtually straight down (east) to Forcella della Grava and several dairy farms. Either turn right (southeast) on n.557 via Casera della Grava (refreshments only) and continue on the jeep-width track to the village of Chiesa - only 3.5km from Dont in Val Zoldana (buses) or 4.5km from Passo Duran (2 refuges). Otherwise head north (left) on n.586 or n.585 to Pecol in Val Zoldana, the starting point of this itinerary. A good few hours should be allowed for each of these possibilities.

The descent continues to be rough - worthy of a dotted line ie. difficult on the map, even though the 25,000 shows it as easy-going path - until around 2050m, when you veer left (north) to coast around a rock base. There are several tricky points here which can be slippery. The cable for R. Torrani's goods supply is overhead. Another 30mins at the most will see you on a more decent path and there is soon another turn-off down towards Val Zoldana - signposted Pian del Crep (40mins in descent). After a low grassy crest a spectacular massive scree-strewn amphitheatre opens up with broad expanses of old snow, under the immense rock walls of the east-facing side of the Civetta. There is soon a turn-off (left) leading to R. Torrani. Keep straight ahead and follow the orange-painted "R. Coldai" indications which appear now. The first says 2h30mins to the refuge, but allow more. There is soon a gentle ascent and over to enter another grandiose amphitheatre - of glacial origin - the Busa del Zuiton. Old snow cover is extensive here, and following previous walkers tracks is often a sensible rule. Test snow depth if it looks newly-fallen. A further ascent left around an outlying rock point takes you to 2400m and the main access point to the famous "via ferrata degli Alleghesi" (experts only).

Indications here say 1h to R. Coldai. Coast around another 30mins to a rocky outcrop and steep descent hugging the rock. There is a variant, but it's best to follow the most recent waymarking - keep right at first to descend then bear left at the bottom where it rejoins the scree. Up again bearing right to the Crodolon at 2329m - just after a metal plaque with prayers in both Italian and German.

This next section, known as the "Sentiero Tivan" includes several partially aided and difficult stretches, though here again the 25,000 map does not acknowledge the fact. Take a rest first, if time permits. The descent, hidden from view at first around the corner, starts with an aided stretch (metal cord fixed to the rock face). There is a small metal plaque at the top in memory of a climber who died after having been struck by lightning there in 1987. The cable is not long, and you're soon left to your own devices on the rock face. Don't let the climbers returning late afternoon to the valley hurry you on, take your time and it won't be problematic. When you're back with the solid normal walking path beneath your boots once more, you have yet another 30mins coasting with infinite ins and outs, ups and downs. R. Coldai has been visible since some way back, but it never actually seems to get any closer. Allow 7h total.

Stage Four: descent via Casera di Pioda (30mins),
Pian di Pezze (45mins) to Alleghe (1h)
On path n.556 you descend west then north to the Casera di Pioda - see Stage One for the route description. To make this a complete round trip you can of course continue the same way and return to Pecol.

From the Alpine Club signposting at the Casera take n.564 for the Forcella di Alleghe, ie. the path furthest left (looking downhill). Very soon. nearby you'll come to an old wooden signpost "Per Alleghe" (To Alleghe) near a large boulder and a path intersection. Take the right branch down (north) between the grazing cows and over several muddy stretches of ground with wonky planks lain over them. The path leads down an idyllic green valley with old timber huts and the Cima di Coldai is up left. The path moves on to becoming a wide gravel track (winter ski run) then returns to the woods for a while. Path numbering is nonexistent, but when you arrive at the top station of a chair lift and see buildings below on the slopes, head for the Ristorante Fontanabona. Then, keeping to the track, proceed on to cross the torrent next to the chair lift station (1470m, 45mins this far). Just before the car parking area (and the beginning of traffic access), you turn down left into the wood - signposted "Per Alleghe" once more. Dark rocks, raspberry canes and pink rosebay willow-herb flowers are along the way. There are excellent views of the north face of the Civetta with its small eternal glacier known as its "eye", and you can just make out R. Tissi's flag flying on the highest point of the Col Rean hillock. There is a turn-off left soon, but it tends to be concealed by undergrowth. Should you miss it and reach an old farm house with fresh running water and where the gondola-car lift from Alleghe passes overhead, turn left here instead. You follow a grass-covered track once used for carts, as the buildings you're heading for on the stream-side were once the mills that served the township of Alleghe. There is still plentiful evidence of the former activity in the way of discarded equipment and mill stones. The main water wheel on the stream was broken by the weight of heavy snow only recently. Take the path down in front of the house which is still inhabited and you descend to the stream. There are 2 sturdy wooden bridges to be crossed as the path winds down and around. Some 45mins from Pian di Pezze will bring you out at the first houses of Alleghe, then its' another 15mins to the main road and town centre. Turn left for the Tourist Office and bus stops, and straight down for the lakeside.

Alternative b): R. Vazzoler to R. Carestiato (3h30mins) and to Passo Duran (40mins)

This stretch is wilder and more solitary than the previous stretch from R. Coldai. From R. Vazzoler go down the dirt track in the direction of Capanna Trieste and Listolade, past the Biv. Moiazza turn-off, further down to "Alta Via 1" signposting (1430m) and path n.554. It runs beneath the great eastern cliffs of the Spiz della Mussai before ascending rather steeply through wood to Col de l'Ors (1800m) a good panoramic point (1h45mins this far). On the next section you cut across a scree slope then there is another ascent to Forcella del Camp (1932m) (another 45mins). North next briefly, before bearing east past the turn-off to the Moiazza's long "via ferrata", and through wood again to R. B. Carestiato (1834m). It stands in a good sunny position, with an excellent terrace looking down (southwest) into Agordo's Cordevole valley, hopefully without too much of the typical summer haze obscuring the view. The panorama also ranges across (east) to the San Sebastiano and Tamer peaks, and around north to the Pelmo with the Antelao to its east. Vipers are not uncommon here, and sunsets are very pink.

In less than an hour you can reach Passo Duran (1605m) by following the vehicle-width track.

A summer bus connection with Agordo from the pass is in the pipeline for the hopefully not-too-distant future, pending completion of the necessary road work.

PRACTICAL INFORMATION

R. B. CARESTIATO TEL:(0437)62949. Alpine Club, Agordo section.
Sleeps 38.
R. SONINO AL COLDAI TEL:(0437)789160. Alpine Club,
Venice section. Sleeps 88.
R. SAN SEBASTIANO (PASSO DURAN) TEL:(0437)62360. Private.
Sleeps 30.
R. TOME (PASSO DURAN). Alpine Club, Agordo section. Sleeps 25.
R. A. TISSI TEL:(0437)721644. Alpine Club, Belluno section.
Sleeps 58.
CAPANNA TRIESTE TEL:(0437)660122. Private. Sleeps 28.
R. VAZZOLER TEL:(0437)660008. Alpine Club, Conegliano section.
Sleeps 80.
TOURIST OFFICE AGORDO TEL:(0437)62105.
TOURIST OFFICE ALLEGHE TEL:(0437)523333.
TOURIST OFFICE FORNO DI ZOLDO TEL:(0437)787349.

✳   ✳   ✳

WALK 28 (see sketch map M, page 190)

SCHIARA

via (Belluno) Bolzano Bellunese - Case Bortot (45mins) -
R. 7° Alpini (3h) - Forcella Pis Pilón (45mins) -
Forcella Càneva (45mins) - Caiàda (2h) - Faè-Fortogna (1h30mins)
TABACCO MAP NO.4 scale 1:50,000
TABACCO MAP NO.024 scale 1:25,000
(2 days suggested)

The Schiara group stands in the far southeastern corner of the Dolomites
and includes the sheer-sided Schiara mountain itself (2565m) as well as
adjacent Monte Pelf (2506m). It is one of the lesser-known and visited
Dolomites, and is more a climbers' mountain with a wealth of "vie ferrate".
The surrounding area (Nature Reserve) is characterised by thickly
vegetated deep and darkish valleys, rugged scenery and abundant plant
and animal life. The origin of the name Schiara has been traced back to
a Celtic word meaning 'ring' (the area was invaded by Celts some 1,000
years B.C.) and probably refers to their custom of using iron rings as

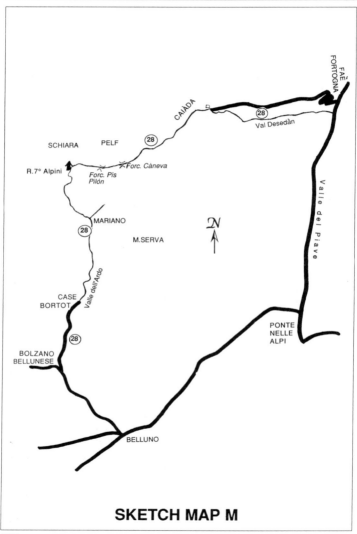

SKETCH MAP M

boundary markers.

Though it is a pity to miss an overnight stay at the refuge, the following itinerary can be adapted as a 1-day return walk, and car access is possible as far as the Case Bortot. Note that parts of Stage Two (which is more panoramic) are often snow-covered, and it has a couple of rough sections including a very steep scree descent from the Forcella Càneva.

Access by way of public transport is no problem: northbound trains from Padua and Venice (Calalzo line) connect with Belluno, and run through Faè-Fortogna, the finishing point (just south of Longarone), though they do not always stop there - check the timetable beforehand. Buses can also be used.

Stage One: via Case Bortot (45mins) to R. 7° Alpini (3h)
This stage follows motorable road as far as the Case Bortot locality. From the city of Belluno (probably of Celtic origin as "Beleno" was the sun goddess), take the suburban bus the 3.5kms northwest up the Ardo River valley to the village of Bolzano Bellunese (541m). Set out uphill and pass the few shops. At the intersection near the church, Alpine Club signposting indicates the downhill road (straight ahead) through another hamlet (Gioz) and down across a largish stream (457m). Then it's uphill past a small chapel where the road narrows then winds up steeply. At the end of the surfaced road is the tavern Osteria Pavèi (no accommodation) and the Case Bortot (700m), a cluster of characteristic stone houses which has seen generations of shepherds, woodcutters and chamois hunters (45mins from Bolzano Bellunese).

A little further up is a clearing for parking and the upper limit for cars. A painted map board of the Schiara and surrounding valleys shows pathways, numbering etc. A clearly marked path (n.501) enters the wood straight off - mostly beech and a profusion of flowering cyclamens. This itinerary is particularly beautiful in autumn with the bright leaf colours, but summer walkers should be wary of snakes particularly on the clear sunny stretches of pathway as the Belluno zone is infamous for its vipers.

Ignore the signed fork off left (n.506 to Forcella Mompiana) and keep straight on in gradual ascent (north) before a decisive downward curve left where there are good views of the Schiara and Pelf to the left up the valley (north) and Monte Serva on your right (east). Soon after this are roughly chiselled words in the rock face in memory of a wartime muledriver who lost his life when he fell into the ravine underneath. The path, in fact, is often a rock ledge (not exposed) under M. Terne and has a plunging edge down into the beech wood, sometimes reinforced by stones piled up underneath. You'll pass a rubber hose pipe rigged up for drinking water - particularly appreciable in summer as these lower reaches can still have the muggy heat of the plains.

After 45mins is a concrete bridge (Mariano, 681m) and stream junction and the Schiara is visible up to your left. The odd rock needle is known as the "Gusèla del Vescovà". Ten more winding mins further on are the ruins of houses burnt down in 1944 during a 'roundup'. Keep left at the signed path junction (still on n.501) and follow the right bank of the stream climbing quite steeply in parts. Keep an eye out for roe-deer crashing around in the wood above. After 1h in mixed wood (including birch, hazel and the common silver fir), you reach 1037m and you cross another concrete walkway-bridge to the left side of the river and start to see more of the white cascading waters and crystal clear blue water pools in this wild and romantic valley. The terrain is still scarred from when the water pipeline was laid and after a crossing to the right side, the track follows the conduit up loose rocky slopes.

Enormous boulders and overhangs characterise the next part, before a crossing to the left preceding the last ascent up the so-called "Calvario" - a steep grassy and beech-wooded hillside. At the top, there's a small substation for the water works, then as you come out of the wood you are greeted by the welcome sight of R. 7° Alpini (1490m). (The '7°' in the name of the refuge stands for 'settimo' which means seventh). It is set against the backdrop of the impressive southern-facing rock wall of the Schiara and Pelf (the easternmost part), which you can contemplate as you settle down with a cool drink served by the friendly people who run this homely refuge. After a rest, wander up behind the refuge and you'll probably find wild flowers including delicate alpine varieties of the tiny mouse-ear, forget-me-not and avens.

Stage Two: to Forcella Pis Pilón (45mins) then Forcella Càneva (45mins) and descent via Caiàda (2h) to Faè-Fortogna (1h30mins)
As the majority of walkers who visit the Schiara are rock-climbers who now go north or west to the various "vie ferrate", this stage is relatively solitary and animal sightings (such as chamois) more likely. There is a good chance of finding snow on the early sections of this stage, so check at the refuge beforehand if in doubt.

Head east on path n.505 under a rocky outcrop (used for rock-climbing practice) and cross the valley that descends from the Forcella del Marmol which separates the Schiara and Pelf. The path climbs quite steeply on rough rock and rubble to a small pass with low mountain pines (look back for good views of the Schiara) before dropping briefly across grassy hillocks to Forcella Pis Pilón (1733m). There may be snow in this area even in late summer. More excellent views from here back west onto the Schiara group. After the forcella the going is level beneath M. Pelf, and a path joins up from the right. The next desolate stretch runs beneath the Sas de Mel and the path climbs to the narrow passage of Forcella Càneva (1840m). The steep gully ahead in descent can be very tricky with its loose scree, and care is needed. Open terrain follows as you bear northeast. There is another path junction and then you enter a wood. After some buildings in ruins (Casera di Càneva at 1509m), a stream crossing and more descent, the path widens and proceeds through the Caiàda forest. After yet another path junction (with n.509) keep straight ahead (still n.505) down on the forestry track which is soon motorable. You soon reach a grazing clearing, carpeted with flowers in spring and summer, and hosting small holiday cabins and some malgas (dairy farms). As well as the vast forest, this brief plain is also known as the Caiàda (1157m), and the name derives from a reference to the area's traditional cheese-making activities (cagliata = curds).

The splendid backdrop to the north is made up of the Caiàda and Cimon mountain chains and the eastern wall of the Pelf is still visible up the valley. A secondary asphalted road starts here, and has some interesting sections lower down that cross ravines or that are cut into the rock face. It is usually busy on weekends so can be avoided by taking the signposted path that turns right and down (essentially east) towards the valley floor of Val Desedàn (another 1h30mins to go). After a winding stretch down through beech and silver fir wood it comes out at a small dam, downstream of unsightly landslide scars. At the far end of the dam wall is the start of an old path which runs up to the left, cut into the high southern bank of the valley. At the time of writing it was impassable, so you'll probably have to take the alternate (and more direct) path due east alongside the stream bed. It proceeds through a sort of mini canyon lined with rubble and gravel all the way down to where it widens out before the rail bridge and main road at the village of Faè-Fortogna (440m). The railway station is on the left, just back up behind the road. (Total 5h from R. 7° Alpini).

PRACTICAL INFORMATION
R. 7° ALPINI TEL:(0437)941631. Alpine Club, Belluno Section. Sleeps 70.
TOURIST OFFICE BELLUNO TEL:(0437)940083.

WALK 29 (see sketch map N, page 195)

ANTELAO / MARMAROLE
via (Pieve di Cadore) Pozzale - Forcella Antracisa (2-3h) -
R. Antelao (30mins) - Forcella Piria (1h) - Val d'Oten (2h30mins) -
R. Chiggiato (2h30mins-3h45mins) - R. Baion (2h30mins) -
R. Ciareido (1h) - R. Marmarole (30mins) - Lozzo (2h-2h30mins).
TABACCO MAP NO.016 scale 1:25,00
TABACCO MAP NO.1 scale 1:50,000
(3 days suggested)

This route covers the entire northwestern side of the Cadore valley and connects a series of refuges all situated at particularly panoramic points, each with direct access from the valley floor. It is described here in a south-north direction, but can easily be adapted for short sections or day-trips. Alternate access from San Vito di Cadore in the Boite valley is also given to allow slotting into Stage Two.

During the years of the Venetian Serenissima, the timber in the Cadore conifer forests, along with that of the Zoldo and Agordo valley areas, was essential for the construction of the Republic's galleys at the Arsenale, the shipbuilding yards capable of turning out a galley a day. The logs were transported in raft form down the River Piave all the way to the Venice Lagoon by workers under the command of expert "zatèr" or "raft-masters", and the practice is known to date back at least 500 years.

Furthermore, the Cadore was another key point in the hostilities between Italy and Austria during the First World War. Though the Austrians blew up as much as possible as they were leaving in 1918, evidence of the barracks, forts and cannon positions that once ringed the valley still remains today, as do some military roads constructed with local labour for access and supply. Examples include the fortifications on Monte Tranego (see Stage One), military barracks on Pian dei Buoi (Stage Three), and Monte Tudaio (see Stage Four), as well as the frequently followed mule-tracks.

The starting point is the gracious town of Pieve di Cadore, where you can visit the birthplace of the famous artist Titian.

Stage One: via Forcella Antracisa (2-3h) to R. Antelao (30mins)
From Pieve di Cadore (880m) (bus connections with Belluno, Cortina,

SKETCH MAP N

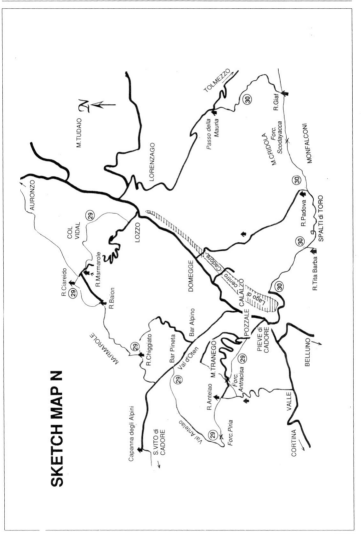

Auronzo, train south from Calalzo) up to the village of Pozzale (1045m) you can drive, take the occasional bus or walk - from the magnificent town square of Pieve di Cadore go uphill (north) straight through the main shopping block, and up the first of two long flights of steps. After a short stretch of road, next to a roadside shrine on the right, is a natural wood sign "Pozzale" pointing up a walkers-only path. In all it's about 30mins to the village square.

There are several possibilities for this next stage as far as Forcella Antracisa (1690m):

a) n.252, signposted to R. Antelao, straight up from the village square in Pozzale, starts off as a road then becomes a good 4WD track. It winds around to the right (north) via Monte Tranego (1847m), has numerous short cuts and wide-ranging views back down to the Cadore valley and across to Monte Cridola and the Monfalconi and Spalti di Toro chain. Allow 2h15mins in all, not counting time for hazelnut and raspberry gathering stops and squirrel watching.

b) Another worthwhile but slightly longer route is via R. PraPiccolo (1450m). It is signposted from Pozzale and begins on surfaced secondary road, becoming a walking track (n.250) on the final stretch, prior to joining the others at Forcella Antracisa, (2h30mins).

c) However, the best walkers-only track is n.253 which takes 2h. It is well-trodden and has great views, though it is slightly steeper in parts than the previous two. Starting out in the square in Pozzale, ignore the most obvious signposting for R. Antelao and walk along to the left, past a restaurant and you'll see the red and white waymarking. You go up briefly past lilac trees then bear left and the way becomes a wide dirt track. Keep left and cross the ski slope to a yellow sign affixed to a tree for R. Antelao. The wide path climbs through woods to another cleared slope - pass under the ski lift and fork obliquely up, still climbing. After more beech and firwood, with brief glimpses towards the Boite valley, by winding right you come out at the top of the chair lift. At the fork, keep left of the tree with red and white waymarking, and climb steeply to a large barn-like timber hut (about 40mins so far). Keep right here (signposted) and the path narrows as it enters a tall perfumed spruce wood. With high earth sides and lined with pine needles, the path goes north, giving excellent views of the Cridola-Monfalconi line-up, east beyond Lago Cadore.

Waymarking is regularly seen, as are alpine snowbells. Pink heather, on the other hand grows thickly along the exposed grassy crest (Costa Nuda) you soon reach. This terminates in a small saddle, with a brief view west of the Antelao's pyramidal peak, then the path turns west across scree and thinly wooded slopes. There are some narrow steepish stretches across grassy slopes, before you coast up to 1693m and Forcella Antracisa and Capanna Tito Panciera (a bivouac hut but always locked). Here you join up with the jeep track, numbered n.250, from now on. There's a new artistically carved drinking trough and tap. Turn left (west) at signposting and it's only 30mins further on through abundant patches of raspberry canes and north-facing dampish woods to R. Antelao at 1796m.

The refuge can also be reached by 4WD vehicles and the area is consequently popular with hunters on weekends from late September on. It is open virtually all year round, and is very well-run, offering interesting local culinary specialities such as "canedui" (or "canederli" in Italian) - a sort of small light dumpling (not at all stodgy) made of bread, flour, lard or salami and egg, served in a consommé or with a tomato or meat sauce. If available, you should also try the "fricò", fried cheese.

It's worth overnighting here to catch the dawn and sunrise's added magnificence in illuminating the surrounding peaks, the 'sea of clouds' effect too if you're in luck.

The pyramid of the Antelao peak (3263m) is visible behind the refuge standing out to the left (west). According to a local legend, there was a handsome giant called Antelao who was in love with a maiden called Pomauria. Unfortunately, as these legends tend to go, a witch had put a curse on him to the effect that, should he fall in love, he would be turned into stone. When the giant realised the curse was taking effect, he rushed desperately across the Marmarole mountains and hurled himself down into the plain that there used to be between the Boite valley (the one leading to Cortina) and the Oten valley (down to Calalzo). There his heart melted and his body turned into a huge petrified mountain with a glacier blue as the colour of forget-me-not flowers.

Alternate descent:
Should you wish to make this refuge part of a round trip, a pleasant return is via the small chapel of S.Dionigi (top marks for position) perched on a hill-top at 1946m (50mins south from R. Antelao). Continue, heading down via n.251 past R. Costapiana/Ugolini (1560m) past the village of Valle (779m) on the main road only 3.5kms from Pieve di Cadore (bus stop). (Total time 3h.)

Stage Two: via Val d'Oten (3h30mins) to R. Chiggiato (2h30mins-4h15mins)

Start out on path n.250 leaving from behind R. Antelao. There is an easy and gradual climb up under the Crode di S.Pietro, then you bear left towards a pleasant airy zone called "La Baranciada" with its low-growing, elastic "baranci" ie. mountain pines. After about 30mins from the refuge, there's a fork leading up right to the Pian dei Cavalli and its pass. This 20-min detour offers a glimpse of the Antelao's glacier and its permanent snow. Back down on n.250 you continue coasting around west admiring the views across the valley and due south to Monte Rite with its strategic World War I fort, and the Bosconero group, until Forcella Piria is reached. This is an ample saddle at 2096m, and the Antelao appears before you. (1h so far). Waymarking on this next stretch is not so frequent or clear but the terrain presents no difficulty, being a mixture of stones and grass and the general direction is down. After the first 50 metres in descent, a track goes off to the left (to Forcella Cadin and hence in descent to Vinigo). You bear right and down, with low scrubby bush cover, including bilberry shrubs. Soon an alternative track cuts across on the left mountain side, leading to the Antelao and its "via ferrata" across the glacier. Your lower track, n.258, soon reaches a white rock area and a stream bed. You may need to spend a little time hunting for the correct way down here - there are old red and white paint patches on rocks and occasional numbering. Do not cross the stream bed but keep on its right and go down (east). There is a steepish narrow stretch down through an overgrown wood before the valley opens out with a couple of log cabins and a luscious grazing plain.

This is the Val Antelao, a delightfully tranquil valley, wide and green and relatively unfrequented. It's a good place for photographers to take shots back up the valley of the Antelao peak with a corner of its glacier in sight. It's 1h30mins from Forcella Piria to the further end of this valley. Then a steepish, but easy track winds down through beech woods with an occasional cascading mossy stream, and comes out in Val d'Oten at a place called Praciadelan and the Bar Pineta (1100m). (3h30mins total to here.)

Should you wish to end your walk here, proceed down the road to Calalzo (1h30mins) for railway connections and buses.

There are 2 main tracks north up to R. Chiggiato from Val d'Oten. One is slightly further upstream from Bar Pineta (1100m) - after 5mins

(From Forcella Piria) looking south towards the Bosconero group

walking, turn off to the right (n.260). It follows the Diassa torrent for a short way to then branch off and up in steep zigzags through tall mixed evergreen woods (can be muddy after heavy rain). Some thoughtful soul has rigged up a pipe 'delivering' drinking water just off the track about two-thirds of the way up (signposted) - fill your water bottles here as the refuge water (if any) is not suitable for drinking purposes. This scenic way will take you about 2h30mins.

The other alternative is considerably longer, but more pleasant (and advisable if you're starting out from Calalzo). From Bar Pineta turn right down the valley (Calalzo direction) and go as far as the Bar Alpino (897m) (30mins) (n.255). Clear signs point you left up the road into narrow Valle Vedessana (n.261). Driving will save you this next, not unpleasant hour, accompanied by an accessible rocky stream, but you'll miss the raspberries all along the road. From where the surfaced road ends the track starts climbing by old huts and later cool woods, soft and springy underfoot. It's 2h15mins to R. Chiggiato. (Total 3h15mins from Bar Alpino, 3h45mins from Praciadelan/Bar Pineta). As you come panting out of the woods onto the flowered

199

meadows you have to get your map straight out to start identifying the mountain groups and peaks visible all around. Don't neglect the view down to Calalzo and its lake. The refuge is at 1950m in a superb position.

Alternate access : San Vito di Cadore - R. Galassi (3h) -
R. Chiggiato (4h)
There is clear signposting at the main bus stop in the town's square (1010m) for track n.228, the secondary and partially asphalted vehicle track leading up east to the private R. Scotter at 1580m (meals and refreshments only). This is just over halfway, and from here you need n.229 which zigzags relentlessly up the scree slope to join n.227 (from R. San Marco). Then proceed to 2120m and the Forcella Piccola, a wide saddle directly south under the Antelao. R. Galassi, originally constructed as a military barracks, stands a little further down on the northern side, at 2018m, and the total time from San Vito is 3h.

In descent in a northerly direction now you follow n.255 and in 1h will reach the cascades and the Capanna degli Alpini (1395m), meals and refreshment stop in Val d'Oten. From here it's down by road - but avoid summer weekend days as it's a popular family picnic area and the traffic can get heavy. Some 3.5kms and 45mins will see you at the turn-off path n.260 north for R. Chiggiato - see above for the description, and allow about 4h in all from R. Galassi to R. Chiggiato.

Stage Three: to R. Baion (2h30mins) then R. Ciareido (1h)
Track n.262 to R. Baion leaves this idyllic spot from the back of the refuge and bears north. This stage does not involve many ups and downs and coasts along mostly at the upper edge of the tree line, contouring the southeastern flanks of the Marmarole group. It provides a non-stop sweeping panorama across to the other side of the Calalzo valley. Waymarking is frequent and clear - but there are many junctions off left to higher cols (forcelle) - if you have time and feel like a new view, check your map for the climb involved and try one.

After the first stretch through tall pine forests and flowered grass areas, the terrain becomes rocky, with low bushy cover (dwarf pines) and the track narrows. At about 40mins from R. Chiggiato there is an aided passage (fixed metal cord) around an exposed rock face, and another shorter stretch in descent further on, but neither are particularly difficult and have reliable footholds. The first one, in fact, has a placard above it testifying to the fact that His Holiness Pope John Paul II walked this track. After a short stretch crossing some enormous boulders, blinding white in strong sunshine, there's a slight descent across meadows with the omnipresent alpine cows and their far-reaching jangling bells, a slight rise and you arrive at R. Baion (1850m) (2h30mins so far). This is another welcoming refuge with the characteristic indoor open fireplace surrounded by wooden bench seating for warming those weary limbs on a cold day. The adjoining partially converted cow sheds are no longer used as such, but have interesting flooring made from cut-off sunk trunk sections.

Alternate ways to reach this refuge include driving up the 15 kms of rough old military road from the village of Lozzo, or walking from Domegge on track n.265/264 (4h).

Facing the refuge, after the cow sheds on the right, you'll find the path (no number) which leads up and north at first then over to R. Ciareido (though the lower dirt road goes some of the way too). It's an easy 1h walk across scattered rubble and through low springy mountain pines, other scrubby vegetation and grazing cows. After the path descends slightly and the refuge comes into sight, there is a brief final climb between enormous rock slabs carved for the passage of the World War I track, up to the dominating rock stronghold at 1969m. Previously a military barracks (constructed 1890) it was restored and equipped as a refuge in 1973. It looks out over Pian dei Buoi (Plain of the Oxen) with its active dairy farm at 1825m, often referred to on waymarking signs. The refuge specialises in roaring evening fires, homestyle cooking, panoramic dormitories and breathtaking sunsets reflected onto Monte Tudaio (east) and its adjacent ranges.

Legends tell of the ancient inhabitants of the Marmarole range, the stone-hearted Crodères. Their queen Tannes (complete with her azure diadem and palace of ice) however, had a human heart and preferred the company of mortals. In fact, she forbade rockslides and avalanches to fall on them, ordered torrents to run more gently, and created lush pasture land. The rugged grey points of the Marmarole used to be pure white, due to the effect of all the snow and ice suspended up there on the Queen's orders. However, Tanna's heart too was turned to stone with bitterness when betrayed by men, and she returned to her icy realm, thus releasing the captured snow and ice from its obligations.

Alternate access: Auronzo - R. Ciareido (4h)

An alternate access path to R. Ciareido (could be used as exit too) leaves from Auronzo (864m) in the Ansiei valley and takes 4 hours. The track begins at the south, non-town end of Lago di S. Caterina. Cross the dam and take the path that leads steeply straight up into the towering pine forest. At first there is no signposting, but the characteristic red and white paint stripes and n.268 are soon obvious and clear to follow. Plenty of squirrels around. Further up there may be fallen trees or cut timber obstructing the track, necessitating detours - ensure you're back on the correct, marked track before proceeding. It is inadvisable to come this way after heavy rain as it can be very muddy in spots.

The occasional clearing with secondary undergrowth (typically stinging nettles and dock leaves) indicates former human settlement - the map, in fact, shows huts, probably used by timber cutters, but these are no longer standing. These clearings constitute useful indications for orientation.

After a good 650m climb southwest, 2 signposted junctions going left down to Cima Gogna and Lozzo, and 2 hours walking, you'll come across a sturdily constructed house, Casone Campediei (1500m). Its position offers views of the Marmarole range to the southwest, and there's a gushing stream below it. From here it's another 1h30mins through some beech and mixed woods (bilberries and wild strawberries) and the track brings you out onto the open pasture land of Pian dei Buoi at 1825m. Keep on n.268 across the fields, making a brief detour to the right (north) onto a low crest for worthwhile views over to the Tre Cime di Lavaredo and Sesto Dolomite group. Bearing left you join up with the narrow bitumen road for a brief stretch as far as the car parking area, then proceed up (west) rather more steeply among the characteristic elastic mountain pines and enormous rock slabs, winding up to reach the rock outpost where the refuge stands (30mins more).

Stage Four: via R. Marmarole (30mins) and descent to
Lozzo (2h-2h30mins)

Take the signposted path (World War I mule-track) that winds down under the massive square blocks of rock under the refuge, to the small car park, verdant pastures, and stretch of bitumen road. At 1825m, just 30mins from R. Ciareido stands an old military barracks (being restructured as a hotel at the time of writing) and just below it, the well-reputed private

R. Marmarole which also offers accommodation.

The mule-track (n.267) continues down to the valley village of Lozzo (750m), but has now become a reasonable, though roughish in parts, vehicle road. Traffic (particularly heavy on weekends) can be avoided by simply taking the numerous (clearly signposted) short cuts which of course eliminate the long zigzags. Though you may be tempted to curse the thick layer of fallen beech leaves which can make for slippery walking, particularly after rain, it is panoramic and will take you about 2h (from R. Marmarole).

A preferable walkers-only alternative however, can be followed by taking the left fork (also signposted n.267) of the secondary dirt road at the fountain (delicious fresh water) just above R. Marmarole. It contours on a level heading in the direction of Col Vidal (World War I fort to the northwest). After 15mins there's a short curving tunnel, then a stretch above cleared ground with obvious levelled areas for wartime buildings and encampments. Roe-deer are likely to be seen around here. After a bend it brings you to a wide saddle (with signposting), and there are more ruins and an excellent view northwest to the Tre Cime di Lavaredo (30mins from R. Marmarole). The distinct pyramid shape of Monte Antelao is seen to the southwest as well.

For the Col Vidal fort, by all means continue straight on (about 20mins more), but the descent to Lozzo now begins as the path turns off down to the right (southeast) at this point - signposted n.268. It's a steepish but easy descent through conifer and mixed deciduous woods. There are several clusters of old dark timber "tabià" huts, kept in good condition and used as holiday cabins. This path is particularly recommended for its close-ups of Monte Tudaio east directly across the valley seen from the openings in the wood - the tightly zigzagging mule-track leading up to its strategic World War I fort can be seen clearly. Waymarking is clear and frequent, and there are stretches cut into the rock, or levelled out. After about 1h10mins, following a stream closely through beech wood for the last stretch, you'll come out onto tarmac for the last 20mins to the village of Lozzo di Cadore (754m) and its numerous lovely artistic fountains, characteristic of the villages here.

(If you do this section in ascent (3h30mins), follow black and white signposting for "Pian dei Buoi" from Lozzo's small village square. Once out of the built-up area, after 30mins (and about 100m ascent) there are some wooden benches next to a stream and path n.268 (signposted) branches off right (north) to begin its steady climb).

At this point, you can continue with walk 30 which does a semi-circle covering the groups to the southeast of the Cadore valley and lake. Otherwise there are bus connections north to Auronzo and Tre Cime, or Cortina, or south to Calalzo railway station and beyond.

PRACTICAL INFORMATION

CAPANNA DEGLI ALPINI - accommodation
R. ANTELAO TEL:(0435)75333 Alpine Club, Treviso Section. Sleeps 26. (*)
R. BAION TEL:(0435)76060 Alpine Club, Domegge Section. Sleeps 50.
R. CHIGGIATO TEL:(0435)31452 Alpine Club, Venice Section. Sleeps 46.
R. CIAREIDO TEL:(0435)76276 Alpine Club, Lozzo Section. Sleeps 44.
R. COSTAPIANA/UGOLINI TEL.(0335)8115470 Private, sleeps 13.
R. GALASSI TEL:(0436)9685. Alpine Club, Mestre. Sleeps 100.
R. MARMAROLE TEL:(0435)76138 Private, sleeps 23.
R. PRAPICCOLO TEL:(0435)32496 Private, sleeps 15.
R. SCOTTER TEL. (0436)99035 - accommodation
TOURIST OFFICE AURONZO TEL.(0435)9359
TOURIST OFFICE CALALZO TEL:(0435)32348/32349.
TOURIST OFFICE DOMEGGE TEL:(0435)72078 seasonal.
TOURIST OFFICE LOZZO TEL:(0435)76051 seasonal.
TOURIST OFFICE TAI DI CADORE TEL:(0435)31644.
TOURIST OFFICE VIGO TEL:(0435)77058 seasonal.
(*) possible extended opening.

* * *
WALK 30 (see sketch map N, page 195)

CRIDOLA / SPALTI DI TORO / MONFALCONI
via Passo della Mauria - R. Giaf (2h30mins) -
Forcella Scodavacca (1h45mins) - R. Padova (2h15mins) -
Casera Vedorcia (2h) - R. Tita Barba (30mins) -
Pieve di Cadore (3h30mins)
TABACCO MAP NO.016 scale 1:25,000
TABACCO MAP NO.1 scale 1:50,000
(2-3 days suggested)

This itinerary covers the southeastern reaches of the Cadore valley, and can also be linked with walk 29.

Stage One: Passo della Mauria then R. Giaf (2h30mins)
From Calalzo station it's easy to catch a bus north then east as far as Lorenzago (from the Roman name "Laurentus"). However, you may have to walk or hitch-hike the last 8km up to Passo della Mauria (1298m) as buses connecting the Cadore with Forni di Sopra and the Ampezzo valley (continuing to Tolmezzo in Carnia), are less frequent.

A hotel stands at the pass, and just behind it is a signboard for the start of path n.341, an easy track. You gradually ascend a wide valley to the south. Below, in the woods, is the source of the River Tagliamento which flows down southeast into Carnia to the coast, coming out between the lagoons of Venice and Grado on the upper Adriatic. At the path intersection with n.348 (up to Monte Cridola) keep left and continue around through a lovely beech wood, now within the bounds of the Carnia Nature Park. Cross a white rock strewn valley and stream, taking care not to go off the marked track. You then zigzag quite steeply up and around the east flank of Monte Boschet first through more beech which later gives way to dwarf pine and larch woods. The last stretch is across the Torrente Giaf (stream) and up through more woods to R. Giaf (1408m). A dirt road (track n.346) also connects it with the valley village of Chiandarens (1h30mins in ascent) 3kms up road from Forni di Sopra. This refuge used to be a 'malga', mountain chalet - shepherd's summertime hut, and was converted by one of the shepherds with the help of his family.

Stage Two: Forcella Scodavacca (1h45mins) then R. Padova (2h15mins)
If you have overnighted at R. Giaf, there's a steep, 600m sweaty climb awaiting you west up path n.346 to Forcella Scodavacca (2043m) first thing this morning. After some 200m, path n.340 forks off right (north) to Forca Cridola then proceeds down to Lorenzago (4h). The first stretch is through dwarf pine and larch wood and, as the sun will probably be beating on your back as you puff up the non-shady part later, by all means make the most of the patches of wild fruit (predominantly bilberries) on the way up, as an excuse for a rest. There's a cirque as you come out of the woods, offering splendid views up to Cridola peak on the right, and Giaf to the left.

Now you start zigzagging up the scree, and shortly after a knoll at 1958m which, from below, looked deceptively like your forcella, you

Calalzo and its lake with the Spalti di Toro

arrive at Forcella Scodavacca, (1h45mins from R. Giaf) and a well-earned rest. The 2h15mins descent to R. Padova then crosses more detritus, after which the Pra di Toro valley and refuge should be visible (southwest), as well as the sweep around to the left (further south) of the Monfalconi and Spalti di Toro ranges. There's a wooded stretch among dwarf pines, then an open tract, more beech and silver firs, a stream to cross and its course is followed for a little way. Descending more and more steeply, but without difficulty, you meet up with the vehicle track from Domegge in the Calalzo valley (n.342, 3h on foot via R. Casera Cercena at 1050m - meals only, no accommodation) and a little further on you arrive at R. Padova (1278m). As well as being a picturesque, particularly well-run and homely-style oasis, it stands in an idyllic position surrounded by meadows, with the backdrop of the Spalti di Toro and Monfalconi peaks (southwest to south). The original building and alpine garden from 1909 were destroyed by an avalanche in 1932 and had to be rebuilt, slightly downhill, with its adjacent chapel.

This area abounds in colourful legends: the Spalti di Toro are said to have been named after the God Thor. Giaf, on the other hand, is short for Giaffredus, who was a hunter and shepherd sent to the Talagona

Valley in the 1300s from Auronzo, to establish grazing lands. After he survived various struggles with bears and wolves, the turn of historic events brought a platoon of invaders to the valley. Giaffredus fled up to the Forcella Scodavacca where he drove back the enemy with a landslide of massive boulders. This, unfortunately, also buried the beasts he had taken with him - only the tail ("coda" in Italian) of the cow ("vacca") was visible - hence the name of the forcella!

Stage Three: via Casera Vedorcia (2h) to R. Tita Barba (30mins)
Path n.350 leads off west from R. Padova through quite dense mixed wood and there's a steepish climb, then a brief gradual descent. However, less than an hour away is the promise of delicious bathing in a gushing icy stream (Torrente Talagona) with a cascade and pool almost out of sight of the main track, with a convenient grass area suitable for picnics alongside. Path n.350 crosses the stream then follows its right bank up a short way to where a wooden hut (1360m) stands. Turn right at the path junction you soon come to.

Alternate access at this point is possible from the rough road (n.342) from Domegge south in the direction of R. Padova and takes 45mins to here.

Next is another steepish climb through pine and larch wood, to where, after another hour the Casera Vedorcia (1707m) dairy farm stands with its vast pastures. You are rewarded with the splendid sight of the Spalti di Toro and Monfalconi in front of you (southwest) and Monte Cridola further west. Now, taking care to follow signposting, (often signs attached to tree trunks) as the path changes direction often, proceed northwest via a fountain (drinking water), jeep track and various holiday log cabins and small chalets, then southwest, and in another 30mins you come out at hospitable R. Tita Barba. It stands in its private meadow clearing at 1821m, and though there's no running water in the building, you can wash at the pump outside. Capercaillie can sometimes be sighted in the undergrowth in the surrounding woods.

Stage Four: Descent to Pieve di Cadore (3h30mins)
This last stretch involves a long 1,000m+ descent, but with no difficult parts, you'll have time to enjoy the scenery. Follow path n.350 north back over to the log cabin area you branched off at in the last stage, and go straight ahead ie. down (north). The descent follows a rough vehicle track

virtually all the way, so orientation and waymarking are clear. After tall forest, the occasional meadow and more holiday chalets and log cabins, the track emerges at the Cadore Lake, near the Miralago Bar Chalet. Give yourself about 2 hours this far. Then, on the road, walk left (south) around to the end of the lake and cross the dam wall to the village of Sottocastello. Following the road straight up, another 1h or so will bring you out on the main road at Pieve di Cadore. From here you can catch a bus back to Calalzo and its station, to Cortina, or south towards the Venetian plain.

PRACTICAL INFORMATION
R. GIAF TEL:(0433)88002 Alpine Club, Forni di Sopra Section. Sleeps 47.
R. PADOVA TEL:(0435)72488 Alpine Club, Padua Section. Sleeps 55.
ALBERGO PASSO DELLA MAURIA TEL:(0435)75034.
R. TITA BARBA TEL:(0435)32902 Private, sleeps 22.
TOURIST OFFICE CALALZO TEL:(0435)32348/32349.
TOURIST OFFICE LORENZAGO TEL:(0435)75042 seasonal.
TOURIST OFFICE LOZZO TEL:(0435)76051 seasonal.
TOURIST OFFICE PIEVE DI CADORE TEL:(0435)31644/31645.
TOURIST OFFICE VIGO TEL:(0435)77058 seasonal.

* * *

WALK 31 (see sketch map O, page 209)

BRENTA GROUP
via Madonna di Campiglio - R. Vallesinella (1h) -
R. Casinei (45mins) - R. Tuckett & Sella (1h30mins) -
R. ai Brentei (1h30mins) - Bocca di Brenta (1h15mins) -
R. Pedrotti & Tosa (15mins) - R. Selvata (1h45mins) -
R. Malga di Andalo (50mins) - Molveno (1h30mins).
TABACCO MAP NO.10 scale 1:50,000
(2-3 days suggested)

The Brenta Group, lying northwest of Trent, is separated physically from the main eastern block of the Dolomites by the Adige River Valley. It is,

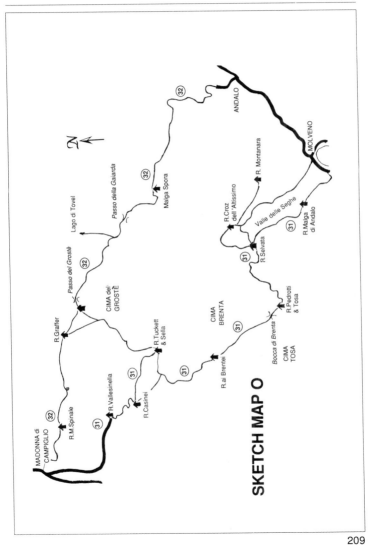

SKETCH MAP O

nonetheless, legitimately included here, as it consists principally of the characteristic light-coloured sedimentary dolomite rock. The Adamello and Presanella Groups further east, on the other hand, are igneous. The whole area is a Nature Park and attracts hosts of visitors. August is best avoided for reasons of crowding as well as the fact that visibility can be spoilt by the haze from the humid air masses which typically rise from the valley floors at this time of year.

The Park proudly hosts some of the last brown bears in Europe, though you shouldn't expect to see these solitary creatures as they prefer the outlying zones not even crossed by walking paths. They are very carefully protected, and apple cultivators in bordering valleys such as the Val di Non (in the northeast) are compensated should their trees and property be damaged by bears who descend to the valley in search of food. Other wildlife including chamois, roe-deer, eagles and several types of grouse is more easily seen.

Another interesting feature of the Brenta Group is the presence of numerous hanging glaciers, referred to as "vedretta" on maps in Italian. These are not glaciers in the true sense of the word as they do not advance slowly valleywards, and are generally smaller. They are essentially masses of permanent ice found on very steep mountain sides.

A small perennial snow-field is crossed in Stage Two. Deep snow could make it problematic. Snow cover naturally varies from year to year, and while both the winters of '88-'89 and '89-'90 in Italy were unusually dry, it's a good idea to check at the nearest refuge if in doubt, particularly early in the season. Immediately following this point is an aided rock climb, but without exposed points, and under normal conditions (free from snow and ice) is easily tackled.

A final note concerning map terminology - a "bocca" (literally "mouth") in the Brenta Group is used to refer to a pass or saddle, more commonly called "forcella" in other parts of the Dolomites.

Brenta refuges tend to close up around the 3rd week in September, but, as usual, check beforehand if planning to go at the extremes of the season. As far as reservations go, each refuge has different 'rules'. R. Tuckett & Sella for example, only usually accepts same-day bookings, and R. Pedrotti & Tosa will only keep reserved places until 6.30pm.

Stage One: via R. Vallesinella (1h), R. Casinei (45mins) to
R. Tuckett & Sella (1h30mins)
Madonna di Campiglio (1522m), a prestigious resort in both winter and

summer, is served by coach lines from Trent (southeast) and Malè (northeast) - which also has a railway - as well as some seasonal direct services to various Italian cities. From the main bus stop in the town centre, go down (east), across the stream and through the park, heading towards the departure station of the Monte Spinale chair lift. Just below it, turn right along the road and down past the south end of the small lake, then left at the intersection at Palù - signposting for R. Cascata (10mins this far). Continue past the last hotels and houses to the end of the road, and a fork: a dirt track leads off down right to R. Cascata di Mezzo, whereas you keep straight ahead on the main (now dirt but still with cars) track for R. Vallesinella.

A walkers-only variant: shortly after this point, red and yellow waymarking (but no signposting) points up left into the wood and links with the "Sentiero dell'Orso" (the Bear's Path) n.376, that skirts east in a wide loop around the valley and rejoins this itinerary at R. Casinei.

The track (n.375) can be dusty in mid-summer, but it's a very pleasant 50min stroll through shady woods of beech and pine, and you are treated to several promising glimpses of the pale mountains east. After 30mins walking you cross into the Adamello-Brenta Nature Park, then another footpath branches down right to R. Cascata di Mezzo, and you can hear the crashing of the cascades and even see them occasionally through the trees. Keep straight on. Unless you arrive towards evening and decide to overnight at R. Vallesinella (1513m) (which also runs a mini-bus taxi from Madonna di Campiglio), fill up your water bottle and move on towards the log cabin on the opposite side of the enormous car park.

Signposting indicates the well-trodden path in brief descent to the neat timber bridge across the stream, then the 45min climb begins. The wood is cool and peaceful, and bilberry shrubs abound. Polished tree roots and rocks on the path n.317 testify to its frequent use, but also to its strategic importance for access. You climb and wind (southeast) to R. Casinei (1826m) set in a tranquil clearing. Facing the hut, keep left and take n.317, with a milder gradient now. Go around to the east through tracts of wild raspberry canes, a water spout (probably dry), until you round a corner for your first decent view - the Castelletto Inferiore is straight ahead (east, slightly south), and two small hanging glaciers are visible to its right on the Cima Brenta. The path traverses a patch of tall nettles and dock leaves, then in gradual ascent, the wood thins down to a few larches, then dwarf mountain pines and alpenrose shrubs. You meander amongst enormous long-fallen boulders, which dwarf walkers ahead, who appear as coloured specks. Nearby, the substantial pylons of R. Tuckett & Sella's cableway carry the cables which run parallel to the path, and you pass under them later on. The Brenta Group extends out both north and south at this point, and above the tree line now gives a wonderful sensation of space. As you climb further up onto solely rock terrain, the Bocca del Tuckett is seen to the east - one of the few strategic passes for access to the other side, and as you reach the refuge, the hanging glacier (looking more like a snow-field here) immediately beneath it comes into sight.

R. Tuckett & Sella (2272m) consists of 2 buildings - the older one is now used as supplementary sleeping quarters. Quintino Sella was the founder of the Italian Alpine Club, and British climber Francis Fox Tuckett - with Freshfield and Devouassoud, the guide - was the first to scale Cima Brenta (3150m), then thought to be the highest peak in the Group. The water in the refuges is piped directly from the glacier, and is classified unsuitable for drinking (see the Introduction on this subject).

Marmots are often seen on the rubble terrain above the refuges.

Alternate accesses:
The following 2 alternatives save you climbing energy by making use of mechanical lifts (discounts for members of the Italian Alpine Club and the Alpenverein). However you also see the devastation caused by the ski runs and lifts in the valley below Passo del Grostè, though at least it is all concentrated here and has not been allowed to spread to other areas of the Park.

a) via Passo del Grostè (1h45mins)
Take the gondola-car (departure station just north of Madonna di Campiglio, before Passo Campo Carlo Magno) to the arrival station and restaurant (no accommodation) just below Passo del Grostè (2442m). Path n.316 (south) will take you down briefly to the path junction with n.331, to then traverse beneath the western flanks of the Brenta (where eagles are known to glide). The path is mostly on a level, and passes among great fallen rock masses beneath the Cima del Grostè, Torrione di Vallesinella and Castelletto Inferiore. Allow 1h30mins from the gondola-car arrival station to R. Tuckett & Sella.

b) via Monte Spinale (3h)
Another possibility is via the Monte Spinale chair lift to R. Monte Spinale (2104m), then 1h on foot (path n.331 in ascent east) to R. Graffer (2261m). Then, still following path n.331 you soon arrive at

At R. Tuckett & Sella looking up towards Bocca del Tuckett

the path junction with n.316 - from Passo del Grostè, thence as above. Allow another 1h45mins from R. Graffer.

Stage Two: via R. ai Brentei (1h30mins) and Bocca di Brenta (1h15mins) to R. Pedrotti & Tosa (15mins)

A labyrinth of irregularly shaped boulders and a river of pebbles down left, characterise the initial stretch after you leave R. Tuckett & Sella on path n.328 (signposting just below the hut). The path (with the occasional red paint stripe) winds its way around then down briefly (west) to grass, wild flower and shrub cover with mountain pines. This area is known as the Sella (saddle) del Freddolin. Bearing left the path crosses a slippery oblique rock slab with vertical channelling gouged out by water run, and joins n.318 from R. Casinei (35mins this far). Now you move southwards and enter the Val Brenta Alta, with some ups and downs but mostly on a level. Some 30mins on, the ample path is cut into the steep cliff side, and there are several cable handrails and very easy aided stretches. There follows a narrow shallow gorge that houses a Madonna statue and a shrine complete with candles, then a brief rock tunnel. This is the "Sentiero Bogani", and a plaque recalls the long-standing president of the Monza section of the Alpine Club. The refuge's chapel soon comes into view up valley, as you continue climbing under the western walls of the Punta di Campiglio. Soon, as the goods cableway then refuge building come into view, a red arrow saying "acqua" (water) points you briefly down right off the main path. It's a good idea to make the most of the spring water, as hereafter only glacier-derived water (classified unsuitable for drinking) is available. The detour quickly rejoins the path again among clumps of edelweiss, just before R. Maria & Alberto ai Brentei (2182m). Run by Bruno Detassis, a famous Italian mountaineer, it occupies yet another wonderful inspiring location. The Crozzon di Brenta stands to the southwest, then virtually due south is Cima Tosa the highest peak (3173m), with Cima Margherita the next one to the east, before the Bocca di Brenta pass southeast. There are also several small hanging glaciers up between the peaks.

Even if you don't overnight here, take a moment or two to visit the open chapel on your way up the valley. It houses numerous plaques in memory of mountaineers who perished on these and other more distant peaks.

Waymarking from now on is red and white, and tends to be more frequent. The path (n.318) makes its way up the left hand side of the valley along the mountainside across scree and rubble, and follows a natural rock ledge for some while. After some 45mins slow climbing you reach the permanent snow-field. Up left (north) is the slender graceful pointed shape of the Campanile Basso. It offers extremely difficult climbing and has attracted mountaineers from all over the world, including a king of Belgium. If the snow looks clean and relatively fresh, check the depth (with a ski stock for instance) and if in doubt, detour around left clambering across fallen rocks. If the winter has been mild there may only be a corrugated sheet of old dirty ice and snow with running rivulets of snow-melt. You can easily walk straight across its soft surface. Head for the large red painted spot and asterisk on the rock face opposite, which indicate the start of the aided climb.

If preferred, the next section can be avoided by scrambling up the steep rubble and scree gully to the left, but the rock presents no problems under normal conditions. Tackle the initial easy "chimney" any way you like, if the metal cable (on the left) is loose, as it was at the time of writing. The rest is very well-anchored and provides psychological rather than physical aid. You climb up to a rock terrace, and cross over left, but not as far as the cliff where a "via ferrata" starts. Your path (red and white waymarking) heads straight up (southeast)' across more snow-ice, which, if too slippery, can be easily detoured by scrambling across the detritus bordering it left. The pass - Bocca di Brenta (2552m) - is quickly reached, and the grey rock building of your next destination immediately obvious. Cloud permitting, you will see the towering shape of the Croz del Rifugio mountain backing the refuge.

It's only another 15mins down then right along the wide rock ledge (with the water pipe) to R. Pedrotti (2491m). (Total 1h30mins from R. ai Brentei). Below it, standing on a more sheltered rock platform is R. Tosa (2439m), now used to provide supplementary accommodation. Another superb location, and there is even a series of smooth sloping white rock slabs for sunbathing, or picnics, just behind the main refuge. These 2 huts have a rather curious history: the lower one was opened in 1881 by 2 local brothers, whereas the larger higher building was the work of the German Alpine Club. As the land was considered to be the property of the Trent Alpine Club (SAT), the dispute was taken as far as the Supreme Court of Vienna, which ruled in favour of Trent, so the refuge was transferred to local hands. It was later looted during World War I, just to complete the story.

The chapel this time, with all respect, is somewhat incongruous here, and has even been likened to a cable-car arrival station.

Stage Three: descent to R. Selvata (1h45mins),
R. Malga di Andalo (50mins) to Molveno (1h30mins)
From R. Pedrotti take path n.319 leaving from the downhill side of the building. There is a series of steps cut into the rock face to facilitate access to the older R. Tosa, and you descend in a northeasterly direction. N.303 - Sentiero Osvaldo Orsi (a local mountaineer and enthusiast) - soon branches off left to connect with the Bocca del Tuckett. You keep on straight down through the rock garden with its miniature yellow and white blooms (such as blue-leaved saxifrage), winding around a rock outcrop down to the grassy flats and a small hut. Left (west) is the line-up beginning (south) with Cima Brenta alta, then Cima d'Armi, Cima di Molveno and so on, with the various "bocchette" (little saddles) traversed by the famous "via ferrata" of the same name. Around 1h walking and you'll reach the stone ruins of an old shepherds hut under the Massodì ("midday") mountains (north). As the path veers around to the right (east) the sheer orangey-black flank of the Croz dell'Altissimo appears ahead. The gradient is steeper now, down a narrow gully and across a watercourse. As you descend among low mountain pines and pink flowering alpenrose shrubs, check the surrounding rocks for the small, rare lilac-coloured alpine flower - Devil's-claw. It has a series of elongated,

pointed flowers together in a sphere, and grows solo in rock (limestone and dolomite) crevices, that appear totally devoid of soil. R. Selvata (1630m), visible for some time during the descent, is set among towering pines and is particularly peaceful.

The most pleasant and characteristic descent from here (n.332) leaves R. Selvata on the path signposted "Malga di Andalo" on the right of the refuge building (facing downhill). It drops down through damp woods, and 10mins below the refuge there is a passage along a rock ledge made more secure on the last brief crumbly stretch with the aid of a metal cable - nothing difficult. Now the wood begins seriously, principally beech, but also with various pines and deciduous trees. 50mins or so will bring you out at the pasture clearing where picturesque R. Malga di Andalo stands (1356m). Look back up the valley due north and the Bocca della Vallazza pass is visible between the various peaks. There is drinking water just below the building, by the ruins of fair-sized cow stalls.

The path to Molveno is clearly indicated, and continues through woods, now carpeted with delicate cyclamen flowers all the way down, as well as entire banks of yellow and purple cow-wheat flowers. Walk as quietly as possible, and you may see startled pairs of red-headed black grouse or even the larger dark capercaillie which frequent this valley to feed on its conifers. Waymarking and signposting are easily followed and the path cuts across old forestry tracks in several points. The valley down the western side of which you are descending, is called Valle delle Seghe (meaning "saws") referring to the traditional timber cutting and still active sawmills. There are glimpses of a surprising milky blue-green lake below. After gradual descent, the path bears right and the last stretch is much steeper again and rather tiring with loose stones. As you come down close above the camping ground, there is a path junction - take the left branch (n.326), and you'll come out shortly at the road. Cross straight over and continue briefly down to the lakeside camping ground and car park. Then go straight up to cross the torrent to the bus stops and kiosks (5mins). 2 bus lines service Molveno - covering both directions - ie. southwest then connecting with Madonna di Campiglio or Trent, as well as northeast for Mezzocorona and train connections, including Trent. Most buses use the village centre though, so you might have to walk up the road to the hotel and shopping centre and follow signs for the "autostazione" (10mins). Allow approx. 4h total from R. Pedrotti & Tosa all the way to Molveno.

Alternate descent routes from R. Selvata are:
a) (1h30mins) the fastest descent route for Molveno - path n.319 from

R. Selvata that cuts through the wood and drops straight down to join the forestry vehicle track in Valle delle Seghe proceeding southeast to Molveno (1h30mins).

b) (2h) a slightly longer alternative is via path n.340 to R. Croz dell'Altissimo (1431m) (20mins) - which also runs a jeep-taxi to Molveno. N.340 continues contouring the cliff-side (without descending to join the valley bottom forestry track) to link up with R. Montanara (1525m) (1h30mins to here) which provides mechanised transport in the form of a chair lift, and to Molveno. Roe-deer and deer are known to inhabit the areas north of Molveno towards the Croz dell'Altissimo.

PRACTICAL INFORMATION

R. MARIA & ALBERTO AI BRENTEI TEL:(0465)441244. Alpine Club, Monza section. Sleeps 100.

R. CASINEI TEL:(0465)442708. Private, sleeps 33.

R. CROZ DELL'ALTISSIMO. Private, sleeps 16.

R. GRAFFER TEL:(0465)441358. Alpine Club, Trent section. Sleeps 64.

R. MALGA ANDALO. Private, sleeps 12.

R. MONTE SPINALE TEL:(0465)441507. Private, accomm.

R. PEDROTTI & TOSA TEL:(0461)948115. Alpine Club, Trent section. Sleeps 120.

R. SELVATA TEL.(0330)239227. Private, sleeps 26.

R. TUCKETT & SELLA TEL:(0465)441226. Alpine Club, Trent section. Sleeps 80.

R. VALLESINELLA TEL:(0465)442883. Private, sleeps 30.

TOURIST OFFICE MADONNA DI CAMPIGLIO TEL:(0465)442000.

TOURIST OFFICE MOLVENO TEL:(0464)586924.

*   *   *

WALK 32 (see sketch map O, page 209)

BRENTA GROUP

via Madonna di Campiglio - Passo del Grostè (10mins-3h) -
Passo della Gaiarda - R. Malga Spora (2h30mins) - Andalo (2h).
TABACCO MAP NO.10 scale 1:50,000
(1-2 days suggested).

See the opening comments to walk 31 for an introduction to the Adamello-Brenta Nature Park.

This easy itinerary starts out with a panoramic crossing of the rocky part of the Brenta Group then descends to the pastoral peace of the dairy farm, Malga Spora before penetrating thick larch woods in a silent valley with an interesting rock ledge passage. It is not as popular as walk 31, thus quieter.

As far as wildlife goes, several bears were sighted recently (by very determined and patient observers) northeast of Passo del Grostè; an area not far north of the path followed here. Your chances are much better of seeing wood grouse and even deer, especially on the final descent towards Andalo.

Stage One: via Passo del Grostè (10mins-3h) and Passo della Gaiarda to R. Malga Spora (2h30mins)

Like the last itinerary, this too is a west-east crossing of the Brenta Group, so it's an advantage to use public transport instead of your car, unless you leave it at a convenient valley centre which you can return to. The starting point, Madonna di Campiglio (1522m) can be reached by bus from Trent (southeast), Malè (northeast) (which also has a railway), as well as from some northern Italian cities with seasonal connections. When you get off the bus in the town centre, go down (east), across the stream and through the park towards the departure station of the Monte Spinale chair lift. By all means make use of the chair lift (discounts for members of the Italian Alpine Club and the Alpenverein) as it saves a rather uninteresting 600m and 1h30min ascent (paths n.384/385) to the modern and impersonal R. Monte Spinale (2104m). Don't waste time here, but head straight off (east) on n.331 in slight descent across rolling grasslands with scattered stone and wild flowers, past the lake (2036m) then in ascent. Ignore all the turn-offs and stick to n.331 all the way to newly-restored R. Graffer (2261m) (1h). Its position, almost directly under the gondola-car cables, seems rather incongruous nowadays for an Alpine Club refuge, though it is obviously of strategic importance for winter skiers. The pale rock of Pietra Grande, part of the north-extending reaches of the Brenta Group towers over the building. Continue on, following path n.331 and you'll soon arrive at the path junction with n.316 which you take up to the restaurant (no accommodation) then Passo del Grostè (2442m) (30mins from R. Graffer).

A faster alternative is to take the gondola-car itself (departure station just north of Madonna di Campiglio, before Passo Campo Carlo Magno, discounts as previously mentioned) straight up to the

Cable-car from Madonna di Campiglio to Passo del Grostè, under the Pietra Grande

restaurant just below the actual pass. If you haven't already done so, fill up with drinking water as the malga is a good 2h30mins off.

Now, from the pass, after admiring the surrounding mountains, start off east on path n.301 which is followed all the way to Andalo. Both tourists and walkers are less frequent from now on. You move southeast across a sort of plateau in an area of very strange karstic terrain. There are almost horizontal layers which form a series of massive terrace steps from where you get more excellent views onto the eastern face of the Pietra Grande massif. There is a slight descent to a junction with a path that leads off north (n.314) to Lago di Tovel, (allow 1h30mins-2h in descent - a very worthwhile detour especially if the lake's famous micro-algae have managed to bloom once more. There has been a long absence brought about by serious pollution. It gives the lake a unique red colouring).

You next reach a wide grassy saddle between the towering rock bastions of Monte Turrion basso (left) and Monte Turrion alto (right). Subsequently you cross the upper part of the pastoral area known as Campo Flavona (another possible descent north to Malga Flavona and

Lago Tovel), and climb again briefly to Passo della Gaiarda (2242m) where there is a surprising view onto the interesting stratified Crosara di Fibion, the mountain bordering to the northeast. Allow about 1h45mins this far from the Passo del Grostè. A pleasant 45min descent follows, firstly on scree on the left-hand side of the narrow valley, then further down it crosses the stream (right), and eventually curves and comes out behind R. Malga Spora (1861m) which was hidden from view until the last moment. The refuge and summer dairy farm stands in a deep peaceful amphitheatre with grazing cows, shaded by Monte Ridont and Crozzon della Spora.

Stage Two: descent to Andalo (2h)
Path n.301 leaves the malga due east and crosses the grassy depression to drop over its easternmost edge where it begins an easy and delightful descent among peaceful conifer woods of larch, for the most part. Signposting (n.338) soon indicates the access (left) to R. Cacciatori di Spora (1869m) (privately owned and usually locked up) which you soon glimpse north at the mouth of Val dei Cavai (meaning "horses"). Next is a steepish descent as the path winds down grassy banks with low trees at the head of the Valle Sporeggio. Path n.302 branches off left towards the village of Spormaggiore. Soon, further down, around 1600m, you reach a refreshing spring. The next section, though easy is somewhat unexpected. It consists of a longish passage on a series of rock ledges, mostly on a level, and running under dramatic cliffs on the exposed northern side of Daniola mountain. There are several lengths of metallic cord to reassure walkers on the points with a dizzy side drop.

Still in thick wood, the path proceeds to the beginning of a forestry track for a short stretch before turning sharp right, and past the path turn-off (n.353 to Malga Daniola). You come out at the small village of Pegorar (1053m) on a secondary road, but go literally straight down to the central square of the resort village of Andalo where you'll find the Tourist Office and bus stops for services either down northeast to Mezzocorona then Trent, both with railway stations, otherwise southwest to connect with Madonna di Campiglio.

PRACTICAL INFORMATION
R. GRAFFER TEL:(0465)441358. Alpine Club, Trent section, Sleeps 64
R. MALGA SPORA. Spormaggiore Council. Sleeps 50.
R. MONTE SPINALE TEL:(0465)441507. Private, accomm.
TOURIST OFFICE ANDALO TEL:(0461)585836.
TOURIST OFFICE MADONNA DI CAMPIGLIO TEL:(0465)442000.

Italian – English Glossary

acqua non potabile	=	water not suitable for drinking
albergo	=	hotel
alm	=	German for alpine dairy farm
alta via	=	high level mountain walking route usually connecting several refuges
alto	=	high
altopiano / altipiano	=	high level plateau
aperto	=	open
bagno	=	bathroom, bath, or toilet
baita	=	an alpine hut for shepherds, now sometimes a farm or refuge
basso	=	low
bivacco	=	mountain bivouac hut, unmanned
bosco	=	wood
burrone	=	ravine, gorge
caduta sassi	=	falling rocks
campanile	=	(literally bell-tower), slender Dolomite rock needle formation
capanna	=	hut
carta geografica	=	map
cascata	=	waterfall
casera	=	mountain hut or dairy farm building
chiuso	=	closed
cima	=	peak
col	=	hill or low mountain
croda	=	sheer-sided Dolomite mountain
cuccetta	=	couchette, bunk bed in refuge
discesa	=	descent
doccia calda/fredda	=	hot/cold shower
est	=	east
fiume	=	river
fontana	=	fountain
forcella	=	saddle, mountain pass on walking path
funivia	=	cable-car
ghiacciao	=	glacier
grande	=	large
hütte	=	German for refuge
lago	=	lake

letto	=	bed, used in refuges to refer to a bed with sheets, as opposed to the dormitory bunk beds (see "cuccetta")
malga	=	alpine dairy farm, sometimes run as a refuge.
montagna	=	mountain
nord	=	north
occidentale	=	western
orientale	=	eastern
orrido	=	ravine
ovest	=	west
maso	=	type of alpine hut in South Tyrol
meridionale	=	southern
passo	=	mountain pass
pericolo	=	danger
pian	=	high level plateau
piccolo	=	small
ponte	=	bridge
pronto soccorso	=	first aid
punta	=	point
ricovero invernale	=	winter premises adjoining a refuge
rifugio	=	refuge, a manned mountain hut providing food and accommodation
rio	=	stream or small river
salita	=	ascent
scorciatoia	=	short cut
seggovia	=	chair lift
sentiero	=	walking path
sentiero alpinistico	=	route for climbers
settentrionale	=	northern
soccorso alpino	=	mountain rescue
sorgente	=	spring or source of river
sud	=	south
teleferica	=	aerial cableway
torre	=	tower-like rock part of a mountain
torrente	=	torrent, mountain stream
val / valle	=	valley
vedretta	=	hanging glacier
vetta	=	peak
via ferrata	=	mountaineering passage over rock with fixed aids - experienced climbers only

Useful expressions

excuse me, where is the bus stop / railway station? = scusi, dov'è la fermata dell'autobus / la stazione ferroviaria?

possible answers:

a destra / sinistra = on the right / left

lì in fondo = over there

sempre diritto = straight ahead

good morning (or afternoon) / good evening = buon giorno / buona sera

hello (on the phone) = pronto

help! = aivto!

how long does it take to get to Calalzo? = quanto tempo ci vuole per Calalzo?

how much further is it to the refuge? = quanto manca per il rifugio?

possible answers: dieci minuti / mezz'ora / un'ora / due ore = ten minutes/ half an hour / one hour / two hours

how much does it cost? = quanto costa?

I don't understand, could you repeat that please? = non ho capito, può ripeterlo per favore?

I'd like to book / cancel one bunk / two bunks (bed / beds) for tonight / tomorrow night, please = vorrei prenotare / disdire una cuccetta / due cuccette (letto / letti) per stanotte / domani notte, per favore.

possible answers: mi dispiace, ma siamo al completo / non ci sono posti liberi = sorry, but we're full / there are no free places left

my name is... = mi chiamo...

Is there any snow on the path to Faè-Fortogna? = c'è neve sul sentiero per Faè-Fortogna?

possible answers: si, ce n'è molta, non si passa = yes, there's a lot, you can't get through

si, un po', ma si passa senza problemi = yes, a little, but you can get through with no problems

no, non ce n'è = no, there isn't any

one ticket / two tickets to Cortina, please = un biglietto / due biglietti per Cortina, per favore

single / return = andata / andata e ritorno

thank you, good-bye = grazie, arrivederci

timetable = orario

what time is breakfast / dinner? = a che ora è la colazione / la cena?

what time are meals? = a che ora si mangia?

what's the weather forecast for today / tomorrow? = che tempo è previsto

per oggi / domani?
possible answers:
sarà brutto / nuvoloso / bello = it will be bad / cloudy / good
ci sarà pioggia / un temporale / sole = there will be rain / a storm /sun

numbers:		
	1=uno	2=due
3=tre	4=quattro	5=cinque
6=sei	7=sette	8=otto
9=nove	10=dieci	11=undici
12=dodici	13=tredici	14=quattordici
15=quindici	16=sedici	17=diciasette
18=diciotto	19=diciannove	20=venti
30=trenta	40=quaranta	50=cinquanta
60=sessanta	70=settanta	80=ottanta
90=novanta	100=cento	1000=mille
2000=duemila		

References

The following books were consulted:
Berti A. (1971) *Guida dei Monti d'Italia, Dolomiti Orientali, vol.1, parte 1.* TCI/CAI, Milano.
Berti A. (1973) *Guida dei Monti d'Italia, Dolomiti Orientali, vol.1, parte 2.* TCI/CAI, Milano.
De Candido I. (1978) *Annello del Cadore* Tamari, Bologna.
Frenademez A. (1989) *Guida per l'escursionista Alta Badia* Azienda Autonomo di Soggiorno di Corvara-Colfosco e Badia.
Rossi P. (1982) *Guida dei Monti d'Italia, Schiara.* TCI/CAI, Milano.
Schaumann W. (1984) *La Grande Guerra 1915/18* vols 1 & 2, Ghedina & Tassotti, Bassano del Grappa.
Various authors, (1970) *Da Rifugio a Rifugio, Dolomiti Occidentali,* TCI/CAI Milano.
Visentini L. (1980) *Dolomiti di Brenta,* Athesia, Bolzano.
Wolff C.A. (1987) *L'anima delle Dolomiti,* Cappelli, Bologna.
Wolff C.A. (1987) *I monti pallidi,* Cappelli, Bologna.
Various useful pamphlets and maps kindly supplied by local Tourist Offices.

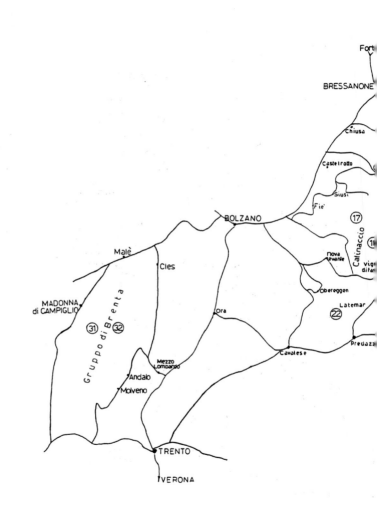